DEMOCRACY
IN THE
MIDDLE EAST

THE WORLD IN FOCUS

THE AMERICAN EMPIRE

DEMOCRACY IN THE MIDDLE EAST

GLOBAL EXTREMISM
AND TERRORISM

DEMOCRACY
IN THE
MIDDLE EAST

JOHN C. DAVENPORT, SERIES EDITOR

CHELSEA HOUSE
PUBLISHERS
An imprint of Infobase Publishing

Library of Congress Cataloging-in-Publication Data
Democracy in the Middle East/[edited by] John C. Davenport.
    p.   cm. — (The World in Focus)
    Includes bibliographical references and index.
    ISBN–13: 978-0-7910-9194-4 (hardcover)
    ISBN–10: 0-7910-9194-5 (hardcover)
1. Democracy—Middle East. 2. Middle East—Politics and government—1979–
3. United States—Foreign relations—Middle East. 4. Middle East—foreign
relations—United States. I. Davenport, John, 1960–   II. Title. III. Series.
    JQ1758.A91D45   2007
    320.956—dc22   2007004197

Text design by James Scotto-Lavino
Cover design by Takeshi Takahashi

Printed in the United States of America

Bang KT 10 9 8 7 6 5 4 3 2 1

Contents Overview

Detailed Table of Contents

———⊶⊷———

Introduction

⊶⊷

The swirl of twenty-first century current events. can easily become overwhelming With unprecedented speed, developments unfold, trends emerge, and crises arise. Every day, there seems to be more information demanding attention. Casual and expert observers alike carry a heavier burden of understanding, a weight made greater by the myriad interpretations of what takes place around the globe on a daily basis. Competing viewpoints crowd the marketplace of opinion; varying analyses of the latest issues vie for audiences and legitimacy. The resulting image of the modern world is thus blurred by abstraction and bias. People today, in short, have more difficulty than ever before in gaining a clear picture of what is going on around them. The challenge facing everyone, then, is to bring the world into focus.

This challenge is taken up in this series, a collection of three volumes that examine some of the most pressing and significant topics at the dawn of the new millennium. Each book plunges the reader into the disputes and debates that surround their subjects, assembling articles and excerpts from a variety of sources, including major books, the internet, and prestigious scholarly journals. Sifting through the various arguments and prescriptions offered by policy advocates, experts, and government agencies, *The World in Focus* examines three specific topic areas: Middle East democracy, American imperialism, and terrorism. The series explores each area in depth, then proceeds to lay out the many options for dealing with the problems associated with them. The arduous tasks of initiating democratic reform within Arab-Muslim society and politics, adapting to the reality of American hegemony, and combating extremism and terror are looked at in detail.

Throughout the volumes, multiple perspectives are reviewed, and a representative sample of contemporary thinking is offered. Authors expressing optimism concerning the chances for democratic change in the Middle East, for example, are coupled with those with more pessimistic outlooks. Supporters of the American assertion of imperial power are paired with its opponents. Writers who differ on the extent of the danger posed by global extremism, and the possible ways to counter it, are placed side by side. The reader will notice many voices in these three books, some more controversial than others. It is hoped that from this collection of analyses and interpretations, a deeper knowledge will be gained that might lead to better decision-making in the future.

DEMOCRACY IN THE MIDDLE EAST

There is perhaps no better place to start this process than the volatile Middle East. Plagued by a history of sectarian violence, repression, and colonialism, political evolution has been a bloody business for the Middle East in the past. Wars, assassination, and intrigue have often been the tools of choice among men and movements seeking to reshape the contours of power throughout a vast region that stretches from Africa to Asia. These struggles take place in an atmosphere charged further by the confluence of politics and Islam, a religion that shapes the lives of over one billion people.

Unsettled for centuries, the Middle East today serves as an arena for a monumental struggle between contesting political philosophies and systems. Traditional forms of autocracy and authoritarianism wrestle for dominance with newly imported strains of democracy. History favors the autocratic and authoritarian regimes that typify the Middle Eastern political landscape, but democracy is building momentum and gaining adherents, all the while being scrutinized for conformity to regional standards. Democracy is attractive to many people, but it must bear up under the strain of proving itself compatible with conservative social and religious norms. Some experts doubt democracy's chances for survival for these reasons; others are more hopeful. All of them, wary of making predictions, are guarded in their assessments.

Democracy in the Middle East presents their arguments and evaluations. It considers the prospects for democratic reform in a region notorious for tyranny, corruption, and inequity. The book's contributors weigh the odds that democratic institutions and political habits of thought can flourish there. Their essays and excerpts look at topics ranging from women's rights to the phenomenon of Muslim democracy. Each outlines and explains the powerful forces for both change and continuity in the Middle East and draws a conclusion as to whether or not democracy can flourish. The volume seeks to answer an important question: is there reason to hope that democracy might ever take root in such a troubled area?

THE AMERICAN EMPIRE

If so, the United States will almost certainly play a crucial role in its establishment. The United States has been and continues to be the most active agent for democratization in the Middle East. As a promoter of democracy, at least in theory, it is unsurpassed. But the American effort to export its political ideas and traditions is not limited to one region. The United States, in fact, is energetically working to reshape large parts of the world in its own image and create a universal political order that is liberal, democratic, secular, and built upon a solid foundation of consumer capitalism. The preferred tools for this job are cultural: movies, music, food, and fashion—but more muscular ones such as public diplomacy and even war are seen as equally valid and often more appropriate. The United States, put simply, has a vision of the world's future that is colored red, white, and blue.

Although viewed as benign or even benevolent by most Americans, many people in other countries wonder why the United States works so diligently to export its beliefs, customs, practices, and lifestyles overseas. They question American motivations and intentions. Perhaps, it is thought, American actions signal a commitment to a better, freer future for everyone. On the other hand, they very well could indicate an insatiable imperial hunger for domination. Is the United States seeking to become a global hegemon? Or is it already a de facto imperial state, an empire in everything but name? What does all this mean for the rest of the humanity?

The American Empire studies these questions and tries to determine whether and to what extent the United States is an empire, what kind it is, and how enduring it will be. The articles and excerpts generally presume America's imperial status, then move on to consider the costs and benefits of such a position. They also seek to place the United States on the continuum of historical empires and come to a conclusion regarding whether the American empire might succeed where so many others have failed.

GLOBAL EXTREMISM AND TERRORISM

Regardless of America's imperial future, its current degree of influence worldwide often generates substantial fear and resentment. Coupled with its championing of Western-style democracy, America's assertiveness creates enemies. For many ethnic and religious groups, the United States' expressions of power evoke memories of European colonialism, exploitation, and oppression. Americans appear, to their eyes, to be just another band of arrogant foreigners bent on controlling the planet, its people, and its resources.

Not surprisingly, forces have emerged in resistance to American goals and objectives. Around the world, movements have sprung up in opposition to everything viewed as either a Western or specifically American import. Usually these movements employ peaceful means of protest. Sometimes, however, driven by local or regional impulses, they devolve into extremism and begin advocating more aggressive forms of reaction, up to and including violence. On occasion, movements transition from words to deeds; they transform themselves into terrorist cells and even transnational terrorist organizations. They adopt violence as both a strategy and tactic for advancing their anti-Western, anti-American agendas. Bombings, kidnappings, assassinations, and executions soon follow.

The third volume in *The World in Focus* surveys the dark and treacherous landscape of terrorism. *Global Extremism and Terrorism* seeks to define, describe, and illuminate the people who have chosen murder and mayhem as weapons in a war against belief systems and ways of life they view as evil. The book leads its readers into a violent netherworld where individuals and groups openly embrace destruction as a vehicle for change. The contributors look at who terrorists are and why they do the things they do. The often twisted motivations and justifications for destruction and the taking of innocent lives are dissected in search of some form of underlying logic. The chosen means of violence, ranging from piracy to suicide bombings, are explored and explained so that the audience can appreciate just how devastating the realization of terrorist plans can be. Lastly, *Global Extremism and Terrorism* weighs the options for counter-terrorist activity. How best to fight terrorism, and end its scourge, is a question for which tentative answers are offered. The world promises to become a far more dangerous place unless the agents of terror and their tools are better understood.

Taken together, the three books in this series sharpen the outlines of the modern world. They help lift the veil of confusion that too often obscures the popular views of current events, and reveal the inner structures of the issues that dominate today's headlines. A degree of blurriness will no doubt persist despite the best efforts of scholars and experts like those represented in *Democracy in the Middle East*, *The American Empire*, and *Global Extremism and Terrorism*. Nevertheless, each book does its part to clarify key global developments and, through close examination, bring them and the world into focus.

John C. Davenport
Series Editor

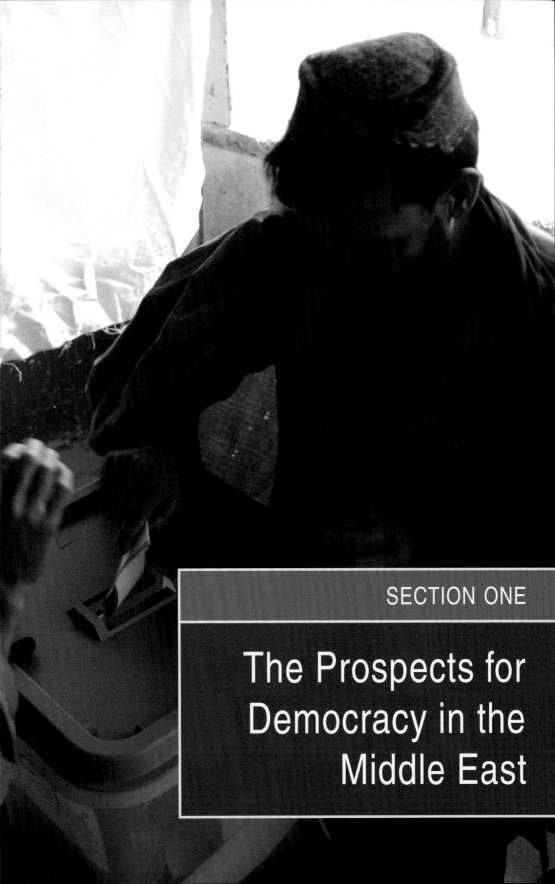

SECTION ONE

The Prospects for
Democracy in the
Middle East

At the center of U.S. policy toward the Middle East is the assumption that democracy is the cure-all for regional ailments that range from discrimination against women to global terrorism. And yet, while democracy's transformative power is routinely proclaimed, it is rarely questioned. Indeed, any inquiry into democracy's ability to bring peace, stability, and freedom to a place that has been plagued by war, unrest, and oppression is usually dismissed as being counterintuitive at best. In some circumstances, efforts to rethink the primacy of democracy are even misrepresented as signs of less-than-perfect patriotism. Democracy, in short, is assumed to be a universal remedy and something that President George W. Bush, speaking on the occasion of his second inauguration, called "the best hope for peace in our world." Alluding to the Middle East, the president reaffirmed his belief that American-style democracy would solve the most pressing international problems. The ideals upon which the United States were founded, he said, had merged with "American's vital interests." Spreading those ideals "is the mission that created our nation . . . So it is the policy of the United States to seek and support the growth of democratic movements and institutions in every nation and culture, with the ultimate goal of ending tyranny in our world."*

Americans have enjoyed the fruits of liberal democracy for almost 250 years, and have credited it with bestowing upon them power, influence, and a historically unsurpassed standard of living. They are justly proud of this accomplishment. Unfortunately, many Americans take for granted that this feat can be replicated quickly and easily in other countries, especially in the Middle East.

But the fact that democracy has served the United States well does not mean that transplanting it intact to a volatile region such as the Middle East would necessarily yield the same results. As scholar Benjamin R. Barber has noted, the goal of the West is to bring freedom to the Muslim world, but "this does not mean exporting American democracy. . . . Trying to make other nations free by exporting American democracy to their shores is unlikely to succeed."** Political liberalization and competitive elections alone, in other words, might not be the keys to security and progress that President Bush and others envision. Acknowledging this possibility in the following article, Marina Ottoway and Thomas Carothers systematically examine and assess popular wisdom regarding democracy in the Middle East. The authors look at, among other topics, common suppositions about Islam and democracy, the nature of American goals and objectives, and the historical obstacles to genuine regional reform. Ottoway and Carothers, in the course of their inquiry, reveal the extent to which each of their target assumptions reflects either sound reasoning, wishful thinking, or utter falsehood. They also suggest that, if democracy did emerge in the Middle East, the impetus for change might come from some unexpected quarters of Muslim society, rather than from an external power such as the United States.

NOTES

*   "President Sworn-In to Second Term." Available online at http://www.whitehouse.gov/news/releases/2005/01/20050120-1.html. Accessed November 27, 2006.

**   Benjamin R. Barber, *Fear's Empire: War, Terrorism, and Democracy* (New York: W.W. Norton and Company, 2003), 169–170.

Think Again: Middle East Democracy
MARINA OTTAWAY AND THOMAS CAROTHERS

People in the Middle East want political freedom, and their governments acknowledge the need for reform. Yet the region appears to repel democracy. Arab regimes only concede women's rights and elections to appease their critics at home and abroad. If democracy arrives in the Middle East, it won't be due to the efforts of liberal activists or their Western supporters but to the very same Islamist parties that many now see as the chief obstacle to change.

"THE MIDDLE EAST IS THE LAST HOLDOUT AGAINST THE GLOBAL DEMOCRATIC TREND"

No. The Middle East is on the wrong side of the global democratic divide, but unfortunately it does not lack company. As Russia slides into authoritarianism, the former Soviet Union is becoming a democratic wasteland with only a few shaky pockets of pluralism, such as Georgia, Ukraine, and Moldova. Central Asia is no better off than the Arab world in terms of democracy. A depressingly large swath of East and Southeast Asia—from North Korea and China down through Vietnam, Laos, and

Burma to Malaysia and Singapore—is a democracy-free zone that shows few signs of change.

Nor was the Middle East immune to the "Third Wave," the decisive expansion of democracy that started in southern Europe and Latin America 30 years ago and subsequently spread to other parts of the world. During the 1980s, several Arab countries, including Egypt, Tunisia, and Jordan, initiated political reforms to permit multiparty competition. These reforms lost momentum or were undone in the 1990s, however, as Arab leaders proved unwilling to risk their own power through genuine processes of democratization. Tunisia, for example, moved back to rigid authoritarian rule.

Today, political reform is percolating again in the region, amid growing public frustration over chronic corruption, poor socioeconomic performance, and a pervasive sense of stagnation. The Sept. 11, 2001, terrorist attacks also created pressure for reform—from both the United States and some Arabs who began to question why their societies were so widely viewed as dangerous political cesspools. Talk about political reform and democracy is rife even in the Gulf monarchies where such issues had been taboo. The steps taken thus far in most countries, however, are modest. Although the Arab world is not impervious to political change, it has yet to truly begin the process of democratization.

"DEMOCRACY IN THE MIDDLE EAST IS IMPOSSIBLE UNTIL THE ARAB–ISRAELI CONFLICT IS RESOLVED"

Wrong. Arab governments curb political participation, manipulate elections, and limit freedom of expression because they do not want their power challenged, not because tension with Israel requires draconian social controls. When the government of Kuwait refuses to give women the right to vote, it does so out of deference to the most conservative elements of its population, not out of fear that voting women will undermine the country's security. Fear of competition, not of a Zionist plot, leads the Egyptian ruling party to oppose competitive presidential elections. When it comes to democratic reform, the Zionist threat is merely a convenient excuse.

Yet failure to resolve the Arab–Israeli conflict prevents the United States from gaining credibility as an advocate of democracy in the Middle East. Liberal Arabs perceive claims by the United States that it wants democracy in the Middle East as hypocritical, pointing to what they see as American indifference to the rights of the Palestinians and unconditional support for Israel. For their part, many Arab governments do not take U.S. pressure to democratize their region seriously, believing that the need for oil and fear of upsetting regimes that recognize Israel will trump Washington's desire for democratic change. U.S. credibility in the Middle East will not be restored—and the unprecedented level of anti-American resentment will not abate—until the United States makes a serious, balanced effort to tackle the conflict. Without such credibility, Washington's effort to stimulate democratization in the region will be severely constrained.

"THE UNITED STATES WANTS DEMOCRACY IN THE MIDDLE EAST"

Up to a point. The democratic transformation of the Middle East emerged as a central objective of U.S. foreign policy during the Bush administration. This new policy is a sharp reversal of several decades of steadfast support for many autocratic regimes in the region, such as those in Egypt, Saudi Arabia, and Jordan. It reflects the new post-9/11 conventional wisdom that Middle East democracy is the best antidote to Islamist terrorism.

Although this desire for democracy may be heartfelt, the United States has a lengthy laundry list of other priorities in the region: access to oil, cooperation and assistance on counterterrorism, fostering peace between Israel and its neighbors, stemming the proliferation of weapons of mass destruction, and preventing Islamist radicals from seizing power.

The newfound U.S. enthusiasm for democracy competes for a place in this mix. Fighting Islamist militants and safeguarding oil still compels the United States to cooperate with authoritarian regimes. People in the region watched as the United States took a tough line against Iran and Syria while failing to push Saudi Arabia, Egypt, Tunisia, or other friendly tyrants very hard. The Bush administration launched new diplomatic endeavors and aid programs to support positive change, such as the Broader Middle East and North Africa Initiative and the Middle East Partnership Initiative. But they consist of mild, gradual measures designed to promote democratic change without unduly challenging the authority of incumbent governments.

Moreover, despite the president's conviction that democratic change in the Middle East is necessary, a great deal of ambivalence remains within the U.S. policy bureaucracy about the prospect of any rapid political openings in the region. This sentiment is particularly true of the State Department and the intelligence community. Some experts worry that, given the political mood of most Arab citizens—who are angry at the United States and sympathetic to political Islam—free and open elections could result in some distinctly unfriendly regimes.

"THE WAR IN IRAQ ADVANCED THE CAUSE OF DEMOCRACY IN THE MIDDLE EAST"

Not yet. The U.S.-led war in Iraq removed from power one of the most heinous, repressive dictators in the region and opened up the possibility that Iraq will one day have a pluralistic political system held together by consensus rather than violence. The actual achievement of democracy in Iraq, however, remains distant and uncertain. The path to that goal will be measured in years rather than months.

The war's political effects in the rest of the region—especially the way it exposed the hollowness of Saddam Hussein's regime—has contributed to increased calls for political reform in many Arab countries. Real progress toward democracy, however, is minimal. In addition, the war provoked some Arab governments, such as Egypt, to limit the already constrained political space they allow as a defensive gesture against public protests and as an excuse for prosecuting opponents.

Regrettably, President George W. Bush's repeated justification of the war as a democratizing mission has discredited some Western-oriented Arab democrats in the eyes of their fellow citizens. Many Arabs have come to view democracy itself as a code word for U.S. regional domination. The unpopularity of the war and the abuses against Iraqis at Abu Ghraib prison have further tarnished the reputation of the United States and fueled Islamist extremism.

Proponents of democratic contagion argue that if Iraq holds successful elections in early 2005, this example will resound loudly in the Arab world. But much of the Arab world will likely view such elections, even if they come off well, as highly flawed. Some parts of the predominantly Sunni areas of Iraq are not expected to participate in the elections, and many Arabs will inevitably accuse the United States of manipulation, because the elections will be held under U.S. occupation. Few Arabs will be dazzled into holding a new view of democracy on the basis of one election. Many countries in the region already hold elections of varying degrees of seriousness and importance, including one in Algeria earlier this year, which a Western observer described as "one of the best conducted elections, not just in Algeria, but in Africa and much of the Arab world."

Promoting democracy throughout the Middle East will require doing away with fantasies of a sudden U.S.-led transformation of the region and taking seriously the challenge of building credibility with Arab societies. Moreover, if the United States is to play a constructive supporting role, it must seriously revise its cozy relations with autocratic regimes, show a sustained ability to apply nuanced diplomatic pressure for political change at key junctures, and back up this pressure with well-crafted and well-funded assistance. Washington must prepare to accept emboldened political forces, and eventually new governments, that are uninterested in doing the United States' bidding. Embracing Middle East democracy in principle is easy; truly supporting it remains an enormous challenge.

"ISLAMISTS ARE THE MAIN OBSTACLE TO ARAB DEMOCRACY"

Think again. The standard fear is the "one person, one vote, one time" scenario: Islamists would only participate in elections to win power and put an end to democracy immediately. Hence, the argument goes, they should not be allowed to participate.

True, the commitment to democracy of even moderate Islamists is uncertain and hedged by the caveat that democratic governments must accept Islamic law. However, the chances of an overwhelming electoral victory that would allow Islamists to abrogate all freedoms at once is remote in the Arab world. During the last decade, Islamist parties and candidates have participated in elections in eight Arab countries (Algeria, Bahrain, Egypt, Jordan, Kuwait, Lebanon, Morocco, and Yemen), always with modest results. (These elections suffered from various degrees of government interference, but there is no indication that the Islamists would have won in a more open environment.) And Turkey, a country where an Islamist party took power with a large majority, is becoming an encouraging example of democratic success.

Although the prediction that Islamist electoral victories would lead to democracy's demise in the Middle East have so far proved unfounded, the possibility cannot be ruled out. Fear of such takeovers remains in many Arab countries and the United States. Many Arab regimes use this fear to justify meddling in elections and placing restrictions on political participation. The presence of Islamist parties thus complicates the process of democratization.

But Islamist parties are also integral to democratization because they are the only nongovernmental parties with large constituencies. Without their participation, democracy is impossible in the Middle East. The future of democracy in the region depends on whether a sufficient number of such parties moderate their political views and become actors in a democratic process, rather than spoilers in the present autocratic states, and whether incumbent governments stop hiding behind the Islamist threat and accept that all their citizens have a right to participate.

"ARAB COUNTRIES HAVE A HISTORIC PROPENSITY TOWARD AUTHORITARIANISM"

Yes. But so what? Most societies have lived under authoritarian rule for some time, often for a long time. Democracy is a relatively recent historical phenomenon. Even in the United States and Europe it was only consolidated through universal suffrage in the last century.

Arab rulers have been highly authoritarian, but no more so than European or Asian rulers for most of history. Arabs developed a political system based on Islam through the caliph, an individual who served as supreme leader of all Muslims. Europeans clung to the concept of the Holy Roman Empire for centuries after it ceased to exist in practice, fought ferocious religious wars for hundreds of years, and adopted the concept of separation of church and state rather late and incompletely. The Arab world, for most of its history, was quite similar to the rest of the world.

Even in the 1960s and 1970s, much of the Arab world was highly representative of the major political trends of the day. Most Arab countries outside the Gulf displayed the combination of nationalism and socialism that constituted typical Third World ideology at the time. Gamal Abdel Nasser in Egypt, alongside Jawaharlal Nehru in India and Marshal Tito in Yugoslavia, was a major champion of this ideology, which waned in the 1980s with the end of the Cold War and the rise of globally connected economies.

To ascribe the lingering Arab absence of democracy to some unique historic affinity for authoritarianism, stemming from Arab culture, Islam, or anything else is thus factually incorrect. It is also politically defeatist, attributing a quality of inevitability that belies the experience of political change in other parts of the world.

"PROMOTING WOMEN'S RIGHTS IS CRUCIAL FOR DEMOCRATIC CHANGE"

False. This myth, a favorite of women's organizations and Western governments, reflects the combination of correct observation and false logic.

No country can be considered fully democratic if a part of its population (in some cases, the majority) is discriminated against and denied equal rights. But efforts to change the status quo by promoting women's rights are premature. The main problem at present is that Arab presidents and kings have too much power, which they refuse to share with citizens and outside institutions. This stranglehold on power must be broken to make progress toward democracy. Greater equality for women does nothing to diminish the power of overly strong, authoritarian governments.

Arab leaders know this truth all too well. Many autocrats implement policies to improve women's rights precisely to give themselves reformist credentials and score points with Western governments, media outlets, and nongovernmental organizations. These efforts, however, often amount to a trick of smoke and mirrors designed to disguise the governments' refusal to cede any real power. In the last few years, several Arab states have appointed women to high positions and hurriedly implemented or proposed reforms concerning marriage, divorce, inheritance, and other personal status issues. These are welcome steps, but they do not address the core issue of promoting democracy: breaking the authoritarian pattern of Arab politics.

"ARAB DEMOCRATS ARE THE KEY TO REFORM"

Paradoxically, no. All Arab countries boast a small number of Westernized liberals who advocate respect for human rights, freedom of thought and speech, and democratic change. But democratic transformation requires more than the ideological commitment of a few individuals. In Western societies, a small democratic cadre sufficed in the distant past, when political participation was the preserve of public-minded intellectual elites and wealthy property owners. But the Arab world of today is not the United States or Europe of the 18th century. The political elite faces a growing challenge by Islamist movements, which are developing a popular support base. As a result, democratic transformation also requires broad-based political parties and movements capable of transforming abstract democratic ideals into concrete programs that resonate with a public whose main concern is survival.

Arab democrats have so far shown little capacity—and less inclination—to translate abstract ideas into programs with mass appeal. Because they talk to Western organizations and each other more than to their fellow citizens, opposition political parties with a liberal agenda find themselves unable to build broad constituencies. This failure leaves the field open to government parties, which can build a following on the basis of patronage, and to Islamist parties, which build their following in the best tradition of mass parties, with a mixture of ideological fervor and grassroots social services.

Government repression and, at times, co-optation have also undermined Arab democrats' effectiveness. Some regimes—notably Saudi Arabia's—move quickly to clamp down on any nascent liberal debate. Others are more tolerant, giving liberals some intellectual space to write and discuss issues openly, as long as their talk is not followed by action. Arab democrats in countries such as Egypt are not a persecuted group. Rather, they tend to be professionals comfortably ensconced in the upper-middle class. Therefore, they are hesitant to demand genuine reforms that might lead to a hard-line takeover and content to advocate democratization from the top.

Under such conditions, it would be a serious mistake for U.S. and European democracy advocates to focus on Arab democrats as the key to political change. These individuals will play a role if democracy becomes a reality. But during this period of transition, they have neither the inclination to push for reform nor the political clout to do so successfully.

"MIDDLE EAST DEMOCRACY IS THE CURE FOR ISLAMIST TERRORISM"

No. This view is rooted in a simplistic assumption: Stagnant, repressive Arab regimes create positive conditions for the growth of radical Islamist groups, which turn their sights on the United States because it embodies the liberal sociopolitical values that radical Islamists oppose. More democracy, therefore, equals less extremism.

History tells a different story. Modern militant Islam developed with the founding of the Muslim Brotherhood in Egypt in the 1920s, during the most democratic period in that country's history. Radical political Islam gains followers not only among repressed Saudis but also among some Muslims in Western democracies, especially in Europe. The emergence of radical Islamist groups determined to wreak violence on the United States is thus not only the consequence of Arab autocracy. It is a complex phenomenon with diverse roots, which include U.S. sponsorship of the mujahideen in Afghanistan in the 1980s (which only empowered Islamist militants); the Saudi government's promotion of radical Islamic educational programs worldwide; and anger at various U.S. policies, such as the country's stance on the Arab–Israeli conflict and the basing of military forces in the region.

Moreover, democracy is not a cure-all for terrorism. Like it or not, the most successful efforts to control radical Islamist political groups have been antidemocratic, repressive campaigns, such as those waged in Tunisia, Egypt, and Algeria in the 1990s. The notion that Arab governments would necessarily be more effective in fighting extremists is wishful thinking, no matter how valuable democratization might be for other reasons.

The experience of countries in different regions makes clear that terrorist groups can operate for sustained periods even in successful democracies, whether it is the Irish Republican Army in Britain or the ETA (Basque separatists) in Spain. The ETA gained strength during the first two decades of Spain's democratization process, flourishing more than it had under the dictatorship of Gen. Francisco Franco. In fragile democratic states—as new Arab democracies would likely be for years—radical groups committed to violence can do even more harm, often for long periods, as evidenced by the Tamil Tigers in Sri Lanka, Abu Sayyaf in the Philippines, or the Maoist rebels in Nepal.

Until very recently, democracy was not a high priority in terms of the U.S. agenda for the Middle East. Throughout the Cold War and the many Arab–Israeli wars, peace and stability were primary in the thinking of American policymakers. Such people were mostly concerned with two specific objectives: one, that Israel remain safe and at peace with its neighbors; and two, that millions of barrels of Arab oil continue to flow unimpeded to the petroleum-thirsty United States. Security and oil took precedent over democracy, even if it meant dealing with corrupt regimes and the occasional dictator.

The terrorist attacks that brought the World Trade Center crashing down onto the streets of New York in September 2001 dramatically altered this equation and raised democracy to a new level on the scale of national interests. As one expert told a Congressional committee looking into terrorism and security issues, "The 9/11 attacks and subsequent terror operations shattered the conventional wisdom that the [Middle East's] stability—anchored by its authoritarian governments—could endure indefinitely and would come at little cost to U.S. interests."* In other words, the United States could no longer pretend that the absence of democracy in the region was of secondary importance. Terrorism pushed democratic reform into the global limelight.

The U.S. government's response, ironically, has been somewhat timid and torn by conflicting perspectives. The urgent need for real democratization in the Middle East has too often competed with the perceived obligation to maintain ties with autocracies that provide sometimes crucial assistance in anti-terrorism operations. Oil, as always, is another consideration shaping U.S. policy. The result of all of this has been essentially half-hearted official support for democratic reform.

"Can the United States really do more?" asks Amy Hawthorne, the author of the following essay. Her answer is a resounding "yes." The policies of the past, Hawthorne contends, were shortsighted and focused too narrowly on regional stability and oil. A longer view is needed, she says: a view that demonstrates American commitment to liberalization and, ultimately, genuine democracy.

NOTES

* Mona Yacoubian, special advisor to the Muslim World Initiative, "Fostering Democracy in the Middle East: Defeating Terrorism with Ballots," statement before the U.S. House of Representatives Committee on Government Reform, Subcommittee National

Security, Emerging Threats, and International Relations, May 17, 2005. Available online at http://www.usip.org/aboutus/congress/testimony/2005/0517_yacoubian.html.

Can the United States Promote Democracy in the Middle East?
AMY HAWTHORNE

The Arab world's democracy deficit has finally captured Washington's attention. The September 11 attacks put an end to Washington's long-cherished illusion that the shortage of democracy in the Middle East was not pressing as long as stability was maintained. Now, President George W. Bush has described the promotion of "freedom" in the Islamic world—assumed to refer especially to the Arab world—as a key element of national security strategy.

Despite this high-level interest, the Bush administration has yet to formulate a realistic democracy-promotion strategy for the Middle East. Ambitious plans to replace current regimes with democratic successors have been proposed for some leaders the United States opposes; elsewhere, a more low-key approach seems to be emerging.

A rapid transformation of internal political conditions in the Arab world is well beyond the United States government's capacity or inclination. At the same time, an overly cautious approach that perpetuates the status quo is unlikely to be effective. What is needed is a sustained policy of high-level engagement with Arab governments, along with support for openings that would bolster reformist groups, and a willingness to accept that genuine political change will be bumpy. Even this modest policy would represent a dramatic and difficult shift for the United States, especially as regional tensions increase.

THE POLICIES OF THE PAST

Democracy has never been a goal of United States Middle East policy. Successive administrations have focused on promoting peace between Israel and its Arab neighbors, maintaining access to oil supplies, and containing radical movements. As long as Arab governments helped achieve these goals, the United States was more concerned about their stability than about their lack of democracy. In fact, stability in this strategically vital region was considered so important that the United States declined to push for democratic change even in "unfriendly" states such as Syria.

But during the 1990s, the United States began to notice political changes occurring in many Middle Eastern countries. The late 1980s had seen many Arab leaders start to allow multiparty legislative elections and greater leeway for nongovernmental organizations. These reforms were not intended to signal a transition to democracy, but to prolong the life of regimes. They aimed to bolster unpopular ruling parties (or leaders), improve the environment for much-needed economic reforms, and dilute the appeal of Islamist groups, which emerged as a major political force in the 1990s, challenging both Arab governments and United States policy. In a decade when the United States actively promoted democracy in other parts of the world, Washington did not want to appear completely indifferent to political reform and human rights in Arab countries. Thus the United States supported Arab governments' cautious reformist moves. It offered verbal and diplomatic support to countries such as Yemen, Jordan, and Morocco that allowed their citizens increased political space.

The United States also funded democracy-assistance programs in nine Middle Eastern countries and the Palestinian Authority (PA). Between 1991 and 2001, the United States spent some $250 million in the region on projects that included strengthening parliaments, improving human rights monitoring, and training judges. These efforts yielded meager results. Some projects were well designed; others were poorly conceived. Their limited impact was due mainly to the inhospitable local contexts in which they were implemented. But these on-the-ground programs were also unconnected to any higher-level United States efforts to encourage democratic change. When Arab governments took actions that undermined the stated goals of American programs (such as Egypt's enactment of a restrictive NGO law when the United States was spending millions to foster an active civil society in the country), the United States often remained silent, especially in strategically critical places such as Egypt or the PA. And, while the United States did raise some human rights issues with Arab governments, it did not pursue a meaningful dialogue to encourage them to take steps beyond their initial reforms.

Indeed, Washington did not want to antagonize regimes whose cooperation it needed to keep the peace process going and the oil flowing. The United States hesitated to press for bolder reforms out of concern for stability and fear of Islamist opposition gains. Occasionally, some officials would recommend a more proactive policy, but were rebuffed by those who argued—compellingly—that the undemocratic status quo was the best the United States could hope for under the circumstances.

RETHINKING THE APPROACH

The September 11 attacks jolted the American foreign policy establishment out of its complacency by providing a terrible example of what the status quo could produce. Washington offered various explanations for the attacks, for the widespread appeal of political Islam, and for anti-American sentiments in the Middle East. Analysts pointed to the Arab world's lack of economic opportunities, to inadequate educational systems that fostered misinterpretations of Islam, and to the unpopularity of American policies in the region. The Middle East's democracy deficit, however, was most often cited as a central explanatory factor. Authoritarian rule created an environment in which Al Qaeda and other militant groups could draw support. Lack of political freedom thwarted peace, prosperity, and modernity. Along with its unpopular regional policies (which the Bush administration did not wish to revise), America's close ties to undemocratic Arab regimes was a source of resentment.

Thus, while democracy promotion previously had been viewed as a pursuit far too idealistic to fit in with the hard, pragmatic core American interests in the Middle East, soon it was portrayed as essential to long-term national security. Undersecretary of State for Global Affairs Paula Dobriansky declared in a speech before the Heritage Foundation that the "advancement of human rights and democracy . . . [is] the bedrock of our war on terrorism. The violation of human rights by repressive regimes provides fertile ground for popular discontent . . . cynically exploited by terrorist organizations. . . . [A] stable government that responds to the legitimate desires of its people and respects their rights, shares power . . . is a powerful antidote to extremism."

Yet although there is now a greater consensus within the Bush administration about the importance of Middle East democracy than before September 11, no coherent rationale has been set forth explaining why the United States should advance democracy in the region. The United States has always had multiple motives for engaging in democracy promotion around the world, but the leading reasons in the Middle East seem especially disparate. Some believe that September 11 demonstrated the need for the United States boldly to remake the Middle East into a zone of pro-American democracies, by coercion or force if necessary. Others view democracy promotion as a way to win

Arab "hearts and minds" in the war against terrorism, and call for public diplomacy programs and democracy aid to this end. Another perspective sees undemocratic governance as the key problem, and recommends engagement with existing governments to promote reform.

FORMULATING NEW INITIATIVES

Democracy-promotion plans are still being formulated. What has emerged so far suggests an awkward combination of three strands: aggressive calls for democracy in certain "unfriendly" regimes, and elsewhere, heavy doses of reaching out to civil society and modest diplomatic engagement.

The boldest initiatives to promote "freedom" target Iraq and the PA, reflecting the influence of those within the administration who favor a coercive approach. The United States has devised grand policies of Iraqi and Palestinian "regime change" coupled with promises of American support for democratic successor governments. The United States repeatedly cites the "liberation" of the Iraqi people from Saddam Hussein's tyranny as a central rationale for a military campaign to disarm Iraq and topple the regime. The administration has also made a rhetorical commitment to establish a "democratic" post-Saddam government, perhaps through an American military occupation similar to that of postwar Japan. In the case of the PA, President Bush has declared that a reformed and democratic government with "new leaders" is a prerequisite for United States support of final status negotiations with Israel and for an independent Palestinian state.

Promoting democracy is not the primary motivation for either policy. Administration officials were pushing for regime change in Iraq long before September 11, and the stance toward Arafat mainly stems from America's conclusion that he is unable to make peace with Israel. Yet in the wake of September 11, in both places the idea of "democracy" can more easily be presented as an appealing by-product of regime change. In addition, new leadership in Baghdad and Ramallah is cast as a catalyst for the broader regional changes that September 11 showed were necessary. As Bush himself stated before the United Nations General Assembly in September, "The people of Iraq can shake off their captivity. They can one day join a . . . democratic Palestine, inspiring reforms throughout the Muslim world." As for democracy promotion elsewhere in the region, the picture is a much less forceful one.

The administrations new multimillion-dollar public diplomacy campaign for the Middle East includes several initiatives to win Arab hearts and minds and to expose Arabs to key elements of United States democracy. Through media outreach, the United States will showcase

"American" values of religious tolerance, open debate, and women's rights. Study tours will bring Arabs to the United States to expose them to American democratic institutions and practices. Fellowships and English-language study programs will help Arabs build personal links with Americans and provide useful "tools" for the modern (democratic) global community.

The State Department will provide up to $10 million in 2003 for new projects in "civil society and the rule of law" across the Arab world (it is seeking significantly more funding for future years). These funds are to come from the new Middle East Partnership Initiative, which will also provide assistance for economic and educational reform.

The United States has suggested it will favor "reformist" Arab governments. "There is already a lot under way in terms of reform—places like Bahrain and Qatar, and to a certain extent Jordan. . . . [W]e want to be supportive of those," national security adviser Condoleezza Rice noted last September. The Bush administration has also taken a few less supportive steps to indicate its new seriousness of purpose. In August, the White House announced it would not honor an Egyptian request for $130 million in supplemental aid to protest an Egyptian security court's July sentencing of prominent Egyptian-American democracy activist Saad Eddin Ibrahim and his colleagues to prison for fraud and defamation. The United States considered the charges and the trial unjust. This was the first time the United States had linked the provision of aid to a human rights case in the Arab world.

AN INADEQUATE RESPONSE

Taken together, these disparate strands do not represent an adequate response to the regional democracy deficit to which September 11 had called such dramatic attention. The expectation that regime change in Iraq or the Palestinian Authority can form the core of a regional democracy-promotion strategy is misguided. Aside from exacerbating regional antagonism, neither is likely to provide a shining, inspirational model of democracy any time soon. Even if the United States succeeds in toppling Saddam Hussein's regime, the development of democracy in a post-Saddam Iraq will be an extremely arduous undertaking given the conditions prevailing inside Iraq, the difficulty of imposing democracy from the outside, and the apprehension of neighboring states about a democratic Iraqi government. Achieving minimal stability and a new leadership amenable to United States interests surely will trump concerns about democracy in the short and medium terms. As for the PA, developments since Bush's June 24 speech calling for a new Palestinian leadership show that political reforms, a reduced role for Arafat, and a democratic structure for a future state—goals that many Palestinians desire—are impossible to accomplish while the conflict with Israel rages and a diplomatic pathway is unavailable. Second, pressing for democracy only in countries where the United States does not like the regime and seems confident it can foster a friendly successor government sends a discouraging message to the rest of the Arab world: "democracy" is about our choices, not yours.

As for the rest of the region, it is unclear if democracy-promotion plans signal a qualitatively new approach, or a continuation of the 1990s efforts, but with more funding and higher-level support. These public diplomacy activities, however valuable, aim mainly to win over Arab publics by promoting a better image of the United States in the Arab world. This is different than focused diplomatic initiatives to encourage Arab governments to open up and to support reformist forces. Increased funding for democracy aid is welcome, but only if new programs do not simply rehash previous initiatives that were ineffective.

Further, it remains to be seen if officials will press governments on democracy and human rights issues in a sustained and comprehensive fashion. The administration's August decision on aid to Egypt represents an important first step in this direction. But it is not clear if the United States will link aid to the broader issues of civil society groups in Egypt beyond this one case, or if it will raise objections to the Egyptian government's treatment of activists who do not have a similar liberal, secularist-oriented platform. Across the region, the comfort level with undemocratic governments remains high. As one senior official remarked recently, "Supporting an authoritarian leader who is a modernizer and is willing to gradually loosen the reins—that essentially should be our policy."[1] Of course, this was the essentially the policy of the 1990s.

Finally, democracy promotion might again become paralyzed over fears about democracy—the United States may still be unprepared to contemplate the possible consequences of democratization where forces opposed to the United States could be the major beneficiaries. In the 1990s, concerns that democratic openings would pave the way for Islamists to impose their own illiberal rule and to pursue anti-American policies led the United States to avoid pushing for such openings. Many American officials are even more wary after September 11. Some believe that the attacks illustrated the need to eradicate all manifestations of political Islam, from Al Qaeda to the Muslim Brotherhood, not to increase Islamist influence, which is what has happened in Morocco and Bahrain, where reasonably free elections have been held recently and

Islamist candidates have scored impressive successes. How the United States will deal with this issue is unclear, but it is likely that the new approach will look much like the old.

OBSTACLES TO DEMOCRACY PROMOTION

Can the United States really do more? Devising a more vigorous yet realistic approach is complicated by both the challenge of democracy promotion in general and by specific features of the United States role in the region.

First, America's ability to influence internal political developments in Arab countries is marginal. Democratic transitions mainly are driven by complex internal factors, with outside forces having a secondary impact at best. In most Arab countries, democracy is not an impossible long-term goal, but current political, economic, and regional conditions are not auspicious. It would be much easier for the United States to intervene in support of popular democratic forces that are already mobilized for change in their own countries, but these forces do not yet exist.

Compounding the problem, domestic groups with a political reform agenda are unlikely to soon become American allies in democracy promotion. Across the region, Islamists remain the main opposition group. But Islamists are not courting United States support—indeed, a major part of their platform is rejection of United States Middle East policies. Nor is the United States likely to provide direct support to Islamists, since it questions their commitment to democratic values. The few existing liberal groups are deeply suspicious of the United States for its past support of autocratic regimes, its policy of regime overthrow in Iraq, and its perceived disregard for Palestinian rights. This is not to say that no individuals or groups would welcome United States support for specific projects, but no significant movements view the United States as their savior or protector.

In addition, many Arab countries have pressing economic needs. With a considerable number of Middle Eastern nations suffering from recessions and rising unemployment, some might ask if the United States should focus so much on "democracy" when many Arabs would like help finding a job or feeding their families.

Finally, United States policymakers remain deeply ambivalent about whether calling for democratic change is truly in America's interest now. Key United States concerns in the Middle East—an uninterrupted, cheap oil supply; political change in Iraq; an Israeli–Palestinian peace settlement; and, more than ever before, help in the war on terrorism—still seem best fulfilled by cooperation with reasonably friendly stable regimes rather than with countries experiencing the turmoil and uncertainties of democratic transformation.

TOWARD A STRATEGY

There is no "one size fits all" answer for Middle East democracy promotion. The approach must be tailored for each country, taking into consideration local conditions. The following four basic recommendations should inform at least the initial stages of a serious United States effort, building on much of what the administration has already devised for beyond Iraq and the PA, but giving it more teeth. First, democracy promotion is a very long-term effort, requiring a consistent series of steps to demonstrate United States sincerity over many years. Toward this end, the United States must shift from zero-sum thinking—that the only alternatives are the status quo or Islamist takeovers—to trying to foster a middle zone of democratization before the question of national leadership is decided. Calling for sudden transfers of power would not lead to democracy or protect American interests. But neither should America endorse cosmetic reforms with the idea that they will suppress grievances or satisfy yearnings for participation and accountability among Arab publics. Every Arab country has a need for some systemic political change, and the longer that steps toward this goal are deferred, the more thorny the problems will become and the more difficult their ultimate resolution.

Interim steps beyond controlled multiparty elections include lifting emergency laws, improving human rights, allowing greater freedom of speech and association, making budgetary processes more transparent, allowing new political parties to form, and granting greater powers to legislatures. As the experience of the 1990s showed, democracy-aid programs, however well intended, have little impact when the broader environment remains stagnant. Further, although economic issues are pressing—and the United States must help Arab governments address them—these problems often have their roots in political distortions, and are unlikely to be resolved without attention to the underlying political structure.

Second, the United States should concentrate its initial efforts on governments, recognizing that if actual democratization takes root, and if regional tensions abate, the United States will have more allies within Arab societies. Arab regimes hold most of the cards in the game of political reform. To the extent the United States has any influence, it is with regimes more than with societies. But even this influence should not be overestimated; in particular, the United States has less leverage with countries that supply it with oil and with those on whom it depends for access to military facilities and counterterrorism support. Nevertheless, since most friendly Arab governments do care what America thinks, the United States must take into account Arab governments' treatment of their citizens when determining the closeness of its ties.

To this end, the United States should issue a high-level policy directive that makes engagement on human rights, political reform, and democracy top priorities. This would empower officials at all levels of the bureaucracy to raise these issues without worrying that they will be left isolated by Washington. In countries where it provides significant economic aid, such as Egypt and Jordan, the United States should explore the feasibility of linking aid to political reforms. But it should introduce these conditions slowly and deliberately, through discussions with each government, rather than impose them abruptly. The United States must also carefully craft the language it uses to talk to and about Arab governments. It should compliment those Arab governments that are taking positive steps, but resist the tendency to overpraise them, as it has in the past. It should speak out, consistently, when governments—even close friends—violate human rights or pursue undemocratic policies. These moves will not change any Arab regime overnight; indeed, they will antagonize some and create a degree of discomfort for the United States. But they would add a new calculation to Arab governments' decision making: the reaction of the United States.

Third, democracy-assistance programs must be taken more seriously. This means conducting honest evaluations to determine what is working and what is not, and avoiding programs that are more about public relations than real change—and more about Washington priorities than the regions needs. It also means understanding democracy aid as just one aspect of a broader effort, not as a substitute for diplomatic action. This is not a call for American officials to interfere in program activities; that would be extremely counterproductive. In the Arab context especially, United States-funded programs must remain at an operational arm's length from Washington. But it does mean that the message delivered at the highest levels should reinforce the stated goals of the activities taking place on the ground.

Fourth, the United States should embark on the long journey of democracy promotion only if it is ready to accept that change is inherent to democratization, and that change may be painful. If Arab governments open genuine political space, many long-suppressed voices will rush to fill the void, some friendly to the United States, many not. But more tinkering at the edges only helps the real problems fester and worsen; specifically, continued repression seems mainly to benefit extremists.

Islamists are now a fact of life in Middle East politics; ignoring this is unrealistic. The goal should be to help create conditions that will not only empower other potential reformers, but also encourage the possibility that moderate Islamist groups (those that accept democratic principles and renounce all violence) could commit to long-term democratic competition. This is key: a democratic transition in any Arab country is certain to involve some kind of pact between moderate Islamists and moderates inside the regime.

AN END TO DENIAL

Taking these steps over the next few years would represent a sea change in American policy. It would require the United States to accept democratic change as a possibility in the Middle East, something it has never seriously contemplated before. It would require tolerating new tensions in American–Arab relations as the United States calls on its Arab friends to take difficult political steps. It would require patient, senior-level attention and ample resources over a period of many years, and in the face of many competing policy demands that involve Iraq, Israeli–Arab relations, the campaign against terror, and unforeseen challenges. It is risky: democracy may continue to be an elusive goal for the region for many years, despite United States efforts. Or, seemingly unshakable authoritarian regimes could crumble, despite United States efforts. The American public, and Congress, must be prepared for the challenge.

Whether Washington will be able or willing to undertake such a commitment to real democracy promotion is unclear. Yet in the aftermath of September 11, the United States has no alternative other than to begin to shift its role in the Arab world from an enabler of authoritarian rule to a supporter of gradual, but genuine, democratic change.

NOTES

1. Richard Haass, director of the Department of State's Policy Planning Staff, quoted in Nicholas Lemann, "Order of Battle: What the War Against Iraq—and Its Aftermath—Might Look Like," *The New Yorker*, November 18, 2002.

Democracy, as it is known in the West, began in ancient Greece and was elaborated upon in ancient Rome and the Renaissance Italian city-states. The English reshaped its contours during the seventeenth century, and finally it was brought to its modern form during the revolutions of the eighteenth century in America and France. Today, democracy is characterized by specific beliefs and practices that never emerged in the Middle East. Therefore, with the sole exception of Israel, which drew heavily on the European tradition in constructing its political system, there are no democracies in the Middle East. Throughout the region, autocracy and authoritarianism reign supreme, crowding out those places where there is, in the words of one scholar, "at best, some fledgling experimentation with democratization."*

The question, then, is this: Can a form of government developed in and for the West be transplanted to the Middle East? Or is such an effort pointless? Many observers argue the latter. The Arab Muslims, they claim, are inherently resistant to the democratic impulse. Steeped in tradition, suffocated within the confines of conservative Islam, and accustomed to authoritarian rule, Muslims are imagined by some people to be exceptionally ill-suited to democratic life. Naysayers argue that democracy, born in the West, will wither in Muslim Middle Eastern society and culture.

Others, however, including Joshua Muravchik, are more optimistic. They believe that democratic values are universal; men and women everywhere want freedom and liberty. Secretary of State Condoleezza Rice is among the optimists. In 2005, she criticized those who think that "somehow the people [of the Muslim Middle East] didn't care about the same freedoms and rights that we enjoy every day. . . ."**

In the following essay, Muravchik, a scholar at the American Enterprise Institute, argues that democracy is possible in the Middle East if the West is patient and lends the proper encouragement. He cites the post–World War II establishment of thriving democracies in Germany, Italy, and Japan as an example of democracy's prospects for success in countries familiar only with tyranny. Furthermore, Muravchik points to some promising steps already being taken in the Middle East, as he attempts to convince his readers that democracy can be brought to the Arab world.

NOTES

* Albrecht Schnabel, "A Rough Journey: Nascent Democratization in the Middle East," in *Democratization in the Middle East: Experiences, Struggles, Challenges*, ed. Amin Saikal and Albrecht Schnabel (New York: United Nations University Press, 2003), 3.

** "03 March 2005: Rice Warns Syria, Iran to Meet International Obligations." Available online at http://usinfo.state.gov/xarchives/display.html?p=washfile-english&y=2005&m=March&x=20050303 1846491CJsamohT0.885235&t=livefeeds/wf-latest.html.

Bringing Democracy to the Arab World
JOSHUA MURAVCHIK

There are 22 Arab countries. Of the world's 170 other governments, 121, or 71 percent, are elected. The number of Arab countries with freely elected governments: 0.

In *The End of History*, Francis Fukuyama likened the nations of the world to wagon trains carrying American pioneers west. Their speeds and routes varied, but they were all headed in the same direction. Are the Arab states the last wagon train to democracy? Or is there something that sets them apart? Are they headed in another direction? Or have their wheels come off, leaving them forever stuck in place?

These are questions to which few Americans—and few American governments—have usually given much thought. But that changed along with so much else on September 11, 2001. Recognizing that a war against terrorism could not be won solely on the battlefield, the United States looked to remove terrorism's underlying causes. To some, such as United Nations Secretary General Kofi Annan, the chief cause is poverty. But for the administration of President George W. Bush, it is tyranny. As the president put it in his address at London's Whitehall Palace in November 2003: "Democracy, and the hope and progress it brings, [are] the alternative to instability and to hatred and terror. We cannot rely exclusively on military power to assure our long term security. Lasting peace is gained as justice and democracy advance. In democratic and successful societies, men and women do not swear allegiance to malcontents and murderers; they turn their hearts and labor to building better lives. And democratic governments do not shelter terrorist camps."

Accordingly, Bush set the goal of spreading democracy to the Middle East as a way to drain the fever swamps in which terrorism breeds. As the president has explicitly acknowledged, his initiative constitutes a break with 60 years of American foreign policy. Until recently, the Middle East had been regarded as exotic and forbidding; Washington's view was that, as long as it pumped oil, the United States had little interest in trying to change the region's ways. Now America is betting its security on its ability to overhaul Arab political culture.

Is this a fool's errand? Are the Arabs capable of democracy? And if so, can Americans be the agents of their transformation? The answer, of course, is that no one knows. The lack of a single democratic Arab government gives grounds for skepticism. The claim that something in Arab culture makes it resistant to democracy cannot be refuted until the first Arab democracy comes into being. But there is reason to be skeptical of the skepticism.

MISTAKEN ASSUMPTIONS

Similar doubts have been expressed in the past about a host of countries and cultures where today democracy seems very much part of the norm. When Mussolini snuffed out Italian democracy in 1922, the historian Arnold Toynbee wrote: "The vague and abstract Greek word 'democracy' by which this peculiar institution of the medieval kingdom of England and its political offspring had come to be known, slurred over the fact that parliamentarism was a special local growth which could not be guaranteed to acclimatize itself in alien soil."

After democracy fell in Italy, it collapsed in countries across southern and eastern Europe, almost all with Roman Catholic majorities. The notion took hold that democracy was congruent only with Protestantism. Catholicism, so it was said with perfect sociological logic, teaches its adherents obedience and hierarchy, and it has an infallible ruler at its head. Only Protestantism, with its belief in an unmediated relationship between the believer and God, fosters the kind of egalitarian habits of thought that democracy requires. Today more than 90 percent of countries where Catholics predominate have democratically chosen governments.

Toward the end of World War II, President Harry Truman received a briefing about what the United States could hope to do with Japan once the imperial power had been defeated. The briefer was Joseph Grew, the State Department's leading authority on Japan who had been America's ambassador to the country until the war broke out. Grew instructed the president that "from the long range point of view, the best we can hope for is a constitutional monarchy, experience having shown that democracy in Japan would never work."

Similar ideas were aired about India's capacity for democratic self government prior to its independence and about democracy's supposed dissonance with Confucian culture in the days before Taiwan and South Korea became democratic. (Today, ironically, the political success of these two Asian "tigers" is often explained by their remarkable economic growth, but a couple of generations ago when they were desperately poor their poverty, too, was sometimes explained by reference to the habits instilled by "Confucian culture.")

Indeed, within living memory, it used to be argued that large numbers of Americans were not ready for self government. U.S. Senator Strom Thurmond suggested in a 1957 address to the Harvard Law School: "Many Negroes simply lack sufficient political consciousness to spur them on to participate in political and civic affairs . . . [A] great number of those who lack this political consciousness probably also lack certain other qualities prerequisite to casting a truly intelligent ballot." A generation later, Thurmond's spokesmen liked to boast that he was the first Southern senator to hire a Negro as a professional aide.

In light of this history of misjudging the readiness of Negroes or Confucians or Hindus or Roman Catholics for democracy, how much weight should be given today to analyses that find something in Islamic culture that does not mesh with democracy? To be sure, the Muslim world lags in this respect. Only nine (20 percent) of the predominantly Muslim countries have elected governments. Still, these nine—Turkey, Albania, Bangladesh, Indonesia, Nigeria, Mali, Senegal, Niger, Djibouti—prove that democracy is possible in a majority Muslim country.

SOMETHING ABOUT THE ARABS?

Could it be that something particular to the Arab world makes it especially allergic to democracy or incapable of practicing it? As I have said, it is impossible to refute this supposition categorically until we have our first functioning Arab democracy. But two pieces of evidence inspire confidence that that day is not far off. First, the world has seen an Arab democracy, namely Lebanon. From the time of its independence around the end of World War II until the mid 1970s, Lebanon was essentially democratic. It was an odd democracy, to be sure, with offices carefully parceled out to the various religious and ethnic groups that make up the national mosaic, but the government rested on elections, free debate, and parliamentary give and take. Foreign intervention by Palestinians, Israelis, and Syrians destroyed this relatively successful system. Today Lebanon remains a Syrian suzerainty, but for roughly three decades it afforded a glimpse of Arab democracy.

Second, increasingly forceful voices can be heard within the Arab world urging democratization. These include not only dissidents such as Egypt's Saad Edin Ibrahim but also members of ruling governments. The kings of Jordan and Morocco have taken steps toward democratization, as have the rulers of most of the small Persian Gulf states. Perhaps most important, a team of several dozen Arab scholars from many countries working under the auspices of the United Nations issued the *Arab Human Development Report* in 2002. This report, which decried three "deficits" in the Arab world—freedom, knowledge, and women's participation—created a sensation that had not yet abated when the authors struck again. They issued a second report in October 2003 elaborating on the knowledge deficit and linking it directly to the absence of "social and individual freedoms." The authors also announced that two more reports are in the works, each to focus on one of the other "deficits."

The two reports point to numerous indicators of social development in which the Arab states have lagged badly. Could it be that their relative poverty accounts for the lack of democracy? It has been well established, at least since the publication of Seymour Martin Lipset's *Political Man* in 1960, that democracy is highly correlated with economic development and other benefits that flow from it, such as literacy. Perhaps the Arabs cannot be democratic until they advance further economically? One problem with this supposition is that the wealthiest of the major Arab countries is Saudi Arabia, which is also arguably the farthest from democracy. Another is that democracy has gained considerable footholds in sub-Saharan Africa, which is on the whole far poorer than the Arab world. What appears to be lacking is political change itself, not some precursor.

FOMENTING DEMOCRACY

This leads to the question of whether America can be the instigator of that change. Intuitively, since democracy means self-rule, it would seem that this is something people must do for themselves, not something that can be introduced by outsiders. But history contradicts this intuition. America, the first modern democracy, has been a powerful engine spreading democracy elsewhere. At its most active, America has done this by force of arms; at its most passive, simply by setting an example from which others have borrowed. In between these two extremes, the

United States has intervened on behalf of democracy by nonviolent means: with diplomacy, foreign aid, international broadcasting, and even covert political manipulations.

Germany, Japan, and other members of the Axis alliance of World War II are democracies today thanks to U.S. military occupation. The states of the former Soviet bloc are mostly democracies in part because of American efforts to undermine Soviet power. U.S. broadcasting that kept truth and hope alive behind the iron Curtain and U.S. financial and technical assistance that aided the transition from communism also contributed to this outcome. The states of Latin America are almost all democracies in part because of diplomatic pressures by the Carter and Reagan administrations that delegitimated military dictators. Much the same can be said of the Philippines, South Korea, and Taiwan.

To foment democracy in the Middle East, overthrowing the regime of Saddam Hussein was a good start. His was the most entrenched, recalcitrant, murderous, and dangerous of the Arab tyrannies. And historically Iraq stands second only to Egypt as a pole of influence in the Arab world. If U.S. efforts to implant democracy in Iraq take hold, as they did so successfully elsewhere in the post–World War II occupations, this will greatly encourage democrats in the other Arab countries. And it will greatly increase the pressure for concessions felt by their rulers. It will have just as much effect on neighboring Iran, not an Arab country but one that significantly influences and is influenced by its Arab neighbors. The replacement of Iran's theocracy by a genuine democracy would also reverberate loudly across the region.

Beyond the mission in Iraq, it is not likely that subsequent U.S. moves to spur democracy will consist of military measures. What impelled the use of force in Iraq was the combination of the threat that America felt—Iraq's long history of developing and using weapons of mass destruction, its support for various terrorist groups, its aggression against neighbors—and the belief that there was no other way to achieve regime change given Saddam's ultra-repressive methods. The other nondemocratic regimes of the Middle East seem either less threatening or (in the case of Iran, which outdistances Saddam's Iraq in its nuclear programs and support for terrorists) more susceptible to change by other methods.

Outside of Iraq, America will use such nonmilitary methods as diplomatic pressure, foreign aid, increased international radio and television broadcasting, and direct assistance to democracy advocates. By these means it will try to foster a regional tide of democratization that will bring the Middle East into sync with the rest of the world.

A dramatic revolution in the methods by which people are governed has taken place this past 30 years. In this brief span of time, the proportion of states ruled by governments elected (in meaningful, competitive elections) by their citizens has gone from less than one-third to nearly two-thirds. Democracy, or at least its rudiments, has suddenly become the norm—a norm that one day will extend to the Arab world.

The United States has had frustratingly little success in fostering the development of democracy in the Middle East. According to a recent study, of the 16 Arab countries in the region, not one qualifies as even a partial democracy. The Arab-Muslim Middle East, moreover, is the only part of the world that has become *less* free over the last 30 years. In fact, democracy scholars Daniel Brumberg and Larry Diamond have concluded that the past record "does not provide fertile ground for optimism about the democratic prospect in the Middle East."* Beneath all this, many observers believe, lies the stubborn resistance of entrenched elites unwilling to reform their governments, as is the case in Saudi Arabia and other oil-rich states.

Multiple and varied attempts have been made during the years to batter down the walls that exclude democracy from the Middle East. Sanctions, embargoes, and exile from the international community have all been tried, but to no avail. Threats and even armed interventions have similarly come to nothing; in nations like Afghanistan and Iraq, such actions have actually proven to be somewhat counterproductive. Initiating change through enhanced military aid and tighter business ties has failed as well.

Yet, there is some reason for optimism. In the next article, Steven A. Cook claims that the failures of the past do not necessarily mean that democracy has no hope of a home in the Middle East. Remedies exist. Cook writes that "the old approach is broken. It's time for a fix." The author's prescription is a simple one: the United States must lead the way in providing new and abundant financial incentives to Middle Eastern nations willing to commit to serious democratization programs. Cook, in short, advocates "buying" democratic reform in places where there is a desperate need for both money and democracy.

NOTES

* Larry Diamond, Marc F. Plattner, and Daniel Brumberg, eds., *Islam and Democracy in the Middle East* (Baltimore: The Johns Hopkins University Press, 2003), xxvi.

The Right Way to Promote Arab Reform
STEVEN A. COOK

LEARNING HOW TO HELP

Since taking office four years ago, President George W. Bush has often spoken of the need for political reform in the Arab world. Ordinary Arabs, however, have had good reason to be skeptical of his much discussed "forward strategy of freedom in the Middle East." After all, their region has been mired in political stasis for years, thanks in part to U.S. support for many of the Middle East's dictators. For most of the last five decades, Washington has done little to promote Arab democratization, relying instead on the autocratic leaders of Egypt, Saudi Arabia, and other countries to help protect vital U.S. interests in the neighborhood.

This skepticism, however, may no longer be warranted. On the morning of September 11, 2001, U.S. priorities in the Middle East changed. Suddenly, the Bush administration came to see democratization, which it had previously ranked below security and stability in its list of concerns for the Arab world, as the critical means by which to achieve these other goals. Indeed, the toppling of the World Trade Center and the attack on the Pentagon fundamentally shifted the underlying assumption of U.S. Middle East policy. Arab authoritarianism could no longer be viewed as a source of stability; instead, it was the primary threat to it. To "drain the swamp" that had incubated Islamist radicals such as Osama bin Laden, it became critical to promote political liberalization, even democratization, in the Middle East, and this goal became a central feature of U.S. national security policy.

Even before this shift, Washington had already begun to try to promote reform in the Middle East—albeit quietly, and never with anything like Bush's rhetorical zeal or fixation on democracy. The United States had, in recent years, pursued three different approaches toward the Arab world: punishing its enemies with diplomatic isolation, sanctions, and invasion; bolstering civil society; and promoting economic development in friendly states. Assuming that these last two tactics would gently drive political liberalization, the United States funded good-governance programs in Egypt, promoted industrial zones in Jordan, and provided various forms of economic assistance to the Palestinian Authority and, more recently, Yemen.

Unfortunately, none of these policies proved very effective, and the failure of the United States to generate political reform in the Arab world before now should serve as a source of caution. Washington's poor track record, however, must not dissuade U.S. policymakers from trying again; the cost would simply be too high. Although the process may be difficult and fraught with risk, promoting the rise of liberal democratic political systems in the Arab world is the only way to reduce, over the long run, the odds of another attack on Americans by Middle Eastern terrorists. It is time, therefore, for Washington to refocus on the challenge: How can it best foster an environment in the Middle East that is conducive to reform? And how can it do so without sacrificing its key interests?

To answer these questions, U.S. policymakers need first to consider what exactly hinders Arab political development, and then to think about what will convince Arab leaders to change. As they build a new strategy, one principle should guide U.S. leaders: punitive policies have proven, time and again, to be of limited value or even counterproductive. Washington needs, instead, to adopt an incentive-based approach, one that will lead Arab countries to fundamentally revise their institutions.

ERRONEOUS ASSUMPTIONS

If the United States hopes to craft a more successful prodemocracy strategy for the Middle East, U.S. officials will have to abandon two central tenets of their past and present approach: reliance on civil society and pressure for economic reform, both of which, it has long been thought, contribute to democratization in authoritarian states.

"Civil society" is political science shorthand for private voluntary groups, including nongovernmental organizations dedicated to issues such as human rights and good governance. Within both the scholarly and policy communities, civil society is often seen these days as a leading force for democratization. As such groups proliferate, the argument runs, individuals become more assertive in demanding their political rights. Once these demands reach a certain pitch, authoritarian leaders are forced to make meaningful changes or risk being swept away. The policy implications of this theory are neat and tidy: to encourage liberalization in repressive states, simply encourage the growth of civil society.

This philosophy has, in fact, been the lodestar of U.S. democratization policy toward the Middle East for some time. One of the primary goals of the Middle East Partnership Initiative (MEPI), launched by the Bush administration in 2002, is to "strengthen democratic practices and civil society." Throughout the 1990s, in addition to providing much-needed technical and economic assistance to friendly Arab countries, the U.S. Agency for International Development (USAID) pursued programs to encourage the development of civic groups in Egypt, Jordan, and the Palestinian territories. Federally funded U.S. organizations such as the National Democratic Institute and the International Republican Institute also worked hard to do the same.

The U.S. faith in civil society dates from the end of the Cold War, when such groups played a major role in toppling communist regimes in the Soviet Union and Eastern Europe. Unfortunately, however, there is little evidence to suggest that such groups are likely to play a similar role in the Arab world today. To begin with, although many Arab countries are already awash in civic organizations (according to one study conducted in the late 1990s, Egypt alone boasts some 19,000 of them), these countries remain oppressive. Civil society in Arab countries may provide critical social services, such as medical care, education, and legal representation, but many of the groups involved, such as those affiliated with radical Islamist movements, are decidedly undemocratic. Others have proven too willing to cooperate with local nondemocratic regimes: Egyptian human rights activists, for example, serve on the government-created Egyptian National Council for Human Rights, which has no power to compel the government to change its predatory practices and serves only as window dressing. Likewise, in Algeria, Syria, Tunisia, and other Arab countries, labor unions and business organizations enjoy government patronage in return for collaboration with the state.

Washington's effort to promote democracy through civil society has run into another problem as well, one related to the United States' dismal image in the Arab world. Put simply, many local activists refuse to work with Americans. Washington's policies toward the region—from the Iraq war and the war on terrorism to its support for Israel—are so unpopular that Arab activists cannot embrace the United States, or even be seen to cooperate with it, without compromising their credibility within the communities they serve.

Washington's second major misapprehension about how to spur democracy—through economic development—stems from a confusion of correlation with causation. Economic development and democratization may in fact often go hand in hand, but this does not mean that the former causes the latter. In fact, social science research indicates that, although economic growth is critical to sustaining democracy, it is not enough to create it. Yet Washington acts as though it is: programs run by the Partnership for Progress (an initiative by the G-8 group of highly industrialized countries plus Russia to promote political change in the

Middle East), MEPI, and USAID are all predicated on the assumption that economic development produces new entrepreneurs, who inevitably demand greater political openness.

The Middle East, however, has refused to conform to this model. Whenever Arab leaders have reformed their economies—as during Egypt's much-vaunted *infitah* (opening) in the late 1970s or Algeria's version of the same in the 1980s—the result has been economic liberalization without either the institutionalization of market economies or the emergence of democracy. As expected, economic development has given rise to new classes of entrepreneurs. But these business leaders, whose fortunes have remained tied largely to the state, have been easily co-opted by local repressive regimes.

Not only have these two approaches failed to achieve the intended result in the Middle East, so have Washington's more punitive alternatives. Over the last decade, the United States has subjected Libya, Iran, and, most famously, Iraq to military, economic, and diplomatic sanctions in an effort to contain their rogue governments and, it was hoped, to compel them to alter their behavior. Although one can argue that containment stopped some problems from getting worse and even helped produce positive results in some cases (such as Libya's move away from radicalism), it cannot be said that punitive measures (short of invasion) actually resulted in any political liberalization. In fact, sanctions have tended to be counterproductive, with Saddam Hussein having been particularly adept at manipulating them to stoke nationalist resentment and rally Iraqis behind his regime.

Of course, the ultimate punitive policy instrument is war, and, as its code name suggests, "Operation Iraqi Freedom" was, among other things, intended to bring democracy to Iraq and the greater Middle East. It is far from clear, however, that the war has contributed anything to the drive for democracy in places such as Amman, Cairo, Damascus, or Riyadh. The arrival of U.S. troops in Iraq may alter the behavior of some states on the country's borders, but this does not mean that the new Iraq will somehow act as a catalyst for political liberalization and democracy in the region. In fact, as security in Iraq continues to deteriorate, many Iraqis are starting to think fondly of the benefits—such as stability and order—that a strongman can provide. With Iraq's transformation into an ostensibly liberal pluralist state growing ever bloodier, democracy—imported at the tip of an M-16 rifle—is looking less and less appealing to many Arabs.

Punitive measures have been no more successful with U.S. allies in the region. Congress, under the prodding of Representative Tom Lantos (D-Calif.), has recently considered measures such as shifting $325 million of the funds currently given to Egypt for military assistance to economic support. Rather than prompt reform, however, the proposal has caused an uproar in Cairo, with Hosni Mubarak's government portraying the measure as a cut in U.S. aid designed to weaken Egypt. (The fact that Lantos is a long-time supporter of Israel and did not propose similar cuts to Jerusalem's aid package did not help.)

INSTITUTIONALIZED

The reason that the promotion of civil society, economic development, and sanctions have not led to political reform in the Arab world is that none of them addresses the real obstacles to change in the region: flawed institutions. Institutions are the organizations, arrangements, laws, decrees, and regulations that constitute the political rules of the game in any given society. Contrary to conventional wisdom, Arab states boast such institutions in spades; the problem is not with their number but with their nature. In the Arab world, these institutions are designed to ensure the authoritarian character of the regimes. Rather than guarantee rights or give citizens a voice, Arab political institutions tend to restrict political participation, limit individual freedom, and vest overwhelming power in the executive branch of government.

So far, all of the discussion about Arab reform seems to have achieved more talk but not much institutional change. Minor modifications have been made, but authoritarian politics prevail throughout the Middle East. Bahrain, for example, kicked off an experiment in political liberalization in 2002. But authorities recently closed the country's leading human rights organization and jailed its leader (he was eventually released, and his organization reopened, after much political wrangling). Citizens of Qatar, meanwhile, have enjoyed greater political rights since the promulgation of a new constitution in September 2004, but that same constitution also institutionalized the absolute power of the emir and his family.

As such examples suggest, U.S. policymakers have yet to come up with a way to press such countries to liberalize their institutions. And indeed, such change is hard to effect. But it is also critical to the emergence of democratic politics in the Arab world. Washington should therefore focus on coming up with ways to make it easier for democratic politics to emerge. Although this might be easier said than done, with some creative thinking, Washington can figure out how to use its massive financial, military, and diplomatic resources to drive institutional change.

The best way to do so would be to move away from negative pressures and toward more positive, incentive-based policies. In the abstract, such policies involve getting others to do what you want by promising them something valuable in return. In this case, the United States can use the prospect of increased aid or membership in international clubs and organizations as levers to encourage Arab progress toward the establishment of pluralism, the rule of law, power sharing, property rights, and free markets.

To start the ball rolling, the United States should offer Arab states additional money, contingent on their undertaking reform. The advantage of this approach is that nothing is coerced. Countries are not forced to change—they are invited to, in exchange for serious financial rewards.

U.S. relations with Egypt—the second-largest recipient of U.S. economic and military aid—were once based on this principle. In 1978, Washington promised Cairo that if Egypt would make peace and normalize relations with Israel, the United States would underwrite the modernization of Egypt's armed forces and economy. Egypt complied, and ever since, it has technically upheld its end of the bargain by keeping the peace—albeit a frosty one—with Israel. The United States, however, should demand more for its money. Even as Washington continues to send Cairo billions of dollars annually, Egyptian-Israeli relations have deteriorated precipitously (although they have improved somewhat since the death of Yasir Arafat). And such aid has become institutionalized: the $2.2 billion Egypt gets each year has morphed from an incentive for the Egyptians to maintain good relations with Israel into a vested bureaucratic and legislative interest.

Elsewhere in the Arab world, Bahrain, Jordan, Morocco, and, more recently, Algeria and Yemen have enjoyed U.S. support without being asked to make any reciprocal commitment to the United States. Some policy experts have argued that Washington cannot afford to put conditions on these gifts: to do so would jeopardize key U.S. priorities in the region, such as access to the Suez Canal, Riyadh's general cooperation, and Amman's constructive role in Arab-Israeli peacemaking. But this argument underestimates the importance of the United States to the countries in question. Washington's Arab friends need it as much as, if not more than, the United States needs them. Could Cairo really afford to deny U.S. warships transit through the Suez Canal?

Precisely because the United States is the predominant foreign power in the Middle East—and because the Arab states have no alternative ally—Washington is well positioned to implement new incentive-based policies. Apart from Egypt, other strong precedents exist to show just how effective such an approach can be. In the 1990s, for example, the United States employed incentives to encourage Ukraine to abandon the nuclear weapons it had inherited from the Soviet Union. Washington promised Kiev economic aid, investment, joint research and development programs, and a guaranteed share of the space-launch market if the latter would create credible export-control mechanisms for sensitive materials and technologies, cancel its plans to upgrade its missiles, and renege on an agreement to supply Iran's nuclear program; Ukraine, eager for Western aid, quickly complied.

Perhaps the best example of a successful incentive-based approach is with Turkey, which has long sought to join the European Union. When Turkey petitioned the EU for membership, Brussels responded by setting clear political, economic, legal, and social standards for Ankara to meet first. The huge benefits offered by EU membership created a vast constituency for reform in Turkey. As a result, the Turkish parliament has been able to pass eight reform packages in the last three years. Turkey's Islamists have come to support the program, which they see as their best chance for securing formal political protections. The Islamists have cleverly recognized that, since the EU demands that its members institutionalize freedom of religion, Turkey, to become a candidate, will have to loosen government control on religious expression and Islamist political participation. Meanwhile, Turkey's long-dominant military has also signed on to the reform project. Although some of the changes demanded by Brussels will reduce the military's influence, Turkey's general staff has realized that it cannot oppose the project without looking like an enemy of modernization—something the inheritors of Mustafa Kemal Atatürk's legacy cannot afford.

MORE HONEY, LESS VINEGAR

Of course, the United States cannot offer the Arab world anything equivalent to EU membership. Still, it is important for U.S. policymakers to recognize how effective Brussels' approach to Ankara—based almost exclusively on incentives—has been.

The Bush administration has, in fact, already embraced a more honey-than-vinegar approach to democracy promotion through the Millennium Challenge Account (MCA). This initiative, announced in 2003, promises to reward poor countries with increased aid if they meet 16 different standards on issues ranging from good governance, the rule of law, and public education to health care and economic transparency. The MCA has the potential to become a powerful new tool for promoting democracy in the Middle East and beyond. But Washington has yet to emphasize the program or to apply it systematically to countries in the Middle East.

Here again, the Bush administration should draw lessons from the Turkey-EU story. Although Washington cannot offer Arab countries membership in its own exclusive club, the United States does have a number of bilateral and multilateral policy levers it could use. Such a new approach would not require major new financial investment. It would, however, demand a significant amount of political will.

On the bilateral front, Washington should start by reconfiguring its military assistance to Egypt. Given the importance of this largesse, changes in how it is disbursed would put serious pressure on Cairo. At the moment, Egypt gets $1.3 billion from the United States each year for its military. This money comes with no strings attached. To help jump-start reform, Washington should actually up the offer to $2 billion. Of this amount, $1.3 billion, or the current total, would remain free from any conditions. But to get the extra $700 million, Cairo would have to embrace a range of reforms, ensuring, for example, greater transparency, government accountability, and wider political inclusion. This would give Egypt strong incentives to comply—especially since Cairo's aid package, which has remained constant for 26 years, has actually decreased by more than half when adjusted for inflation; $700 million more per year would go a long way toward rebalancing the figure. Such a program would offer a number of benefits both to the United States and to Egypt. First, restructuring U.S. military assistance in this manner would safeguard U.S. interests in the region by helping ensure that Egypt's military becomes technologically advanced and capable. Second, this new way of doing business would give Egyptians a more dignified role in their relationship with the United States: Cairo would be encouraged to undertake reform, but the ultimate choice would be theirs. Moreover, putting subtle pressure on the Egyptian leadership to reform will bolster U.S. credibility with the Egyptian public and help assuage general Arab skepticism toward Washington—which has long talked about political progress in the region while doing painfully little to make it happen.

Reconfiguring the U.S. aid package to Egypt would also reduce the risk of a rift developing between the two countries. Relations between Washington and Cairo have been strained in recent years by the war on terrorism, the invasion of Iraq, and the Arab-Israeli conflict. Cutting military aid now, as some have suggested—or even transforming military aid into economic assistance—would create a serious backlash in Cairo that could lead to a major break. Washington could ill afford such an event: Egypt can often be a fractious ally, but the pursuit of U.S. interests in the Middle East would become immeasurably more difficult if the Egyptian leadership decided to actively oppose them.

In the multilateral arena, the United States could offer to sponsor Arab participation in clubs such as the World Trade Organization (WTO), NATO's Partnership for Peace, or a new Community of

Democracies—if, that is, Arab states first agreed to conduct serious political liberalization and economic reform. With the WTO, for example, the United States, in concert with its European allies, could require potential Arab members to embrace specific reforms—beyond what the WTO already requires—in return for U.S. and European support for their candidacies. Such reforms might include changes to electoral and political party laws to broaden participation, or penal code reform that would improve human rights by guaranteeing due process and instituting safeguards against torture. Arab leaders might complain that this requirement is unfair: after all, no one put such conditions on China, with its deplorable human rights record, when it joined the WTO. Like it or not, however, Arab leaders would retain the choice of whether to comply or not.

To be realistic, there are limits to what incentive-based policies can achieve. Offering new military aid will be more effective with Egypt and Jordan than with Morocco or Saudi Arabia, for example. Saudi Arabia needs the money much less and has such a critical strategic position that it can better resist pressure from the United States. As for Morocco, it is one of the few Arab states that has a viable alternative to the United States as a patron: Europe.

Consequently, U.S. policymakers interested in pursuing an incentive based approach with such countries will need to look to other areas where the United States can leverage its influence to encourage political and economic change. In the Saudi case, the answer might be a free trade agreement or a U.S. promise to sponsor Saudi membership in a variety of international organizations.

Caveats aside, the fact remains that incentives are a critical—and critically underused—tool for effecting reform and spurring democratization in the Arab world. Current U.S. policy is based on a mix of defective assumptions: about the role of civil society, about the transformative effect of economic development, and about the efficacy of punitive policies to force change. If it is serious about finally spurring progress in the Middle East, the United States needs to focus more explicitly on political targets and embrace a more positive set of means. An incentive-based approach offers a more coherent, less intrusive, and ultimately more promising strategy toward the Arab world. As the attacks of September 11 showed, the old approach is broken. It's time for a fix.

Reprinted by permission of FOREIGN AFFAIRS, (March/April 2005). Copyright 2007 by the Council on Foreign Relations, Inc.

Perhaps the greatest gamble in the overall plans for bringing democracy to the Middle East is in expecting collaboration from authoritarian regimes. Historically, they have proven to be resistant to change, but the West is increasingly relying on undemocratic governments that at most, according to a writer in *Middle East Times*, "are prepared to consider some reforms so long as power is not given to the people."* The fate of democracy, then, is at least partly in the hands of autocrats with no incentive to reform and a vested interest in maintaining the status quo.

It is risky to wager that strongmen, dictators, and oligarchs will put themselves out of work for the sake of liberty and freedom, but Daniel Brumberg contends that it is a risk that must be taken. Brumberg claims that the regimes the West seeks to change are far less secure in their dominance than one would imagine. Autocracies from Saudi Arabia to Iran seem deaf to calls for democracy, but in reality they are under intense pressure, from within and without, to liberalize. As these leaderships make essentially cosmetic changes in their political and social policies, Brumberg writes, opportunities for real reform will materialize. Such openings might be fleeting, but, according to him, they can be exploited. The key is for the West, led by the United States, to press democracy's case harder. The world's established democracies, in Brumberg's opinion, must not allow the Middle East's autocratic states to halt their progress at the point of liberalization. They must push these regimes over the crest toward genuine democracy. If the West eases its pressure, it would indeed fall into the trap of accepting liberalized autocracy, while deeper and more lasting change is the goal.

NOTES

*   Abe W. Ata, "Opinion: Western Democracy Stillborn in Mideast." *Middle East Times*, 13 June 2005. Available online at http://www.metimes.com/print.php?StoryID=20050613-073346-9623r. Accessed November 27, 2006.

The Trap of Liberalized Autocracy
DANIEL BRUMBERG

Over the past two decades, the Middle East has witnessed a "transition" away from—and then back toward—authoritarianism. This dynamic began with tactical political openings whose goal was to sustain rather than transform autocracies. Enticed by the prospect of change, an amalgam of political forces—Islamists, leftists, secular liberals, NGO activists, women's organizations, and others—sought to imbue the political process with new meanings and opportunities, hoping that the "inherently unstable" equilibrium of *dictablandas* would give way to a new equilibrium of competitive democracy.[1]

It is now clear, both within and far beyond the Middle East, that liberalized autocracy has proven far more durable than once imagined.[2] The trademark mixture of guided pluralism, controlled elections, and selective repression in Egypt, Jordan, Morocco, Algeria, and Kuwait is not just a "survival strategy" adopted by authoritarian regimes, but rather a *type* of political system whose institutions, rules, and logic defy any linear model of democratization.[3] And while several of the authors who write about the Middle East in this issue of the *Journal of Democracy* argue that political liberalization is moving forward, Jillian Schwedler's essay on Yemen and Jason Brownlee's article on Egypt—as well as the recent experience of Jordan—suggest that in fact *deliberalization* may be underway.

Perhaps these states will join the ranks of Bashar Assad's Syria, where the door was opened a crack and then quickly closed, and countries such as Iraq, Tunisia, and Saudi Arabia, where the rulers have never risked even the most controlled liberalization. Certainly, the outrageous August 2002 decision of Egypt's Supreme Court to uphold the conviction of Saad Eddin Ibrahim and his young colleagues appears to support the notion that Middle East regimes are becoming less rather than more autocratic. Yet what we are witnessing is probably *not* a return to full authoritarianism, but rather the latest turn in a protracted cycle in which rulers widen or narrow the boundaries of participation and expression in response to what they see as the social, economic, political, and geostrategic challenges facing their regimes. Such political eclecticism has benefits that Arab rulers are unlikely to forgo. Indeed, over the next few years Bahrain and Qatar may swell the ranks of Arab regimes dwelling in the "gray zone" of liberalized autocracy.[4]

In the Arab world, a set of interdependent institutional, economic, ideological, social, and geostrategic factors has created an adaptable ecology of repression, control, and partial openness. The weblike quality of this political ecosystem both helps partial autocracies to survive and makes their rulers unwilling to give up *final* control over any strand of the whole. But there is more to the story than wily rulers and impersonal "factors," for the governments of Algeria, Morocco, Jordan, Kuwait, and even Egypt receive a degree of acquiescence and sometimes even support from both secular and some Islamist opposition groups. Such *ententes* can take the form of arrangements that give oppositionists a voice in parliament or even the cabinet, and may also involve a process of "Islamization" by which the state cedes some ideological and institutional control to Islamists.

This ironic outcome reminds us that while liberalized autocracies can achieve a measure of stability, over time their very survival exacts greater and greater costs. Because they have failed to create a robust *political* society in which non-Islamists can secure the kind of organized popular support that Islamists command, these hybrid regimes have created circumstances under which free elections could well make illiberal Islamists the dominant opposition voice, leaving democrats (whether secularist or Islamist) caught between ruling autocrats and Islamist would-be autocrats. Hence the great dilemma in which substantive democratization and genuine pluralism become at once more urgently needed and more gravely risky.

While the solution to this dilemma may lie in gradualism, any reforms worthy of the name must address the weakness or even absence of political society in the Arab world. This will mean promoting independent judiciaries; effective political parties; competitive, internationally observed elections; and legislatures that represent majorities rather than rubber-stamp the edicts of rulers. Such changes will demand bold initiatives from Arab rulers, as well as U.S. readiness to support a policy of democratic gradualism whose purpose is to help liberalized autocracies carefully move beyond the politics of mere survival.

While it is true that the Arab world boasts no democracies, some of its autocracies are decidedly less complete than others. To understand this variation, and to grasp why some partial autocracies are better than others at sustaining survival strategies, we must ask how the rulers perceive the threats they face, and we must look at the institutional, social, political, and ideological conditions that tend to intensify or reduce such threats. The importance of threat perception lies in the very logic of partial autocracies: To endure, they must implicitly or explicitly allow some opposition forces certain kinds of social, political, or ideological power—

but things must never reach a point where the regime feels deterred from using force when its deems fit. If a regime can keep up this balancing act, reformists within the government will find it easier to convince hard-liners that the benefits of accommodation outweigh the costs. Conversely, where it is hard to make this case, rulers will prefer total autocracy. As to the conditions that encourage a choice in favor of one or the other, these can be summarized as follows: States that promote competitive or *dissonant* politics will tend to feel surer that Islamist ambitions can be limited and so will be more willing to consider accommodating opposition, while states that promote hegemonic or *harmonic* politics will tend to invite more radical "counterhegemonic" Islamist opposition movements whose presence increases the expected cost of political liberalization.

THE DEAD END OF HEGEMONY

Iraq, Saudi Arabia, and Syria are total autocracies whose endurance is often attributed to three conditions, each of which bears a word of comment. The first, oil money, is necessary but not sufficient: Some other Arab countries receive oil income but are not *total* autocracies. The second condition is the "harmonic" foundation of legitimacy: Total autocracies spread the idea that the state's mission is to defend the supposedly unified nature of the Arab nation or the Islamic community (the danger that Islamists might "outbid" the regime on the second score should be obvious). The third condition is the hegemonic reach of state institutions: Total autocracies create powerful organizations whose main job is to absorb or repress rival political voices. Here too there is a potential danger for the regime. As the ambivalent alliance between the House of Saud and the Wahabi religious establishment shows, state control of Islamic institutions is both central to this hegemonic strategy and a threat to it. Because Islam is a transcendent religion that can never be fully coopted, governments must cede some autonomy to state-supported religious institutions or elites, thereby raising the prospect that elements of the religious establishment could defect to the Islamist opposition.

To deter this and all other possible rebellions, total autocracies have large and brutal security agencies. Yet the more force is used, the longer grows the list of revenge-seeking enemies—a drawback that is especially acute when the rulers belong to ethnic or religious minorities (in Syria, Alawites; in Iraq, Sunni Arabs). Harmonic ideologies and their pretenses of "Islamic" or "Arab" unity may aspire to hide such narrow power bases, but the reality of minority rule is apparent enough, further alienating key religious groups and making the expected costs of reform that much higher.

One way out of this vicious circle might be to emphasize instrumental over symbolic legitimacy—by handing out more oil rents to key groups, for instance. Such strategies have obvious limits. An alternative (or complementary) approach is to rob your neighbor's bank, as Iraq tried to do by invading Kuwait in 1990. But barring such desperate measures, some leaders might conclude that a limited political opening is worth the risk. After all, what value is there in maintaining decades of hegemonic rule if the instruments of domination cannot be used to ensure the ruling elite's continued good health?

This was certainly the motive behind Algeria's dramatic political opening in 1989. At the time, Algeria was a classic harmonic state. For nearly 30 years, its generals and ruling-party hacks had been absorbing all potential opposition into a quasi-socialist order that celebrated the alleged harmony of "the Algerian people." Islamic leaders and institutions were drafted into this hegemonic project, thereby ironically ensuring that, in the wake of liberalization, populist Islam would emerge as *the* counterhegemonic force. The Islamic Salvation Front (FIS) and its revolutionary—if nebulous—vision of an Islamic state galvanized an estranged generation which had come to believe that the rhetoric of unity spouted by the ruling National Liberation Front (FLN) was mere window-dressing for the corrupt rule of a minority that was more French than Arab, or more Berber than Muslim. Despite this growing estrangement, in 1991 the FLN foolishly wagered that it could reproduce its hegemony through competitive elections. While a proportional system might have limited the FIS's electoral gains and thus made some kind of power sharing possible, the FIS's revolutionary ideology created so grave a perceived threat that no such arrangement could likely have survived the military's quest for total certainty, or the preference of many secular would-be democrats for the protection that the generals promised.

This illusory quest for safety set the stage for a civil war that has claimed some 100,000 lives. In the wake of this disaster, Algeria's leaders tried to put together a power-sharing system in which the identity claims of Berbers, secularists, Islamists, and (implicitly) the military would be recognized, institutionalized, and perhaps negotiated. But the mixed system that was born with the 1997 parliamentary elections produced mixed results. It certainly provided unprecedented opportunities for elites with opposing ideologies to pursue dialogue.[5] But to give such a system credibility, regimes must promote genuine (even if circumscribed) representation, while leaders must project an understanding of the populace's elemental fears and aspirations. President Abdelaziz Bouteflika got off to a good start in 1999, but the high abstention rate in the 2002 parliamentary elections suggests that much work remains to be done if the regime is to consolidate whatever gains it can claim.

Algeria's recent experience suggests that leadership and political learning can play a role in helping regimes and oppositions to exit autocracy, but the lesson seems lost on some. Syria's brief opening is a case in point. When President Bashar Assad assumed the reigns of power from his late father in June 2000, observers wondered if the son would honor his public promises to open up the system.[6] The answer was clear by the autumn of 2001, when some liberal intellectuals were arrested for holding informal meetings to discuss democracy. Thus was the door slammed shut on the briefest Arab-world political opening to date.

What did Assad fear? His security chiefs probably convinced him that the tiniest reform was a slippery slope to oblivion. While the regime had decimated its radical Islamist opposition in 1982 by massacring 10,000 citizens in the town of Hama, and while it had coopted some businessmen from the Sunni merchant elite, a combination of economic crisis, anger at corruption, and a growing contempt for "Baathist socialist" ideology and Assad's contrived cult of personality all gave the regime reason for concern.[7] In the face of these and other worries, the new president could not pin his hopes on a few liberal intellectuals with no organized following. These knowns and unknowns, as well as the imposing shadow of his late father, proved far more relevant than Bashar's optometry studies in London or his exposure to the Internet. With oil rents still flowing in, it seems a wonder that it took so long for him to conclude that full autocracy was the only option.

While Tunisia's President Ben Ali has reached a similar conclusion, the origins of total autocracy in his country differ from those in Saudi Arabia, Iraq, or Syria. Instead of oil money and ideology, there is Ben Ali's obsession with power and the determination of business interests and the ruling elite to emulate the Asian model of state-driven, export-oriented industrialization. With a small population whose well-educated workers and professionals include a large percentage of women, Tunisia had significant constituencies *within and outside* the regime that chose not to contest the "nonideological" hegemony of the ruling Democratic Constitutional Rally (RCD). The spectacle of the bloodshed next door in Algeria helped to cement this tacit consensus against rocking the boat.

By the late 1990s, the effort to create an "Asian-style" economic miracle in North Africa had run into many obstacles, not least of which has been the regime's abuse of civil and human rights. Moreover, in the absence of accountability and the rule of law, state-driven industrialization was feeding rent-seeking and corruption.[8] By 1999 there was clearly a demand for political opening, but the voting that year ended with the RCD controlling 92 percent of the seats in the Chamber of Deputies and Ben Ali winning another term with a claimed mandate of 99.4 percent of the vote. Islamists remained banned, revealing the regime's continued anxieties about threats from that quarter. Since then, Ben Ali has rammed through a set of constitutional amendments to extend his term from four to six years and arrested human rights activists, thereby signaling his determination to maintain total power.

WHY "DISSONANCE" IS GOOD

Total autocracy is the exception rather than the rule in the Arab world. Most Arabs live under autocracies that allow a measure of openness. Three factors have generated and sustained such regimes. First, the rulers of Morocco, Egypt, Jordan, Kuwait, and Lebanon have not tried to impose a single vision of political community. Instead, they have put a certain symbolic distance between the state and society in ways that leave room for competitive or *dissonant* politics. By not nailing the state's legitimacy to the mast of one ideological vessel with a putatively sacred national or religious mission, they have helped to short-circuit the growth of counterhegemonic Islamist movements. Second, partial autocracies are *nonhegemonic*. Within limits, they allow contending groups and ideas to put down institutional roots outside the state. This ensures competition not only between Islamists and non-Islamists, but among Islamist parties as well. The more such contention there is, the likelier it is that rulers will risk an opening. Third, partial autocracies have enough economic development and competition to free the state from obsessive concern with any single interest, class, or resource. In many such regimes, for instance, one finds public-sector employees and bureaucrats vying with independent professionals and private businessmen for the state's political and economic support.

Such economic and political dissonance facilitates the juggling act that is central to regime survival. Rulers of liberalized autocracies strive to pit one group against another in ways that maximize the rulers' room for maneuver and restrict the opposition's capacity to work together. Yet such divide-and-rule tactics also give oppositionists scope for influence that they might not have in an open political competition that yields clear winners and losers. Consensus politics and state-enforced power sharing can form an alternative to either full democracy or full autocracy, particularly when rival social, ethnic, or religious groups fear that either type of rule will lead to their political exclusion. In Kuwait, Lebanon,

Jordan, Morocco, and to some extent Egypt, the peaceful accommodation of such forces depends in part on the arbitrating role of the ruler.

No ruler is completely autonomous in relation to society. The kings of Morocco and Jordan may have a better perch from which to arbitrate conflicts than do Arab presidents, whose fates are usually tied to a ruling party or its interests. But since both monarchs derive their legitimacy at least *partly* from their purported lineage ties to Mohammed, they are, as Abdeslam Maghraoui notes, at once modern leaders of a nation (*watan*) and traditional patrons of the Islamic community (*umma*). Similarly, while Egypt's rulers long ago distanced themselves from the Arab-nationalist rhetoric of Gamal Abdel Nasser, they have not fully repudiated the basic ideological premises of the populist state that he founded. The legitimacy of the Egyptian state still rests partly on its role as a defender of communal Islamic values.

That the rulers of some liberalized autocracies are both the chief arbiters within society and the major patrons of religious institutions is central to these regimes' survival strategies. As arbiters, those who hold power in Egypt, Morocco, and Jordan use cultural, religious, and ideological dissonance to divide the opposition. As patrons of religion, these same powerholders use their ties to Islamic institutions to limit the influence of secular political forces. Over time, this Islamization strategy has led to acute dilemmas. For in their efforts to coopt conservative Islamic ideas these regimes have hindered the creation of alternatives to the illiberalism that is characteristic of *mainstream* (and not merely radical) Islamism.

Consider the case of Egypt, where indulging Islamist sensibilities is an old art form. With parliamentary elections looming in the fall of 2000, the culture minister, backed by the top religious authorities at the leading state-funded Islamic university, banned the obscure Syrian Haidar Haidar's novel *A Banquet for Seaweed* on the grounds that it dangerously departed from "accepted religious understanding" and threatened "the solidarity of the nation." Having thus defended the faith, the government then shut down the very opposition newspaper that had exposed the offending book![9] However cynical, the move made perfect sense. The political party that published the paper had close ties to the mainstream Muslim Brotherhood, and the state was out to underscore its own role as the supreme arbiter of matters Islamic (for good measure, the authorities had two hundred Muslim Brothers arrested). In a stinging judgment that actually understates the problem, Max Rodenbeck observes that the cumulative effect of actions like this has been to "compel an 'orthodoxy' that is both amorphous and restricted, preventing Islamist thought from moving beyond denunciation of heresy and repetition of formulas from the Koran."[10] Even El-Wasat—a party led by Islamists who advocate a more pluralistic vision of Islam—has had its application for party certification repeatedly turned down. Egypt's rulers are not interested in promoting a liberal Islamic party, either because they fear that radicals might capture it or because they do not want a successful liberal Islamist party to ally with secular parties in ways that might undermine the regime's strategy of survival through a delicate balancing act.

Variations of this Islamization strategy can be found in other regimes which, unlike Egypt's, permit legal Islamist parties. Partial inclusion is a more useful way of buttressing liberalized autocracies because it requires Islamists to renounce violence, act openly, and most importantly, play by what are ultimately the government's rules. Yet the Islamists may reap advantages, since even limited participation in parliaments or cabinets gives them means to extend their influence. Following the 1991 unification of North and South Yemen, for example, the General People's Congress (GPC) became the ruling party by cutting a deal with the tribal-cum-Islamist Islah party, whose religious wing thereby gained control of public education. Indeed, in 1994 President Ali Abdallah Salih "gave money to Sheikh Abdel Meguid al-Zindani, an Afghan veteran and former associate of Mr. Bin Laden's, to build Al Eman University on government land near Sanaa."[11] Still, once the deal with Islah had served the purpose of marginalizing the South, the GPC engineered an election in 1997 that ushered many of Islah's Islamists out of parliament while leaving the tribal members with their seats. More recently, the government has tried in the wake of September 11 to assert more control over Islah's schools.

By comparison with other hybrid regimes, Yemen's experience is unique. While a patrimonialist vision of authority colors public education in much of the Arab world, there is little evidence that the governments of Egypt, Jordan, Morocco, and Kuwait promote a particularly radical or anti-Western vision of Islam. Yet neither do they imbue their curricula with anything like liberal democratic values. Absent such a positive effort, the state-sponsored "traditional" view of Islam (with its emphasis on state authority and the claims of community) will remain vulnerable to the allure of radical Islam. Periodic attempts to placate Islamists by unleashing state-subsidized clerics against "apostates" can produce the same result. Apart from the danger that such efforts may backfire—as they did when the ceding of the Jordanian education ministry to Islamists in 1994 provoked an uproar from liberals—over time Islamization strategies undercut the careful juggling acts at the heart of regime survival strategies.

THE NEED FOR POLITICAL SOCIETY

One way of escaping the dilemmas created by partial autocracies might be to advocate liberal Islam. But no leader has embraced this option, for obvious reasons. Liberal Islam, moreover, constitutes a limited intellectual trend that has thus far not sunk organizational roots in Arab societies. Nor have civil society organizations been able to pierce the armor of liberalized autocracy. On the contrary, in Egypt, Morocco, and Jordan the sheer proliferation of small NGOs—riven by fierce ideological divisions and hamstrung by official regulations—has made "divide and rule" easier.

By themselves, civil society organizations cannot make up for the lack of a functioning political society, meaning an autonomous realm of self-regulating political parties that have the constitutional authority to represent organized constituencies in parliaments.[12] Autocratic rulers know this, of course—their survival strategies are designed to *prevent* the emergence of any effective political society. Partial autocracies use patronage as well as laws governing parties and elections to stop opposition elites from creating organic political parties. As a result, most Arab-world political parties are better at negotiating with powerful rulers than at articulating the aspirations of each party's disorganized followers. Under such conditions, apathy reigns, while elections rarely attract more than 35 percent of the potential voting public.

As for legislatures, constitutions hobble rather than bolster their authority, as does the lack of a rule of law (which is not the same thing as a state that makes lots of laws). Such constitutions are rife with loopholes that "guarantee" freedoms of speech and assembly so long as such liberties do not infringe upon "national" or "Islamic" values. Indeed, what used to be said of the old Soviet Constitution can be said of most Arab constitutions: They guarantee freedom of speech, but not freedom *after* speech. Arab "reformers" since Anwar Sadat have been great advocates of "a state of laws," by which they have meant laws passed by compliant legislatures and upheld by compliant judges in order to legitimate the regime's survival strategies. Such laws not only inhibit democratization, they give legal sanction to forms of economic corruption that only further delegitimate the so-called capitalism of liberalized autocracies.

Because the absence or presence of political society is largely a function of official policy, it will not emerge unless Arab leaders redefine the relationship between citizen and state. Sadly, it is now clear that the new generation of leaders in Jordan and Morocco are not up to this task. Indeed, insofar as survival strategies have increased the perceived costs of democratization while not providing for effective economic development, the young kings of these lands have shown themselves unwilling or unable to cross anxious hard-liners in the military, the security forces, and the business community. Thus while Morocco's King Mohamed VI spoke early on of shifting to a "new concept of authority," he soon fell back on one of the hoariest defenses of partial autocracy, pleading lamely that "each country has to have its own specific features of democracy."[13]

"REFORM" VERSUS DEMOCRATIC GRADUALISM

If an exit from liberalized autocracy to competitive democracy is improbable, can we detect movement in the opposite direction? As noted above, events in Egypt and Yemen as well as Jordan—where there has recently been a crackdown on the press—seem to suggest that the answer is unfortunately "yes." This "deliberalizing" trend, as Jason Brownlee calls it, has at least four causes. First, there is the decline in external rents. This process has pushed regimes to adopt the kinds of structural economic reforms that they had previously skirted in their efforts to accommodate key constituencies. But such reforms have not produced enough "winners" to defend them successfully under conditions of open political competition, so rulers see a need to clamp down on previous political openings. Second, there is the growing influence of *mainstream* Islamism. Radical Islamism may be declining in some quarters of the Arab world, but Islamist movements that seek *peacefully* to advance illiberal cultural projects by playing according to the rules of partial autocracy are getting stronger.[14] Although these movements may not command electoral majorities, the disarray besetting secular democrats means that Islamists would certainly win at least powerful pluralities in any open election. Third, the failure of the Palestinian–Israeli peace process has not only given Islamists across the Arab world a powerful symbol, it has also facilitated the forging of ideologically heterogenous alliances between secularists and Islamists that rulers find increasingly threatening.[15] Finally, in the context of a U.S.-led war on terrorism that requires the support or good will of many Arab leaders, Washington has until very recently evinced a certain tolerance for democracy.

Yet past experience suggests that the deliberalizing trend we are seeing is an inflection point in a long-term cycle. Perhaps the current shift toward tightening will be more protracted than previous ones, but in the longer run rulers and oppositionists are unlikely to forgo the advantages that partial autocracy offers to both. Even in Jordan, with its volatile combination of a Palestinian majority whose most effective leaders are Islamists, a new king who is still establishing his authority, a fragile economy, and the looming prospect of a U.S.-led regional war, it is unlikely that either King Abdullah or the Islamists (who won 20 of the parliament's 50 seats in the 1999 elections) will give up a tradition of uneasy but mutually beneficial accommodation.[16]

Indeed, while Egypt and Jordan may be moving, for the time being, in a more authoritarian direction, there is some evidence that liberalized autocracies might be growing *more* rather than less common in the Middle East. As Michael Herb notes, in 1999 and 2000, respectively, the leaders of Qatar and Bahrain initiated political openings after years of full autocracy. Bahrain will hold parliamentary elections in October 2002 while Qatar will hold parliamentary elections to replace its 35-member Consultative Council in 2003.[17] Morocco, which will be holding parliamentary elections as this article goes to press in September 2002, might also expand the boundaries of liberalized autocracy by creating more space for Islamist opposition. It is not a coincidence that all these countries are monarchies. Arab monarchs have more institutional and symbolic room to improvise reforms than do Arab presidents, who are invariably trapped by ruling parties and their constituencies. That said, and as I have argued, not all monarchies are equally capable of promoting political reform. Totalizing monarchies that rule in the name of harmonic ideologies—one thinks of the House of Saud—engender radical oppositions and thus are unlikely to countenance more than the slightest opening.

As for kings who rule partial autocracies, those who serve as both arbiters of the nation and spokesmen for the Islamic community find themselves constrained by the very Islamic elites whose teachings the kings often echo or encourage. As Abdeslam Maghraoui notes, Morocco's Mohamed VI might confront this paradoxical fact of life as a result of the coming elections. If the Islamist Justice and Development party makes major gains in the upcoming election but does not overplay its hand by rejecting membership in a multiparty majority coalition that limits its ideological reach, Morocco might follow the lead of other Arab states by allowing for partial inclusion of Islamists in a mixed system. But if the Islamists score a large victory and then challenge the king's *religious* authority, Morocco's leaders may eventually decide to move toward less rather than more political openness.

There is no doubt, as Jean-François Seznec observes, that one factor pushing Arab regimes to engage in even modest political openings is that oil just does not pay the way it used to. With external rents declining, the implicit bargain by means of which rulers bought popular acquiescence in return for various forms of petroleum-funded largesse has fallen on hard times. Yet we should be careful not to lapse into structural determinism, for social, institutional, and ideological factors can raise or lower the expected costs of political change in dramatic and unexpected ways.

None of this excuses partial autocrats, of course. After all, they have embraced only such "reforms" as *hinder* the emergence of an effective political society. Moreover, because their survival strategies have often boosted Islamists rather than an expanded political arena as such, these rulers have sustained a cycle of conflict, stalemate, and reform. This makes it hard for even reformers with the best of intentions to envision a different future, and easy for the most cynical to rationalize their opposition to anything deeper than cosmetic reforms. Given the paucity of will and the imposing constraints, there is not likely to be much substantive change until the United States presses its Arab allies to transcend an involuted gradualism whose small steps trace the sad contours of an unvirtuous circle rather than the hopeful lineaments of a real path forward. Such a policy of *democratic gradualism* must not only push for the creation of effective political parties, representative parliaments, and the rule of law; it must also be accompanied by international support for effective monitoring of local and national elections. Without international observers, the silent pluralities of the Arab world—large groups of people who often have little sympathy for illiberal Islamism—will never be able to make their voices heard.

NOTES

1.   Adam Przeworski, "The Games of Transition," in Scott Mainwaring et al., eds., *Issues in Democratic Consolidation: The New South American Democracies in Comparative Perspective* (Notre Dame: Notre Dame University Press, 1992), 109. Przeworski argues that "what normally happens is . . . a melting of the iceberg of civil society which overflows the dams of the authoritarian regime." While he later observes that "liberalization could substitute for genuine democratization, thereby maintaining the political exclusion of subaltern groups" (111), the thrust of his conceptualization is that transitions move forward or back to reach a new equilibrium.

2.   Thomas Carothers, "The End of the Transition Paradigm," *Journal of Democracy* 13 (January 2002): 5–21. Carothers (9) notes that "of the nearly 100 countries considered as 'transitional' in recent years, only a relatively small number—probably fewer than 20—are clearly en route to becoming successful, well-functioning democracies or at

least have made some democratic progress and still enjoy a positive dynamic of democratization."

3. For several excellent discussions of this phenomenon see the essays in the section on "Elections Without Democracy?" by Larry Diamond, Andreas Schedler, and Steven Levitsky and Lucan Way in the April 2002 issue of the *Journal of Democracy*. These articles highlight the *exceptional* character of democratic transitions.

4. Thomas Carothers, "End of the Transition Paradigm," 9. He defines the "gray zone" as one in which regimes are "neither dictatorial nor clearly headed toward democracy."

5. The interviews that I conducted in Algiers in May and June 2002 with members of the 1997 parliament, Islamist and non-Islamist alike, suggest that political learning beyond the merely tactical level took place.

6. See Scott Peterson, "The Grooming of Syria's Bashar al-Assad," *Christian Science Monitor*, 13 June 2002; Susan Sachs, "Bashar al-Assad: The Shy Young Doctor at Syria's Helm," *New York Times*, 14 June 2000. See also "Democracy Glimpses at Syria's Parliament," 27 June 2000, Arabia.com (http://www.arabia.com/article/print/0,4973,23698,00.html).

7. Bassam Haddad, "Business as Usual in Syria?" MERIP Press Information Note 68, 7 September 2001.

8. Christopher Alexander, "Authoritarianism and Civil Society in Tunisia," *Middle East Report*, October–December 1997 (http://www.merip.org/mer/mer/mer205/alex.html.)

9. The party was the Labor Socialists and its newspaper was *Al-Shaab*, which in fact got Haidar's book wrong. See Max Rodenbeck, "Witch Hunt in Egypt," *New York Review of Books*, 16 November 2000, 39. The quotes condemning Haidar come from Al-Azhar University's Islamic Research Academy and can be found in the first note to Rodenbeck's essay.

10. Max Rodenbeck, "Witch Hunt in Egypt," 41.

11. "Yemen's Religious Academies: From Defender of the Faith to Terrorist," *Economist*, 1 June 2002, 48.

12. See Manuel Antonio Garretón and Edward Newman, eds., *Democracy in Latin American (Re)Constructing Political Society* (New York: United Nations University Press, 2001).

13. Lisa Anderson, "Arab Democracy," 55–60. Quote from page 58; originally cited in Roxanne Roberts, "Morocco's King of Hearts," *Washington Post*, 23 June 2000.

14. See Gilles Kepel, *Jihad: Expansion et déclin de l'islamisme* (Paris: Gallimard, 2002).

15. See Dina Shehata, "The International Dimensions of Authoritarianism: The Case of Egypt," paper presented at the Annual Meeting of the American Political Science Association, Boston, 28–30 August 2002.

16. Citing the current political situation in the region, King Abdullah has once again postponed parliamentary elections, which were scheduled for the fall of 2002. It should be noted that the elections were first supposed to be held in November but were postponed because of the second Intifada. Clearly, the failure of the peace process has reinforced the regime's fears about the consequences of further liberalization.

17. The recent decision by the main opposition groups in Bahrain to boycott the parliamentary elections due to the government's failure to address concerns over the narrow boundaries of political reform indicates that a transition to liberalized autocracy is far from inevitable.

Brumberg, Daniel. The Trap of Liberalized Autocracy. Journal of Democracy 13:4 (2002), 56–68. © National Endowment for Democracy and The Johns Hopkins University Press. Reprinted with permission of The Johns Hopkins University Press.

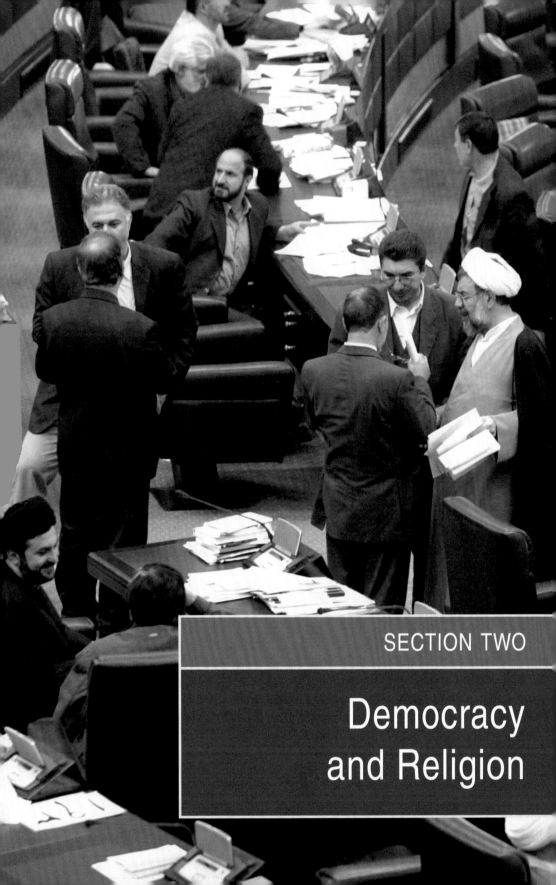

Democracy and Religion

The question of whether or not Islam and democracy are compatible is contentious and by no means easily answered. The first step toward an answer, however, would seem to lie in crafting historical definitions of both terms. One must determine, for example, how Muslims have viewed the West and democracy, over at least the last century or so, and how Islam has tended to respond to Western ideas and influences more generally. It would also be useful to compare Islam and Christianity in terms of how each dealt with the challenges of reconciling religion and politics within the different cultural environments of Europe and the Middle East. The theory and operation of democracy merit examination as well. What is democracy? How has it changed? What does it mean to the people who accept it as the social and political norm? These questions need to be answered before democracy can be recommended to non-democratic states.

Comprehending the historical and ideological details of democracy promises to be heavy work, but it will be a far easier assignment for Westerners than fathoming Islam's depths. Islam, it can be said without exaggeration, created the Arab world as it is known today. If one excludes Israel, Islam *is* the Middle East. More than a set of religious tenets, Islam is a social, political, and cultural force arguably without equal anywhere. Having shaped the history of a large part of the globe, Islam needs to be understood clearly; it certainly cannot be ignored when it comes time to discuss democracy's overall prospects in the Middle East. What has been said about the Prophet Muhammad could readily be applied to Islam as a whole: it exerts a "powerful influence ... over the hearts and imaginations" of all who embrace it.[*]

Bernard Lewis encourages his audience to explore the histories of both Islam and democracy. As a starting point, he provides readers with a brief introduction to the relationship between the two in the following essay. Lewis asks that one looks beyond stereotypes, biases, and glib assumptions. He cautions that democracy and Islam must be examined together in a search for points of intersection as well as divergence. Can Islam and democracy meld, thus creating a new political framework in the Middle East? Perhaps, Lewis argues, but such a synthesis will take time. Change will come, he asserts, and it will be real, but the prerequisite is at least a passing knowledge of the forces at work.

NOTES

[*]   Allama Sir Abdullah Al-Mamun Al-Suhrawardy, *The Wisdom of Muhammad* (New York: Citadel Press, 2001).

A Historical Overview
Bernard Lewis

In a necessarily brief discussion of major issues, it is fatally easy to go astray by misuse or misinterpretation of some of the words that one uses. Therefore, I ought to say first what I mean by the terms "Islam" and "liberal democracy."

Democracy nowadays is a word much used and even more misused. It has many meanings and has turned up in surprising places—the Spain of General Franco, the Greece of the colonels, the Pakistan of the generals, the Eastern Europe of the commissars—usually prefaced by some qualifying adjective such as "guided," "basic," "organic," "popular," or the like, which serves to dilute, deflect, or even to reverse the meaning of the word.

Another definition of democracy is embraced by those who claim that Islam itself is the only authentic democracy. This statement is perfectly true, *if* one accepts the notion of democracy presupposed by those who advance this view. Since it does not coincide with the definition of democracy that I take as the basis of this discussion, I will leave it aside as irrelevant for present purposes.

The kind of democracy I am talking about is none of these. By liberal democracy, I mean primarily the general method of choosing or removing governments that developed in England and then spread among English-speaking peoples and beyond.

In 1945, the victors of the Second World War imposed parliamentary democracy on the three major Axis powers. It survives in all three, precariously, perhaps, in one. In none of them has it yet confronted any crisis of truly major proportions. Among the Allies, Britain and France bequeathed their own brands of democracy—with varying success—to their former colonies during the postwar retreat from empire.

Perhaps the best rule of thumb by which one can judge the presence of the kind of democracy I mean, is Samuel P. Huntington's dictum that you can call a country a democracy when it has made two consecutive, peaceful changes of government via free elections. By specifying *two* elections, Huntington rules out regimes that follow the procedure that one acute observer has called "one man, one vote, once." So I take democracy to mean a polity where the government can be changed by elections as opposed to one where elections are changed by the government.

Americans tend to see democracy and monarchy as antithetical terms. In Europe, however, democracy has fared better in constitutional monarchies than in republics. It is instructive to make a list of those countries in Europe where democracy has developed steadily and without interruption over a long period, and where there is every prospect that it will continue to do so in the foreseeable future. The list of such countries is short and all but one of them are monarchies. The one exception, Switzerland, is like the United States in that it is a special case due to special circumstances. In the French Republic, established by revolution more than two centuries ago, the march of democracy has been punctuated by interruptions, reverses, and digressions. In most of the other republics of Europe, and, for that matter, in the rest of the world, the record is incomparably worse.

In all this, there may be some lesson for the Middle East, where the dynastic principle is still remarkably strong. The most purely Arab and Muslim of Middle Eastern states, Saudi Arabia, derives its name and its identity from its founding and ruling dynasty. So, too, did the Ottoman Empire—the most recent and by far the most enduring of all the Islamic empires. Even such radical revolutionary leaders as Hafiz al-Assad in Syria and Saddam Hussein in Iraq endeavor to secure the succession of their sons. In a political culture where the strain of dynastic legitimacy is so strong, democracy might in some places fare better by going with it rather than against it.

What of our other term, "Islam"? It too has multiple meanings. In one sense, it denotes a religion—a system of belief, worship, doctrine, ideals, and ideas—that belongs to the family of monotheistic, scriptural religions that includes Judaism and Christianity. In another sense, it means the whole civilization that has grown up under the aegis of that religion: something like what is meant by the once-common term "Christendom."

When we in the West today talk of Christian art, we mean votive art, religious art. If we talk of Islamic art, however, we mean any art produced by Muslims or even by non-Muslims within Islamic civilization. Indeed, one can still speak of Islamic astronomy and Islamic chemistry and Islamic mathematics, meaning astronomy, chemistry, and mathematics produced under the aegis of Islamic civilization. There is no corresponding "Christian" astronomy or chemistry or mathematics.

Each of these terms, Islam in the sense of a religion and Islam in the sense of a civilization, is itself subject to many variations. If we talk about Islam as a historical phenomenon, we are speaking of a community that now numbers more than a billion people, most of whom are spread along a vast arc stretching almost 10,000 miles from Morocco to Mindanao; that has a 14-century-long history; and that is the defining characteristic of the 53 sovereign states that currently belong to the Organization of the

Islamic Conference (OIC). For obvious reasons, it is extremely difficult (though not impossible) to make any kind of valid generalization about a reality of such age, size, and complexity.

Even if we confine ourselves to speaking of Islam as a religion, significant distinctions must be drawn. First, there is what Muslims themselves would call the original, pristine, pure Islam of the Koran and the *hadith* (the traditions of the Prophet Mohammed) before it became corrupted by the backsliding of later generations. Second, there is the Islam of the doctors of the holy law, of the magnificent intellectual structure of classical Islamic jurisprudence and theology. Most recently, there is the neo-Islam of the so-called fundamentalists who introduce ideas unknown alike to the Koran, the *hadith*, or the classical doctrines of the faith.

Clearly this last version of Islam is incompatible with liberal democracy, as the fundamentalists themselves would be the first to say: they regard liberal democracy with contempt as a corrupt and corrupting form of government. They are willing to see it, at best, as an avenue to power, but an avenue that runs one way only.

HISTORY AND TRADITION

What then of the two others—historic Islam and Islam as a system of ideas, practices, and cultural traits?

A first look at the historical record is not encouraging. Predominantly Muslim regions show very few functioning democracies. Indeed, of the 53 OIC states, only Turkey can pass Huntington's test of democracy, and it is in many ways a troubled democracy. Among the others, one can find democratic movements and in some cases even promising democratic developments, but one cannot really say that they are democracies even to the extent that the Turkish Republic is a democracy at the present time.

Throughout history, the overwhelmingly most common type of regime in the Islamic world has been autocracy—which is not to be confused with despotism. The dominant political tradition has long been that of command and obedience, and far from weakening it, modern times have actually witnessed its intensification. With traditional restraints on autocracy attenuated, and with new means of surveillance, repression, and wealth-extraction made available to rulers by modern technologies and methods, governments have become less dependent than ever on popular goodwill. This is particularly true of those governments that are enriched by revenues from oil. With no need for taxation, there is no pressure for representation.

Another noteworthy historical and cultural fact is the absence of the notion of citizenship. There is no word in Arabic, Persian, or Turkish for "citizen." The cognate term used in each language means only "compatriot" or "countryman." It has none of the connotations of the English word "citizen," which comes from the Latin *civis* and has the content of the Greek *politês*, meaning one who participates in the affairs of the *polis*. The word is absent in Arabic and the other languages because the idea—of the citizen as participant, of citizenship as participation—is not there.

At the same time, however, we can discern elements in Islamic law and tradition that could assist the development of one or another form of democracy. Islam boasts a rich political literature. From the earliest times, doctors of the holy law, philosophers, jurists, and others have reflected carefully on the nature of political power, the ways in which political power ought to be acquired and used and may be forfeited, and the duties and responsibilities as well as the rights and privileges of those who hold it.

Islamic tradition strongly disapproves of arbitrary rule. The central institution of sovereignty in the traditional Islamic world, the caliphate, is defined by the Sunni jurists to have contractual and consensual features that distinguish caliphs from despots. The exercise of political power is conceived and presented as a contract, creating bonds of mutual obligation between the ruler and the ruled. Subjects are duty-bound to obey the ruler and carry out his orders, but the ruler also has duties toward the subject, similar to those set forth in most cultures.

The contract can be dissolved if the ruler fails to fulfill or ceases to be capable of fulfilling his obligations. Although rare, there have been instances when such dissolutions took place. There is, therefore, also an element of consent in the traditional Islamic view of government.

Many *hadith* prescribe obedience as an obligation of a subject, but some indicate exceptions. One, for example, says, "Do not obey a creature against his creator"—in other words, do not obey a human command to violate divine law. Another says, similarly, "There is no duty of obedience in sin." That is to say, if the sovereign commands something that is sinful, the duty of obedience lapses. It is worth noting that Prophetic utterances like these point not merely to a *right* of disobedience (such as would be familiar from Western political thought), but to a divinely ordained *duty* of disobedience.

When we descend from the level of principle to the realm of what has actually happened, the story is of course checkered. Still, the central point remains: there are elements in Islamic culture that could favor the development of democratic institutions.

One of the sayings traditionally ascribed to the Prophet is the remark, "Difference of opinion within my community is a sign of God's mercy." In other words, diversity is something to be welcomed, not something to be suppressed. This attitude is typified by the acceptance by Sunni Muslims, even today, of four different schools of Islamic jurisprudence. Muslims believe the holy law to be divinely inspired and guided, yet there are four significantly different schools of thought regarding this law. The idea that it is possible to be orthodox even while differing creates a principle of the acceptance of diversity and of mutual tolerance of differences of opinion that surely cannot be bad for parliamentary government.

The final point worth mentioning in this inventory is Islam's emphasis on the twin qualities of dignity and humility. Subjects—even the humblest subjects—have personal dignity in the traditional Islamic view, and rulers must avoid arrogance. By Ottoman custom, when the sultan received the chief dignitaries of the state on holy days, he stood up to receive them as a sign of his respect for the law. When a new sultan was enthroned, he was greeted with cries of "Sultan, be not proud! God is greater than you!"

THE INFLUENCE OF THE WEST

For the first thousand years of its history, Islamic civilization's relationship to Christendom was one of dominance. The loss of Spain and Portugal on the remote western periphery had little impact in the heartlands of Islam, and was more than compensated by the advance toward the heart of continental Europe. As late as 1683, an Ottoman army was encamped before the very gates of Vienna. Earlier in the seventeenth century, North African corsairs were raiding as far north as the British Isles. By the early nineteenth century, however, Islamic power was clearly in retreat as European power grew. Finding themselves the targets of conquest and colonization, Muslims naturally began to wonder what had gone wrong. Islam had always been generally "successful" in worldly terms. Unlike the founder of Christianity, who was crucified and whose followers saw their religion made the official faith of the Roman Empire only after centuries as a persecuted minority, Mohammed founded a state during his lifetime, and as ruler he collected taxes, dispensed justice, promulgated laws, commanded armies, and made war and peace.

Educated Muslims, chagrined by the newfound potency of their European rivals, asked: What are they doing right and what are we doing wrong, or not doing at all? Representative, constitutional government was high on the list. The nineteenth century saw the rise of elected assemblies in a number of Western countries, and democracy in our current sense was beginning to take hold. Many Muslims suspected that here—in this most exotic and alien of Western practices—lay the secret to the West's wealth and power, and hoped that the adoption of constitutions and the creation of elected legislatures in the Islamic world would redress the civilizational balance.

Getting used to the idea was not easy; the first Muslim visitors to the West disliked much of what they saw. The earliest detailed description of England by a Muslim traveller is a fascinating account by Mirza Abu Talib Khan, a Turko-Persian resident of Lucknow who was in England between 1798 and 1803. He watched the House of Commons in action, and his comments are enlightening. The government and opposition MPs sitting on their benches facing each other across the chamber reminded him of trees full of parrots squawking at each other, a common sight back home in India. When he learned that the purpose of the noisy assemblage was to make laws, he was shocked. The English, he explained to his readers, had not accepted a divine law and so were reduced to the expedient of making their own laws, in accordance with the experience of their judges and the requirements of their time.

Later accounts were more positive. The first Egyptian student mission went to France in 1826. Their chaplain, a sheikh from al-Azhar, learned a great deal (probably more than his student wards) and wrote a remarkable book about Paris. In it he discusses the National Assembly and the freedom of the press, among other things, and makes the very astute observation that the French, when they speak of freedom, mean roughly what Muslims are getting at when they talk of justice. With this insight, he cuts right to the heart of a key difference between European political culture and its Islamic counterpart.

To Muslims, the use of "freedom" as a political term was an imported novelty, dating only from the time of the French Revolution and General Napoleon Bonaparte's arrival in Egypt in 1798. Before that, it had only legal and social connotations, and meant simply the condition of not being a slave. For Muslim thinkers, as the sheikh from al-Azhar implied, justice is the ideal, the touchstone by which one distinguishes good governments from bad.

By the latter part of the nineteenth century, Islamic rulers were coming to think of a constitution as something that no well-dressed nation could afford to be without. Just as gentlemen were abandoning traditional garb in favor of Western-style frock coats, neckties, and trousers, so the state would sport a constitution and an elected legislature as essential accoutrements.

Yet the idea of freedom—understood as the ability to participate in the formation, the conduct, and even the lawful removal and replacement of government—remained alien. This notion, which belongs to the inner logic of constitutionalism and parliamentarism, is obviously a troublesome one for dynastic autocracies, which can hardly accept it and remain what they are. The real question, then, was whether constitutions, elections, and parliaments—the institutional trappings of democracy—would be only that, or would actually become means that the governed could use to gain some say in their government.

The first serious elections in the Islamic world were held to choose the parliament called for by the Ottoman Constitution of 1876. This parliament was no doubt meant to be a tame body that would supply the ceremonial ratification of the sultan's authority. But the Chamber of Deputies soon developed a mind of its own. On 13 February 1878, the deputies went so far as to demand that three ministers, against whom specific charges had been brought, should appear in the Chamber to defend themselves. The next day, in response, the sultan dissolved the parliament and sent its members home. It did not meet again until the year after the Young Turk Revolution of 1908. That phase, too, was of brief duration, and a military coup ended the stormy interval of parliamentary rule.

Since then, parliamentarism has not fared especially well in the Islamic world. All too often, elections are less a way of choosing a government than a ritual designed to ratify and symbolize a choice that has already been made by other means—something like a presidential inauguration in the United States or a coronation in Britain. This is not always so—there are intervals and cases where elections mean something, and they become more common in the record as one goes from the nineteenth into the twentieth century, in spite of (or perhaps because of) a number of dramatic moves in the opposite direction.

A ROUGH CLASSIFICATION OF REGIMES

Another complication surrounding the term "freedom" is a legacy of imperialism. When outsiders ruled much, though not all, of the Islamic world, freedom came also, or even primarily, to mean communal or national independence, with no reference to the individual's status within the body politic.

Most of the countries in the Islamic world today are free from external domination, but not free internally: they have sovereignty, but lack democracy. This shared lack, however, does not preclude the existence of very great differences among them. Predominantly Muslim societies (Turkey, as we saw earlier, being the great exception) are ruled by a wide variety of authoritarian, autocratic, despotic, tyrannical, and totalitarian regimes. A rough classification would include five categories.

1) *Traditional autocracies.* These are the countries, like Saudi Arabia and the Gulf sheikhdoms, where established dynastic regimes rest on the traditional props of usage, custom, and history. These regimes are firmly authoritarian in character, but the same traditions that sustain them also bind them: their legitimacy relies heavily on acceptance, and too much open repression would shatter it. Their props are not quite what they used to be, however, having been partly undermined by new ideas and forces. The rulers use modern devices to help maintain themselves, but the same devices—especially electronic communications media—are now also available to those who would overthrow the existing order.

   The Iranian Revolution, which overthrew the Shah in 1979, was the first electronic revolution in history. It will not be the last. Khomeini could do nothing while he was in Iran, and very little from nearby Iraq. But when he went to Paris and began recording cassette tapes and calling Iran via the direct-dial telephone system that the Shah had installed, he reached a vast audience, with results we know all too well. Satellite television, the fax machine, and electronic mail can all carry the message of subversion in ways difficult to prevent or control. The methods used by the Islamic revolutionaries against the Shah are now being used—in a more sophisticated form—by those who seek to overthrow the Islamic Republic. Other dissident groups—ethnic, religious, ideological—are using the same methods against the regimes that rule in their countries.

2) *Modernizing autocracies.* These are regimes—one thinks of Jordan, Egypt, and Morocco in particular—that have their roots in traditional autocracy but are taking significant steps toward modernization and democratization. None really fits the description of liberal democracy as given above, but none is anything like a total autocracy, either. All three are moving toward greater freedom. Difficulties, setbacks, and problems may abound, but the basic direction of change is clear.

3) *Fascist-style dictatorships.* These regimes, especially the one-party Ba'athist governments in Hafiz al-Assad's Syria and Saddam Hussein's Iraq, are modeled on European fascism. In matters of precept, practice, and style, they owe a great deal to the example of Benito Mussolini and, to a lesser extent, Adolf Hitler.

4) *Radical Islamic regimes.* There are two of these so far, Iran and Sudan. There may be others to follow, perhaps in Afghanistan or Algeria, though the latter possibility now seems to be dwindling rather than growing. Egypt has a potent radical Islamic movement, but the Egyptian political class also has a remarkable knack for maintaining itself in power. Moreover, the threat to the sovereign state posed by

pan-Islamic radicalism has been greatly exaggerated. Khomeini used to say that there were no frontiers in Islam, but he also stipulated in the constitution that the president of the Islamic Republic of Iran must be of Iranian birth and origin. In Khomeini's own practice, let alone that of his successors, the Iranian element remained paramount. Elsewhere, there is a similar disinclination among even the most fanatical Islamic groups to sink their national or territorial integrity into some larger whole.

5) *The Central Asian republics.* A final group of countries, classifiable more by history and geography than by regime type, are the six former Soviet republics with mostly Muslim populations, sometimes known nowadays as "the five 'stans" plus Azerbaijan. I can venture no characterization of the regimes in these countries, but will only observe that they seem to be having the same problems disentangling themselves from their former imperial masters as the Egyptians, North Africans, Syrians, and Iraqis had with their respective former masters earlier in this century. After the formal recognition of independence comes the postimperial hangover, a period of interference, unequal treaties, privileges, basing agreements, and so on. The big difference this time, of course, is that the former colonial peoples are dealing not with London or Paris, but with Moscow. This may give rise to different results.

MUSLIMS OUTSIDE THE MIDDLE EAST

There are also hundreds of millions of Muslims in South and Southeast Asia, but space limitations and my own relative ignorance of these lands lead me to offer only a brief and superficial impression of what is happening in them. Pakistan, Bangladesh, Malaysia, and Indonesia all appear to resemble Egypt or Morocco more than Syria or Iraq, which is encouraging. I say that the South Asian countries resemble the Middle Eastern or North African countries (and not vice versa) for a reason. There are almost as many Muslims in Indonesia, for example, as in the whole of the Arab world, but the lines of influence run from the latter to the former. The historical heartlands of Islam have hitherto enjoyed the kind of influence in the Islamic world that the outlying regions could rarely, if ever, achieve. With the overwhelming numerical preponderance of South and Southeast Asian Islam and the growing importance of the Islamic communities in the West, this may change.

Another relatively small group of Muslims who may matter a great deal are those adherents of Islam who have emigrated to non-Muslim countries in Western Europe and North America. These groups are extremely important, not so much because of what is happening in the countries of their present residence, as because of the impact that they have on their countries of origin. As Muslim minorities go, of course, they are a tiny handful. India's Muslim minority (equal to 11 percent of its total population) is by far the largest concentration of Muslims in a non-Muslim country. Indeed, only two other countries (Indonesia and Bangladesh) have more Muslims living within their borders. In the Middle East, there is a sizeable Muslim minority in Israel. Ethiopia, a Christian country whose church traces its origins to apostolic times, has a significant Muslim minority, and many other countries in sub-Saharan Africa have Muslim majorities or substantial minorities.

There are also old Muslim minorities in Europe, in the Balkan states, and above all in the Russian Federation itself, which may be as much as 15 percent Muslim.

Like Khomeini amid the Iranian-exile community in the 1970s, some of the political groups that move among the new Muslim communities in Europe and North America are seeking to recruit support for struggles against those in power at home. The separatist movement of Turkish Kurds, for instance, is highly active among the Kurdish population in Germany. The Islamic-fundamentalist movement in North Africa collects money, buys weapons, and organizes in France, and various movements are now using the United States in the same way.

The vast majority of Muslim immigrants in Western Europe and North America, it should be noted, has no interest in extremist or revolutionary movements. On the contrary, these immigrants are increasingly taking part (sometimes as citizens) in the democratic processes of their adopted societies while remaining in touch with their countries of origin. The views that they form as a result of their experience of democracy may well be among the most significant factors shaping the political future of the Islamic world.

RELIGION AND THE STATE

In Islam, as was mentioned above, there is from the beginning an interpenetration, almost an identification, of cult and power, or religion and the state: Mohammed was not only a prophet, but a ruler. In this respect, Islam resembles Old Testament Judaism and looks quite different from Christianity. Christianity, to repeat, began and endured for centuries under official persecution. Even after it became the state religion of Rome under the Emperor Constantine in the fourth century, a distinction was maintained between spiritual and temporal powers. Ever since then, all Christian states without exception have distinguished between throne and altar, church and state. The two powers might be closely associated, as under the caesaropapism of the Byzantine Empire, or they might be separated; they might work in harmony or they might come into conflict; one might dominate for a time and the other might displace it; but the duality remains, corresponding to the distinction in Christian Rome between *imperium* (imperial power) and *sacerdotium* (priestly power).

Islam in its classical form has no organizational equivalent. It has no clergy or clerical hierarchy in anything like the Christian sense of the word, and no ecclesiastical organization. The mosque is a building, not an institution in the sense that the church is. At least this was so until comparatively recently, for Khomeini during his rule seems to have effected a kind of "Christianization" of Iran's Islamic institutions, with himself as an infallible pope, and with the functional equivalent of a hierarchy of archbishops, bishops, and priests. All of this was totally alien to Islamic tradition, and thus constituted an "Islamic revolution" in a sense quite different from the one usually conveyed by references to Khomeini's legacy.

Islamic civilization has produced a wealth of theological, philosophical, and juridical literature on virtually every aspect of the state, its powers, and its functions. What is not discussed to any great extent is the difference between religious and temporal powers. The words for "secular" and "secularism" in modern Islamic languages are either loanwords or neologisms. There are still no equivalents for the words "layman" and "laity." Jurists and other Muslim writers on politics have long recognized a distinction between state and religion, between the affairs of this world and those of the next. But this in no way corresponds to the dichotomy expressed in such Western pairs of terms as "spiritual" and "temporal," or "lay" and "ecclesiastical." Conceptually, this dichotomy simply did not arise. It has arisen now, and it may be that Muslims, having contracted a Christian illness, will consider a Christian remedy, that is to say, the separation of religion and the state.

Of course, I am well aware that the Reformation was a stage in the evolution of Christendom and the Enlightenment a stage in the history of Europe, and I am not suggesting that the past of the West can somehow be grafted onto the future of Islam. There is no reason whatever why the Muslims can or should be expected to follow precisely the same pattern, by the same route. If they take up the challenge at all, they will have to tackle it in their own way. So far, alas, there is little sign that they are willing to take it up, but one may hope.

Turkey alone has formally enacted the separation of religion and the state. Its constitution and laws declare it a secular republic. In many practical respects, however, Islam remains an important and indeed a growing factor in the Turkish polity and in the Turks' sense of their own identity.

As a rule, gradual and unforced change is better than sudden and compulsory change. Democracy cannot be born like Aphrodite from the sea foam. It comes in slow stages; for that reason, places like Egypt and Jordan, where there is evolution in a broadly democratic direction, seem to offer the best prospects. In Iraq and Syria, an overthrow of the present dictators is unlikely to lead to the immediate establishment of a workable democracy. The next change of regime in those countries will probably just produce less-brutal dictatorships, which might then evolve into reforming autocracies in the Egyptian or Jordanian style. That would not be democracy, but it would be a huge step forward nonetheless.

The places that offer the best prospects for democracy are those where there is a process of gradual change in the direction of freer institutions. Democracy usually evolves out of a movement toward freedom. The liberal democracies of the West certainly did not come about all at once. One need only think of the history of slavery in the United States or the disenfranchisement of women in most of the Western world to see that, even under favorable conditions, democratic progress takes time and effort and may be hard-won indeed.

Imperialist powers deprived most of the Islamic world of sovereignty; the prime demand, therefore, was for independence. Foreign rule was equated with tyranny, to be ended by whatever means possible. But tyranny means different things to different people. In the traditional Islamic system, the converse of tyranny is justice; in Western political thought, the converse of tyranny is freedom. At the present day, most Islamic countries are discovering that while they have gained independence, they enjoy neither justice nor freedom. There are some—and soon, perhaps, there will be many more—who see in democracy the surest way to attain both.

Diamond, Larry, Marc F. Plattner, and Daniel Brumberg, eds. *Islam and Democracy in the Middle East.* pp. 208–219. © 2003 The Johns Hopkins University Press and The National Endowment for Democracy. Reprinted with permission of The Johns Hopkins University Press.

Abdou Filali-Ansary claims that the problem facing the Muslim Middle East is not one of harmonizing Islam and democracy. Filali-Ansary writes that the real issue is how such a question is framed; or, more to the point, why it is posed in the first place. The author believes that merely asking whether or not Islam and democracy are compatible undermines an understanding of either and reveals a subtle but poisonous prejudice. Filali-Ansary, to be specific, sees the specter of "Muslim exceptionalism" hovering over the Islam-and-democracy debate. Muslim exceptionalism is a theory that holds that Islam, by its very nature, is exceptional in being utterly hostile to democracy. Islam, so it is said, is fundamentally unreceptive to liberal democratic core concepts such as individual autonomy, personal freedom, limited government, free expression, gender equality, and a clear separation between church and state. Islam not only resists democracy, but modernity as well. The flat rejection of both democracy and modern life, the theory holds, is a function of the Muslim reverence for tradition and the use of God as a social reference point. As historian Richard D. Brown has noted, modern political systems "never presume to possess an ageless, distant past . . . [and their] origins are human and known rather than divine and mysterious."* Democracy fits this definition. Considering that the past and the divine are central to Islam, it follows that democracy is beyond the grasp of the Muslim mind. Accordingly, if exceptionalism is assumed, it can be expected that the Muslim world and the West will continue to clash until a radical change in Muslim thinking takes place.

As the next essay demonstrates, the historical record does not necessarily bear out the central thesis of Muslim exceptionalism. In fact, history shows that Islamic teachings and values often follow the general contours of democracy. Islam, Filali-Ansary contends, welcomes both modernization and liberal reform in politics and economics and is no less compatible with democracy than Christianity or Judaism. These two world religions have successfully blended with democratic forms of government, despite being bound by tradition. Islam can, too. Filali-Ansary is confident that democracy can flourish in the Middle East if certain specific prerequisites are met.

NOTES

* Richard D. Brown, *Modernization: The Transformation of American Life, 1600–1865* (Prospect Heights, Ill.: Waveland Press, 1976), 13–14.

Muslims and Democracy
ABDOU FILALI-ANSARY

The past is often held to weigh especially heavily on Muslim countries, particularly as regards their present-day receptivity to democracy. I do not dispute that past history has had an overwhelming and decisive influence in shaping the contemporary features and attitudes of Muslim societies. But the past that is most relevant today is not, as is commonly thought, the early centuries of Islamic history, but rather the nineteenth-century encounter of Muslims with the modernizing West.

It is widely believed that the key to understanding contemporary Muslim societies is to be found in a structure of beliefs and traditions that was devised and implemented at (or shortly after) the moment at which they adopted Islam. This view, often labeled as "Muslim exceptionalism," holds that these societies are, as Ernest Gellner has elegantly put it, permeated by an "implicit constitution" providing a "blueprint" of the social order.[1] This view has been subjected to intense criticism by a number of scholars, but it still influences dominant attitudes in academia and, with much more devastating effects, in the media.

This theory rests on two assumptions: first, that the past is ever-present and is much more determining than present-day conditions; and second, that the character of Muslim societies has been determined by a specific and remote period in their past during which the social and political order that continues to guide them was established. This past has allegedly acquired such a strong grip that it can—and does—channel, limit, or even block the effects of technological, economic, or social change. In other words, for Muslims alone a remote past has defined, forever and without any possibility of evolution, the ways in which fundamental issues are perceived and addressed. The ultimate conclusion lurking behind these considerations is that, due to the overwhelming presence and influence of that particular part of their past, the societies in question are incapable of democratization. In other societies history may take the form of continual change, but in Muslim ones history is bound to repeat itself.

Apart from the many other criticisms that have been directed against this set of views, it should be emphasized that it is not based on any solid historical knowledge about the way in which this "implicit constitution" was shaped and implemented or imposed. Some of its proponents refer to a normative system that was never really enacted: They invoke the model of the "rightly guided" caliphate, which lasted, at most, for about three decades after the death of the Prophet. Many others cite instead the social order that prevailed during the Middle Ages in societies where Muslims were a majority or where political regimes were established in the name of Islam. In both of these versions, however, the power of this past to determine the present remains, by and large, mysterious. It is simply taken for granted, with no explanation given about why the past has had such a far-reaching and pervasive effect in these societies. To understand how the belief in these misconceptions was born and came to influence contemporary attitudes so powerfully, we must turn to a particular moment in modern times—the beginning and middle of the nineteenth century.

A TENACIOUS MISUNDERSTANDING

The earliest intellectual encounters between Muslims and Europeans in modern times took the form of sharp confrontations. Jamal-Eddin Al-Afghani (1838–97), one of the first and most prominent Muslim thinkers and activists in the struggle against despotism, became famous for engaging in a controversy against European secularists. He acquired a high reputation, especially for his efforts to refute European critics of religion in general and of Islam in particular. An essay that he wrote in reply to Ernest Renan bore the title *"Ar-Rad 'ala ad-Dahriyin"* ("The Answer to Temporalists"). He used the term *Dahriyin*, which literally means "temporalists," to refer to secularists. The word itself, which is of Kuranic origin, had originally been applied to atheists. Al-Afghani attacked the positivist ideologues of his century, who were deeply convinced that religion was responsible for social backwardness and stagnation and that scientific progress would soon lead to its disappearance. Through his choice of terminology, Al-Afghani implicitly equated these nineteenth-century positivists with the seventh-century opponents of the Prophet. For Muslim readers, this formulation defined the terms of a large and enduring misunderstanding. From then on, secularism was seen as being intimately related to, if not simply the same thing as, atheism. The confusion was taken a step further when, some decades later, other Muslim authors wishing to coin a term for secularism, and either ignoring Al-Afghani's choice of the term *Dahriyin* or feeling that it was inappropriate, chose *ladini*, which literally means nonreligious or areligious.

    These initial choices of terminology gave birth to the opposition in the mind of Muslims between, on the one hand, the system of belief and the social order that they inherited and lived in, and on the other, the alternative adopted by the Europeans. Although the term *ladini* was replaced later by another, *'ilmani* (this-worldly), the bipolar opposition between the two views was already deeply entrenched. The feeling that has prevailed since then among Muslims is that there is a strict and irreducible opposition between two systems—Islam and non-Islam. To be a secularist has meant to abandon Islam, to reject altogether not only the religious faith but also its attendant morality and the traditions and rules that operate within Muslim societies. It therefore has been understood as a total alienation from the constituent elements of the Islamic personality and as a complete surrender to unbelief, immorality, and self-hatred, leading to a disavowal of the historic identity and civilization inherited from illustrious ancestors. It is worth noting that the vast majority of Muslims in the nineteenth century, even those who were part of the educated elite, lived in total ignorance both of the debates going on in Europe about religion and its role in the social order and of the historical changes reshaping European societies. They were not aware of the distinction between atheism and secularism. The consequences of this misunderstanding still profoundly shape the attitudes of Muslims today.

Thus secularism became known to Muslims for the first time through a controversy against those who were supposed to be their "hereditary enemies." The original distinction within Christianity between "regular" and "secular" members of the clergy,[2] which was the initial step in the long evolution toward the establishment of a separate secular sphere, had no equivalent in the Muslim context. Hence the choice of a term for the concept of secularism was decisive. In the latter part of the nineteenth century and early in the twentieth, the confrontation with the colonial powers, thought to be the carriers and defenders of a mixture of aggressive Christian proselytism and of the new secularism, played an important role in strengthening this dualism. In the diverse conflicts that local populations waged to defend their independence, identity and religion became intimately fused. The oppositions between local and intruder, between Muslim and European, between believer and secularist were, in one way or another, conflated. The resulting polarization came to dominate all attitudes and approaches to questions related to religion, politics, and the social order.

One of the most striking consequences of this evolution is that Islam now appears to be the religion that is most hostile to secularization and to modernity in general. Yet intrinsically Islam would seem to be the religion closest to modern views and ideals, and thus the one that would most easily accommodate secularization. "The high culture form of Islam," writes Ernest Gellner, "is endowed with a number of features—unitarianism, a rule-ethic, individualism, scripturalism, puritanism, an egalitarian aversion to mediation and hierarchy, a fairly small load of magic—that are congruent, presumably, with requirements of modernity or modernisation."[3] In a similar vein, Mohamed Charfi observes that, on the level of principles, Islam should favor individual freedoms and the capacity for religious choice. The historical developments noted above, however, caused Muslim societies to evolve in the opposite direction—toward the loss of individual autonomy and total submission to the community and the state.[4]

This evolution gave birth at later stages to such dichotomies as "Islam and the West," "Islam and modernity," "Islam and human rights," "Islam and democracy," and others of the sort, which set the framework within which critical issues are addressed, whether in popular, journalistic, or even academic circles. This framework has imposed a particular way of raising questions and building conceptions, imprisoning attitudes in predefined and static formulas.[5] Muslim exceptionalism seems, therefore, to reside in the ways we raise questions about these matters. Although many studies on religion and its influence in the social and political spheres are undertaken in what were formerly referred to as Christian societies, nobody today poses the issue of "Christianity and democracy" in the same way that this question is formulated with respect to Islam. The fact that we still ask questions such as "Is Islam compatible with democracy?" shows how strong this polarization has become. It also shows that a dynamic was established, enabling the polarization that emerged in the nineteenth century to replicate itself as it extends to new fields or expresses itself in new terms.

FROM SETTLEMENT TO SYSTEM

This polarization, which still determines the type of questions that can be asked, rests on two main prejudices: The first is that Islam is a "system," and should be treated as a structure of rules. The dubious character of this assumption has been clearly pointed out by the eminent scholar of comparative religion Wilfred Cantwell Smith: "[T]he term *nizam* [or] 'system,' is commonplace in the twentieth century in relation to Islam. This term, however, does not occur in the Koran, nor indeed does any word from this root; and there is some reason for wondering whether any Muslim ever used this concept religiously before modern times. The explicit notion that life should be or can be ordered according to a system, even an ideal one, and that it is the business of Islam to provide such a system, seems to be a modern idea (and perhaps a rather questionable one)."[6] Once Islam has been defined in this way, it can be used to assess whether other new or alien concepts can be accommodated within it and to decide the degree of their compatibility with its presumed and predefined content. This stance, however, reflects a particular attitude toward religion, not a particular feature of Islam. In fact, as Leonard

Binder has observed, any of the monotheistic religions, if adopted in this manner, can lead to similar conclusions: "In the light of modern liberal democratic thought, Islam is no more, nor any less democratic than Christianity or Judaism. All three monotheistic religions, if proposed as constitutional foundations of the state, and if understood as providing an ineluctable authority for the guidance of all significant human choice, are undemocratic or non-democratic."[7]

The second prejudice is more insidious. It is based on the confusion of Islam as a religion with Islam as a civilization. This confusion is deeply entrenched, again because of prevailing linguistic usages both in Arabic and in European languages. For Islam, no distinction has been drawn comparable to that between "Christianity" and "Christendom." The same word was, and still is, used to refer both to a set of beliefs and rituals and to the life of the community of believers through time and space. Only recently, thanks to the work of historian Marshall G.S. Hodgson, has the necessity of drawing a sharp line between Islam and "Islamdom" been recognized as essential for explaining key phenomena in the history of Muslims.[8] Islamdom, in its golden age, was a social and political order built on norms adopted from Islamic sources but specifically adapted to the conditions of the time (only at a later stage were these formulated as explicit rules). This enabled Muslims in the Middle Ages to create and maintain a world civilization attuned to the circumstances of the era.

Muslims at that time lived within polities bound by *shari'a*, yet did not consider the political regimes to which they were subjected to be in conformity with Islamic principles. The rulers were considered to be legal but not really legitimate. Even though they were not fully legitimate, they had to be obeyed, but only to avoid a greater evil, the *fitna* (the great rebellion or anarchy). For premodern societies of Muslims, the political model remained the early caliphate, which was not bound by *shari'a*, since *shari'a* had not yet been devised. The ideal was a kind of "republican" regime, where caliphs are chosen by members of the community rather than imposed by force, and where the behavior of rulers is clearly dedicated to serving the community instead of satisfying their personal ambitions. Nonetheless, Muslims came to understand that it was no longer possible to implement the fully legitimate system of *Khilafa rachida*, the virtuous or rightly guided caliphate, that the republican ideal was out of reach, and that they had to accept the rule of despots. They could, however, limit the extent of the power accorded to autocratic rulers by invoking *shari'a*, to which a sacred character had come to be attributed. In this way, at least some degree of autonomy from the political authorities, and minimal protection against arbitrariness, could be attained. This is what one may label the "medieval compromise" or "medieval settlement."

The sacralization of *shari'a* achieved through this process led to another far-reaching consequence: Ever since, Islam has been seen as a set of eternal rules, standing over society and history, to be used as a standard for judging reality and behavior.

In fact, *shari'a* was never a system of law in the sense in which it is understood nowadays. As was noted by Fazlur Rahman: "Islamic law . . . is not strictly speaking law, since much of it embodies moral and quasi-moral precepts not enforceable in any court. Further, Islamic law, though a certain part of it came to be enforced almost uniformly throughout the Muslim world (and it is primarily this that bestowed homogeneity upon the entire Muslim world), is on closer examination a body of legal opinion or, as Santillana put it, 'an endless discussion on the duties of a Muslim' rather than a neatly formulated code or codes."[9]

What happened in the nineteenth century was the transformation of the medieval settlement into a system in the modern sense of the word. The duality of fact and norm was inverted, as *shari'a*-bound societies were confused with fully legitimate Muslim communities and deemed to be fully realizable through voluntary political action, whether of a peaceful or violent character. We see therefore how the confusion between a "model" and a historical system could arise and spread among Muslims at a time when they were confronted by the challenge of modern ideas. The typical attitudes of premodern Muslims had been based on a sharp distinction between the norm (of the virtuous or rightly guided caliphate) and the actual conditions (including the implementation of the *shari'a*) under which they lived. In the face of this duality, people adopted an attitude of resignation, accepting that the norm was, at least temporarily, out of reach. By contrast, some modern Muslims have elevated the actual conditions and rules under which their medieval forefathers lived to the status of a norm, and decided that they too have to live by these rules if they are to be true Muslims.

This has led to the contradictions of the present day: Secularization has been taking place for decades in Muslim societies, yet prevailing opinion opposes the concept of secularism and everything that comes with it (like modernity and democracy). As a historical process, secularization has so transformed life in Muslim societies that religion, or rather traditions built on religion, no longer supply the norms and rules that govern the social and political order. In almost all countries with substantial communities of Muslims, positive law has replaced *shari'a* (except with regard to matters of "personal status," and more specifically the status of women, where the traditional rules generally continue to be maintained). Modern institutions—nation-states, modern bureaucracies, political parties, labor unions, corporations, associations, educational systems—have been adopted everywhere, while traditional institutions are, at best, relegated to symbolic roles. Similarly, prevailing conceptions and attitudes of everyday life are founded on modern rationality and on doctrines influenced by science and philosophy rather than on traditional or premodern worldviews. Most Muslims now have come to accept the "disenchantment of the world," and this has profoundly transformed expectations and models of behavior within their societies. The evolution from the premodern attitude, combining resignation toward despotism with millennial hopes, to the typically modern combination of sharp political determination and desire for this-worldly progress, is clearly a visible consequence of these very changes, that is, of the secularization that has actually been going on in Muslim societies.

Secularism, however, continues to be rejected as an alien doctrine, allegedly imposed by the traditional enemies of Muslims and their indigenous accomplices. Islam is seen as an eternal and immutable system, encompassing every aspect of social organization and personal morality, and unalterably opposed to all conceptions and systems associated with modernity. This creates an artificial debate and an almost surrealist situation. The changes that are evident in the actual lives of individuals and groups are ignored, while ideological stances are maintained with great determination. Secularists and, more generally, social scientists are often pushed into adopting defensive positions or withdrawing altogether from public debates. Frequently they feel obliged to prove that they are not guilty of hostility toward religious belief, morality, and the achievements of Islamic civilization.

As Mohamed Charfi has pointed out, the policies adopted by some modern states under the influence of nationalist ideologies are partly responsible for this state of affairs. The education systems in many Muslim countries have taught Islam not as a religion, but as an identity and a legal and political system. The consequence is that Islam is presented both as irreducibly opposed to other kinds of self-identification or of social and political organization and as commanding certain specific attitudes regarding political and social matters.[10]

ATTITUDES TOWARD DEMOCRACY

We saw that, as a consequence of the inversion of norms that occurred in Muslim societies during the nineteenth century, the traditional rules and usages grouped under the emblem of *shari'a* were transformed into a system and elevated into norms that define the "essence" of being Muslim—that is, simultaneously the ideal status and the specific identity of Muslims. Thus *shari'a*-bound societies are now equated with "truly"

Islamic societies. Implementing the *shari'a* has become the slogan for those who seek a "return" to Islam in its original and pure form, which is held to embody the eternal truth and ultimate pattern for Muslims.

What could the status of democracy be in societies that have evolved in this manner? One first must perceive the difference between a question posed in this way, which attempts to interpret the actual evolution of particular societies and their prevailing conceptions, and the kinds of questions frequently asked by fundamentalists and by some scholars, such as: "What is the status of democracy with regard to Islam?" This latter formulation posits Islam as a system that one can use to evaluate everything else.

One can discern two possible answers to the question of democracy as I have posed it. The first accepts the strict identification between Islam and *shari'a*-bound systems, and thus rules out any possible future for democracy in this particular environment. The second identifies democracy itself with a kind of religious faith or "mystical ideal." As Tim Niblock has noted: "The Middle East related literature purveys a romanticized conception of the nature and characteristics of liberal democracy. This occurs not through any explicit description of liberal democracy, but precisely through the absence of any analysis of the concept and its practical application. The concept hovers, like a mystical symbol, in the background of the discussion on democratization in the Middle East, with an implied assumption that liberal democracy constitutes an ideal polity where the common good is realized by means of the population deciding issues through the election of individuals who carry out the people's will."[11]

There even appears to be a certain trend toward adopting this second attitude. More and more fundamentalists accept the idea that Islam is not opposed to democracy; some argue that by embracing the principle of *shura* (or "consultation"), for example, Islam has always favored the kind of relationship between rulers and ruled that democracy entails. Democracy may even end up being described as a Western adaptation of an originally Islamic principle. Many fundamentalists are prepared to go as far as possible to support democracy—with the notable reservation that it should be maintained only within the limits set by *shari'a*. A "guided democracy" is the system envisioned by many fundamentalists and traditionalists of different sorts. Iran may be considered as a case where this kind of doctrine has been implemented. In addition to institutions common in all democracies, like elected parliaments and executives, it also has a high council of experts and a religious guide who are entrusted with ensuring that the laws and decisions made by democratically elected bodies are in conformity with religious principles and rules.

This shows how much popularity, or rather prestige, democracy enjoys within contemporary Muslim societies. The renowned contemporary philosopher Mohamed Abed Jabri has said that democracy is the only principle of political legitimacy which is acceptable nowadays in Muslim societies, whatever their religious beliefs and attitudes may be. "Revolutionary" alternatives that postpone the implementation of democracy until other conditions are realized no longer seem to be acceptable to the masses.[12] This support for democracy reflects in some cases a realistic recognition that it responds to the needs of contemporary societies, that it is indeed the only alternative that really works and makes possible the peaceful and rational management of public affairs. In many other cases, however, this newly favorable reception of democracy arises from its being viewed as another utopia.[13] While this may have certain immediate advantages, especially in contexts where democratic systems are in place or where democratization is under way, it may also encourage attitudes that are harmful to the longer-range prospects for democratization. For it may lead to democracy's being seen as an alien or unattainable ideal, and thus strengthen the idea that the Islamic alternative is more workable and better adapted to the conditions of Muslim societies. In other words, democracy may be treated in the same way as other modern ideologies, such as nationalism and socialism, that recently enjoyed a brief ascendancy in some Muslim countries. Both nationalism and socialism were indeed endowed with a quasi-religious aura; they were adopted as ultimate worldviews and total beliefs, and considered as magical remedies to all the ills and problems of society. This kind of approach would only deepen the initial misunderstanding on the part of Muslims of both secularization and democracy. The result would be to strengthen the view that Islam and democracy represent two irreducibly separate and opposing outlooks, even if some mixture of Islam and democracy were to be envisaged and tentatively implemented.

REPLACING DEMOCRACY WITH ITS "BUILDING BLOCKS"

What might be an appropriate strategy for democrats in this situation? For those who are convinced that democracy is not a new religion for humanity, but that it provides the most efficient means to limit abuses of power and protect individual freedoms, enabling individuals to seek their own path to personal accomplishment, there can be a variety of approaches. The most effective ones avoid the reified and "utopianized" version of democracy, either by highlighting such concepts as "good governance" or by supporting some of the "building blocks of democracy," that is, conceptions and systems that are linked to or part of democracy.

Replacing highly prestigious and, at the same time, highly contentious notions with terms that refer to easily understood facts and ideas is neither a retreat from conceptual clarity nor a defeatist position. A few years ago Mohamed Abed Jabri was bitterly attacked by a large number of Arab intellectuals for proposing to replace the slogan of secularization with such notions as rationality and democratization. Secularization, he contended, had become a charged issue for Arab public opinion because it was understood as being more or less equivalent to Westernization; its actual contents, however, such as rational management of collective affairs and democracy, could hardly be rejected once they were understood and accepted in their true meaning. In a similar vein, Niblock has observed: "Focusing on the 'big' issue of democratisation has detracted from the attention which can be given to a range of more specific issues which affect populations critically. Among these are the level of corruption, the effectiveness of bureaucratic organisation, the independence of the judiciary, the existence of well-conceived and clearly-articulated laws, freedom of expression, the respect given to minorities, attitudes to human rights issues, and the extent of inequalities which may create social disorder."[14]

In order to avoid a new and devastating misunderstanding that would present democracy as an alternative to religion and make its adoption appear to be a deviation from religious rectitude, it is essential to renounce quixotic confrontations and to accept some "tactical" concessions—especially when the use of appropriate terminology can bring greater clarification without sacrificing substance. Niblock's suggestion, stressing the importance of specific issues relevant to democracy, is one possible strategy, and it is certainly of real usefulness for the cases at hand. Yet it represents an external point of view, one that seems to be directed primarily at politicians and decision makers who attempt to influence political change in Muslim countries from the outside. It does not take into account the attitudes of Muslims themselves, and especially the need to foster their real acceptance and support of democracy. For this purpose, a more "conceptual" approach is required, one that would help present democracy in terms understandable and acceptable to Muslim publics, and thus bridge the gap between a "mystical" representation and a more realistic comprehension. It would answer the need for analytical terms that can clarify the conceptions and adjust the expectations of Muslims regarding democracy, and that can encourage the kind of *political* support that is equally distant from mythical or ideological fervor on the one hand, and egotistical or individualist attitudes on the other.

This approach, which should be understood not as an alternative but rather as a complement to the one proposed by Niblock, aims at clarifying the issue for a specific public that is influenced by particular worldviews and has expectations of its own. Finding the right terms is not easy. Interpretations of democracy and democratization are so rich and diverse that it may be difficult to reach a consensual view on the subject. All such interpretations, however, seem to point to some basic features as being essential conditions for achieving real democracy. It is possible to underscore at least three such conditions that seem to be required for the particular case of contemporary Muslim societies: 1) the updating of religious conceptions; 2) the rule of law; and 3) economic growth.

1) The *updating of religious conceptions* should be understood not in terms of the Reformation that occurred in sixteenth-century Christian Europe, but rather as the general evolution of religious attitudes that has affected Christians and Jews (except within limited circles of fundamentalists) since the seventeenth or eighteenth centuries and achieved its full effects only in the early decades of this century. The Reformation is a singular event in history, linked to a particular environment and to specific conditions. It cannot, as some observers are suggesting nowadays, be "replicated" in the context of another religion and under twentieth-century conditions.

   There is, however, another process of change in religious attitudes that, although it first occurred in one particular environment, is of more universal scope and significance and seems to be related to modernization in general. This process leads the majority of the population to give religious dogmas a symbolic truth-value, and to consider religious narratives as contingent, historical manifestations or expressions of the sacred that are amenable to rational understanding and scientific scrutiny. Religious dogmas and narratives no longer define, in a monolithic way, people's ideas about the world and society, nor do they determine the views that believers are supposed to be guided by in their social and political interactions. This kind of "disenchantment" may discard the literal meaning of sacred words and rituals, but it maintains (and probably reinforces) the overall ethical and moral teachings. Religious attitudes are no longer defined in terms of a combination of strict observance of rituals and the adoption of premodern views, but rather as an informal but deeply felt adherence to principles of morality and a commitment to universal values. Faith becomes a matter of individual choice and commitment, not an obligation imposed upon all members of the community.

An evolution in this direction has proceeded quite far among Christians and Jews, but has made only limited headway among Muslims. The reification of Islam that began in the nineteenth century is the most important obstacle to such progress. Thus it is significant that a number of contemporary Muslim thinkers agree that new attitudes toward religion are now required both by a scrupulous interpretation of sacred sources and by modern conditions. Their teachings imply a strict separation between the sacred message of Islam and Muslim attempts to implement it in the course of history, including the political systems and legislation created in the "golden age." The Egyptian theologian Ali Abderraziq, for example, proposed to consider the early caliphate created by companions of the Prophet not as a religious institution but as a political one, amenable to critical scrutiny in the same way as any normal human institution.[15] Fazlur Rahman and Mohamed Mahmoud Taha suggested a tempered and modernized attitude toward revelation.[16] Mohamed Talbi and Mohamed Charfi introduced and defended a clear distinction between religious principles and the legal prescriptions devised in order to implement them.[17] This trend (if one can so label a collection of otherwise unrelated thinkers who come to similar conclusions) has received little coverage in the media. Its influence has also been restricted by the educational policies of modern states and by intimidation on the part of the fundamentalists.

2) The *rule of law* is a notion that expresses something that Muslims have longed for since the early phases of their history, and have felt to be part of the message of Islam. Muslim travelers to Europe in the nineteenth century were struck by Europeans' adhesion to rules and rule-bound behavior. This made some of them think that these societies were "Muslim" without being aware of it, as Islam was clearly identified with law-abiding attitudes. Fundamentalists claim that the only way of satisfying this aspiration for lawfulness is by implementing *shari'a*, which they present as the sole remedy for the arbitrariness and abuse of power common in most "Muslim" states. This argument can be countered by showing that the modern concept of "rule of law" is clearer, more operational, and easier to monitor, and thus that the dichotomy of "Islam (or rather *shari'a*) vs. despotism" trumpeted by fundamentalist propaganda is not the whole story. Experience has revealed that law-abidingness is rather a feature of truly modernized societies, where individuals feel that they have a voice in the making of public decisions.

3) *Economic growth* here refers to the idea of continuous progress, which is a basic component of modernity, replacing the messianic

hopes and political resignation dominant in premodern societies with the voluntarism and this-worldly resourcefulness of modern times. Democracy, as an expression of the free will of the citizens, cannot thrive if no collective will is allowed to surface or to have a say about the changes that society is compelled to undergo. It is the direct and visible expression of what Alain Touraine called modernization (in contrast with modernity)—that is, the process through which societies take control of their own affairs, mobilize their forces and their resources, and seek to determine the course of their destiny.[18] Economic growth offers the prospect of an improvement in the conditions of life, which seems to be required in every modern society, and all the more so in "developing" ones. No prospect of democratization can be envisaged if no economic growth is actually taking place.

TOWARD A UNIVERSAL RULE OF LAW

It seems obvious that democracy cannot be exported, much less imposed on peoples who are not prepared to accept it and to mobilize themselves to implement it. If great numbers of Muslims today invoke religion rather than democracy as the alternative to despotism, and others consider democracy itself (at least implicitly) as a kind of new religious belief, this is not because of some special characteristics either of Islam or of Muslims. It is rather because of the particular historical circumstances that I have tried to explain. Muslim confrontations with European colonial powers in the nineteenth century gave birth to some great and lasting misunderstandings, as a result of which Muslims have rejected key aspects of modernity (secularization and, to some degree, democratization) as an alienation and a surrender of the historical self to the "Other."

For those who believe that "civilizations" are hard-core realities that last throughout history and that have distinctive and irreducible features, such polarization is understandable, being the "normal" course of history. It should therefore be treated as such, and the appropriate behavior would be to prepare to defend one's own civilization against alien ones in the unavoidable confrontations of the future.

For those, however, who believe that modern history has, for better or worse, put an end to the separate life of different cultures, there can be convergent paths to establishing social and political systems that promote individual freedoms, human rights, and social justice. These convergent paths point to the crucial importance of the international context and especially of the ongoing relationships between established and would-be democracies.

The fact that democracy has been adopted only in some countries (where it defines the ways their interests are promoted) and not in others creates an asymmetry. The collective interests of some communities, and not of others, find a channel for their expression, and therefore for the promotion of their particular national interests. The moral values that prevail within these communities will not prevail in their relationships with others. This asymmetry will fuel deeper antagonism between nations and greater resentment from those who are weaker. It is therefore time to call for a universal rule of law, where law is not considered only as a means for defending selfish national interests, but is respected for its own sake in a "Kantian" way.

We are living, much more than did our ancestors of the nineteenth and early twentieth centuries, in a deeply integrated world. Some form of a "universal rule of law," creating a new balance between the selfish interests of nations and universal principles, would ease the evolution we are seeking. It would help to define a framework—political, cultural, and economic—that is truly compatible with democratic ideals on the scale of humanity, and favorable to their wider acceptance.

NOTES

1. "Islam is the blueprint of a social order. It holds that a set of rules exists, eternal, divinely ordained, and independent of the will of men, which defines the proper ordering of society. . . . In traditional Islam, no distinction is made between lawyer and common lawyer, and the roles of theologian and lawyer are conflated. Expertise on proper social arrangements, and on matters pertaining to God, are one and the same thing." Ernest Gellner, *Muslim Society* (Cambridge: Cambridge University Press, 1981), 1.

2. Those priests who belong to monastic order and live according to its rules are considered "regular" clergy, while those priests living in the world and not bound by monastic vows or rules are considered "secular" clergy.

3. Quoted by Samuel Huntington, "Democracy's Third Wave," in Marc F. Plattner and Larry Diamond, eds., *The Global Resurgence of Democracy* (Baltimore: Johns Hopkins University Press, 1993), 19.

4. Mohamed Charfi, *Islam et liberté: Le malentendu historique* (Paris: Albin Michel, 1998), 191.

5. Richard K. Khuri gives a very comprehensive description of the way this build-up was achieved. See Richard K. Khuri, *Freedom, Modernity and Islam: Toward a Creative Synthesis* (Syracuse, N.Y.: Syracuse University Press), 1998.

6. Wilfred Cantwell Smith, *The Meaning and End of Religion: A New Approach to the Religious Traditions of Mankind* (New York, 1962), 117.

7. Leonard Binder, "Exceptionalism and Authenticity: The Question of Islam and Democracy," *Arab Studies Journal* 6 (Spring 1998): 33–59.

8. Marshall G.S. Hodgson's main work is *The Venture of Islam*, 3 vols. (Chicago: University of Chicago Press, 1974). A summary of his conclusions appeared in a collection of articles published posthumously under the title *Rethinking World History: Essays on Europe, Islam and World History*, edited, with an introduction and a conclusion, by Edmund Burke III (Cambridge: Cambridge University Press, 1993).

9. Fazlur Rahman, *Islam and Modernity: Transformation of an Intellectual Tradition* (Chicago: University of Chicago Press, 1982), 32.

10. Mohamed Charfi, *Islam et liberté* (Paris: Albin Michel, 1998), 228.

11. Tim Niblock, "Democratisation: A Theoretical and Practical Debate," *The British Journal of Middle Eastern Studies* 25 (November 1998): 221–34.

12. Mohamed Abed Jabri, *Ad-Dimuqratiya wa Huquq al-Insan* [*Democracy and Human Rights*] (Beirut: Center for Arab Unity Studies, 1994).

13. Tim Niblock, "Democratisation," 226.

14. Tim Niblock, "Democratisation," 229.

15. Ali Abderraziq (1888–1966) attempted, in a famous and much debated essay published in 1925, to dispel the misunderstanding and confusions surrounding religion and politics in Islam. His demonstration—for it was intended to be a rigorous demonstration—aimed at showing the strict separation between, on the one hand, religious principles and rules relating to social and

political matters and, on the other, the laws and regulations made by theologians and political leaders to implement the faith in the temporal life of their community. He rejected the view, widely held among Sunni Muslims, that the end of the 'rightly guided' caliphate (approximately three decades after the death of the Prophet), which allegedly saw the replacement of the initially religious community by a regular polity and of a religious order by a secular or temporal order, constituted a really basic turn in the history of Muslims. The initiative of Ali Abderraziq was a founding moment in contemporary Muslim thought and politics. It did not succeed in dispelling the "big misunderstanding"; it is, however, the most radical attempt to show that a "new beginning" is possible for Muslims regarding such basic issues as the overall relation between faith and the social and political order. Ali Abderraziq, *L'Islam et les fondements du pouvoir* (Paris: La Découverte, 1994).

16. Fazlur Rahman did so in scholarly and measured terms, while Taha wrote a kind of manifesto calling for a reversal of the order of prominence that Muslims give to Koranic verses: Mahmoud Mohamed Taha, *The Second Message of Islam*, translated by Abdullahi Ahmed An-Na'im (Syracuse, N.Y.: Syracuse University Press, 1987).

17. For Mohamed Talbi, see *Plaidoyer pour un Islam moderne* (Casablanca: Le Fennec, 1996). For Charfi, see *Islam et liberté: le malentendu historique* (Paris: Albin Michel, 1998).

18. Alain Touraine, "Modernité et spécificités culturelles," in *Revue Internationale des Sciences Sociales* 118 (November 1988): 497–512.

Religion and politics evolved together in the West. To put it more precisely, the formative centuries of Christianity and democracy took place on the same European stage. To be sure, church and state often clashed, sometimes with great violence, but in the end they came together to form a composite ideology. Combined, Christianity and democracy produced a set of ideas, values, and principles that allowed each to keep its place and power in society while lending crucial support to the other. This functional agreement contributed significantly, perhaps decisively, to Europe's and, later, America's global dominance. When facing outward, the West thus presented a united religious–political front to the rest of the world. Europe in particular, according to J. M. Roberts, approached foreign societies "not only as a collection of political and economic potentials, but as the centre of a distinctive civilization whose heart was its religion."[*]

This history explains why many Europeans, to this day, can choose to support Christian Democratic political parties. U.S. president George W. Bush, leader of the most powerful democracy on Earth, routinely invokes the name of God in matters that have little to do with religious faith, hence blending the divine and the secular. Vali Nasr, the author of the next article, asks: If a Christian democracy is possible, why not a Muslim one? Why could not a mutually supportive arrangement between religion and liberal democracy not emerge in the Middle East? The resulting hybrid, the author concedes, might not be recognizable to Western eyes, but it would be democracy nonetheless. In fact, as Nasr points out, indigenous blends of Islam and democracy are already emerging in places like Turkey and Pakistan; one could also add Iran. None of these, of course, would be considered thoroughly democratic states, but they are Muslim, and they are moving, however slowly, toward a degree of democracy. It is true that periodic reverses mar progress in liberalizing Muslim countries, but Nasr is convinced that change is possible, and indeed inevitable. When it comes, Muslim democracy will prove to be good for the Middle East and the rest of world.

NOTES

[*] J. M. Roberts, *A History of Europe* (New York: Allen Lane, 1996), 190.

The Rise of "Muslim Democracy"
VALI NASR

A specter is haunting the Muslim world. This particular specter is not
the maligned and much-discussed spirit of fundamentalist extremism,
nor yet the phantom hope known as liberal Islam. Instead, the specter
that I have in mind is a third force, a hopeful if still somewhat ambiguous trend that I call—in a conscious evocation of the political tradition
associated with the Christian Democratic parties of Europe—"Muslim
Democracy."

The emergence and unfolding of Muslim Democracy as a "fact on
the ground" over the last fifteen years has been impressive. This is so even
though all its exponents have thus far eschewed that label[1] and even
though the lion's share of scholarly and political attention has gone to the
question of how to promote religious reform within Islam as a prelude to
democratization.[2] Since the early 1990s, political openings in a number
of Muslim-majority countries—all, admittedly, outside the Arab world—
have seen Islamic-oriented (but non-Islamist) parties vying successfully
for votes in Bangladesh, Indonesia, Malaysia, Pakistan (before its 1999
military coup), and Turkey.

Unlike Islamists, with their visions of rule by *shari'a* (Islamic law)
or even a restored caliphate, Muslim Democrats view political life with
a pragmatic eye. They reject or at least discount the classic Islamist claim
that Islam commands the pursuit of a *shari'a* state, and their main goal
tends to be the more mundane one of crafting viable electoral platforms and stable governing coalitions to serve individual and collective
interests—Islamic as well as secular—within a democratic arena whose
bounds they respect, win or lose. Islamists view democracy not as something deeply legitimate, but at best as a tool or tactic that may be useful
in gaining the power to build an Islamic state. Muslim Democrats, by
contrast, do not seek to enshrine Islam in politics, though they do wish to
harness its potential to help them win votes.

The rise of the Muslim Democrats has begun the integration of
Muslim religious values—drawn from Islam's teachings on ethics, morality, the family, rights, social relations, and commerce, for example—
into political platforms designed to win regular democratic elections.
Challenges and setbacks will almost surely complicate the process, and
the outcome is far from certain. Yet the ongoing dynamics of democratic

consolidation, more than the promise of religious reform and ideological change, are likely to define the terms under which Islam and democracy interact in at least several Muslim-majority lands.

The past decade and a half has witnessed open electoral competition for legislative seats in Bangladesh (1991, 1996, and 2001); Indonesia (1999 and 2004); Malaysia (1995, 1999, and 2004); Pakistan (1990, 1993, and 1997); and Turkey (1995, 1999, and 2002). The length of this electoral era and the changes that it has set in train allow us to go beyond a "snapshot" of Muslim political preferences in order to track broader trends. Such trends suggest the shape of things to come among the political parties and platforms that will most likely dominate the strategic middle ground of politics in these Muslim-majority countries (or that, in the case of Pakistan, would dominate absent military intervention).

A brief rundown of results is suggestive. In Pakistan in 1997, the right-of-center but non-Islamist Pakistan Muslim League (PML) won 63 percent of the seats in parliament, marginalizing the Islamist party, Jamaat-e-Islami (JI). Similarly, in 2001 the Bangladesh Nationalist Party (BNP) captured 64 percent of the seats in parliament to sideline Bangladesh's own JI. In Turkey in 2002, the Justice and Development Party (AKP)—a group with roots in the world of Islamism but which has always abjured such Islamist hallmarks as the demand for state enactment of *shari'a*—won 66 percent of the seats in parliament; voters had a clear Islamist alternative before them in the form of the Felicity Party, and turned it away with no seats. In Indonesia in 2004, a cluster of center-right Muslim parties, the National Mandate Party (PAN), National Awakening Party (PKB), United Development Party (PPP), plus Golkar (the old ruling party), won 53 percent of the seats, as compared to 8 percent for the Islamist Prosperous Justice Party (PKS). In Malaysia in 2004, the United Malays National Organization (UMNO) won 49.7 percent of the seats while the Islamic Party (PAS) managed to pick up only 3.2 percent.

Such results suggest that in these Muslim societies, the "vital center" of politics is likely to belong neither to secularist and leftist parties nor to Islamists. More likely to rule the strategic middle will be political forces that integrate Muslim values and moderate Islamic politics into broader right-of-center platforms that go beyond exclusively religious concerns. Such forces can appeal to a broad cross-section of voters and create a stable nexus between religious and secular drivers of electoral politics.

Muslim Democrats can begin from an Islamist point of departure, as is the case with Turkey's AKP, but may spring as well from nonreligious parties: Consider Pakistan's PML or Malaysia's UMNO. Not all those who have sought to stake a claim to the middle in Muslim politics have succeeded: In Pakistan, the military toppled the PML government of Prime Minister Nawaz Sharif. But the trend is clear, and so far seems to be a case of practice outrunning theory. Muslim Democracy rests not on an abstract, carefully thought-out theological and ideological accommodation between Islam and democracy, but rather on a practical synthesis that is emerging in much of the Muslim world in response to the opportunities and demands created by the ballot box. Parties must make compromises and pragmatic decisions to maximize their own and their constituents' interests under democratic rules of the game.

In working more on the level of campaign-trail practice than of high theory, Muslim Democracy somewhat resembles Christian Democracy. The first Christian Democratic party was founded in southern Italy in 1919, decades before the theological rapprochement that the Catholic Church made with democracy around the time of the Second Vatican Council in the 1960s.

LIBERALISM AND CONSOLIDATION

Muslim Democracy does not always flow from ideas of Islamic moderation, and it may not always act as a liberalizing force. In some cases, Muslim Democratic parties have backed Islamist demands for stricter moral and religious laws (Pakistan in the 1990s, Bangladesh since 2001) or sought to remove limits on Islamic schools (Turkey since 2002). Yet even such overtures to Islamism should be seen as strategic moves aimed at dominating the middle. The extent to which Muslim Democrats have backed the enforcement of Islamic law or restrictions on women and minorities has seemed to be less a matter of deep ideological conviction than of deals made to win votes in societies where conservative Islamic mores run strong.

The depth of commitment to liberal and secular values that democratic consolidation requires is a condition for Muslim Democracy's final success, not for its first emergence. As was the case with Christian Democracy in Europe, it is the imperative of competition inherent in democracy that will transform the unsecular tendencies of Muslim Democracy into long-term commitment to democratic values.[3]

Rather than arguing for changes in or fresh glosses on Islamic teaching as the path to democracy, Muslim Democrats are in the streets looking for votes and in the process are changing Islam's relation to politics. The shifts that Muslim Democracy will spark in Muslims' attitudes toward society and politics will come not from theoretical suppositions, but from political imperatives. The rise of Muslim Democracy suggests that political change will precede religious change.

Evidence now in from the Muslim world can help to identify the contours of Muslim Democracy, what it stands for, who supports it, and what factors have governed its evolution, its successes, and its failures. Muslim Democracy is a nascent force about which much remains to be learned.

Islamist ideology, which has dominated political debates from Malaysia to Morocco for a quarter-century, calls for the creation of a utopian Islamic state that notionally vests all sovereignty in God. This call is based on a narrow interpretation of Islamic law, and promotes an illiberal, authoritarian politics that leaves little room for civil liberties, cultural pluralism, the rights of women and minorities, and democracy. The Islamist surge since the Iranian Revolution of 1979 has led many to argue that well-organized and determined Islamists will use democratic reforms in Muslim-majority societies to seize power (probably through one-time elections) and impose theocracy. Democracy, the argument goes, should therefore wait until liberalization via ideological and religious reform can blunt the Islamist threat.

The assumption here has been that the key historical process which will lead to democracy in the Muslim world is an intellectual one, a moderation of the Islamist perspective, or more broadly, perhaps even an Islamic Reformation. While some reformists and moderates have been influential, more often than not their efforts have lagged behind the ground-level political realities that have been the growth medium of Muslim Democracy. It has not been intellectuals who have given shape to Muslim Democracy, but rather politicians such as Turkey's Recep Tayyip Erdogan, Pakistan's Nawaz Sharif, and Malaysia's Anwar Ibrahim and Mahatir bin Mohamad. They are the ones grappling with key questions surrounding the interaction of Muslim values with democratic institutions, the nature of Muslims' voting behavior, the shape and location of an "Islamic" voter base, and the like.

One should also note that the rise of Muslim Democracy has occurred at the same time as a steady increase of religious consciousness within Muslim-majority societies.[4] The recent "greening" of Muslim societies, in other words, has led not to votes for Islamists but rather to something that looks at least somewhat like the early stages of Christian Democratic politicking in twentieth-century Western Europe. There are substantial differences, of course. Muslim Democracy, unlike Christian Democracy, cannot measure itself against an authoritatively expressed core of political and religious ideas that transcend national boundaries under the aegis of a centralized religious hierarchy such as the Vatican's. Muslim Democrats, not surprisingly, lack a clear, unified message. They seem instead like the inchoate offspring of various ad hoc alliances and pragmatic decisions made in particular political circumstances. Their provisional and experimental character, however, may be one of the reasons for their success: Free of heavy intellectual baggage, they can move nimbly with the changing tides of electoral circumstance. At the same time, the degree of commonality seen across Muslim Democratic movements in countries as far apart as Malaysia and Turkey underlines the likelihood that Muslim Democracy really is a major trend and not just a cluster of unrelated political accidents.

Still, the differences are important too. In each land, the Muslim Democratic experiment has proceeded more or less independently. In Turkey and Malaysia (as in precoup Pakistan), Muslim Democracy is a winning electoral formula that has yet to fully articulate a vision for governing (and it was failures of governance—especially rampant corruption—that helped set the stage for the Pakistani coup). In Indonesia, Muslim Democracy is less a platform and more a space wherein a number of parties are struggling to strike the right balance between secular politics and Muslim values. In Bangladesh, it is still only an ad hoc political alliance between right-of-center and Islamist parties that has captured the middle but has yet to resolve its own internal political and ideological differences.

Experiments with Muslim Democracy could eventually produce a more coherent political platform and Muslim political practice. What is notable at this stage is less what Muslim Democracy has said about Islam and more what has been achieved at the polls. The Muslim Democratic movements could become more like one another, or they could begin to take diverging paths. Muslim Democracy could prove an independent force for moderation within Islam, or it could come to seem a reflection rather than a shaper of society's religious values. For all these reasons, it will bear close scrutiny in the years ahead.

KEY FACTORS

The rise of Muslim Democracy has depended on the interplay of several factors. First, Muslim Democracy has surfaced in countries where democracy emerged after the military formally withdrew from politics, but remained a powerful player de facto. (In Malaysia the military is not a political actor, but the ruling UMNO has played a similar role through its use of extensive authoritarian powers.) The gradual democratic openings in Turkey since 1983 and in Pakistan during the decade between the reigns of General Zia ul-Haq (d. 1988) and General Musharraf (r. 1999–)

were episodes in which the military shaped the opportunity structure in the democratic arena.

Military involvement in politics had three notable effects. First, it limited the Islamists' room to maneuver. Second, it gave all parties an incentive to avoid confronting the military while angling for advantage within the democratic process. Finally, the military's meddling in politics led to more elections, political realignments, and shifts in coalitions, accelerating and intensifying experimentation with new political formulas. Interestingly, the net effect of all this—a boost for Muslim Democracy—was the same in both Turkey, where the military strongly defended secularism, and Pakistan, where the military worked with Islamists. Turkey's Islamists learned to adopt pragmatic policies to avoid the generals' wrath, while Pakistan's right-of-center PML saw Muslim Democracy as the means to strengthen a frail system of elected civilian rule and the party's own standing within it.

Both the AKP and the PML sought to reduce military pressure on politics through a readiness to compromise with the generals as well as through efforts to build broader coalitions that the generals would hesitate to confront. The PML's success was one of the things that led the Pakistani military to stage its 1999 coup aimed at, among other things, stopping Muslim Democracy. The upshot, tellingly, has been that the seat share of Islamist parties in parliament has risen sharply from its negligible 1997 level of less than 1 percent to 20 percent in 2002. By removing the Nawaz Sharif government—and with it Muslim Democracy—General Musharraf has strengthened the Islamists, whether he meant to or not.[5]

While the Indonesian and Bangladeshi militaries have been more circumspect, each has also helped to nudge Islamists and right-of-center parties to explore Muslim Democracy. Malaysia is unique in that change there came not at military prompting, but from within the ruling party. In the 1980s, UMNO's control over national politics allowed it to restrain Islamists with one hand while using the other to reach out systematically to Muslim voters. The Malaysian case aside, it seems clear that Muslim Democracy is more likely to emerge when Islamist and democratic forces sense a common interest in protecting the democratic process from the military.

Second, Muslim Democracy has emerged in societies where the private sector matters. The less state-dependent and more integrated into the world economy a country's private sector is, the more likely is that country to see Muslim Democracy gain traction as a political force. Muslim Democracy, in short, needs the bourgeoisie, and the bourgeoisie needs Muslim Democracy. Muslim Democracy combines the religious values of the middle and lower-middle classes with policies that serve their economic interests.

In Turkey, the success of AKP's Muslim Democratic platform is less a triumph of religious piety over Kemalist secularism than of an independent bourgeoisie over a centralizing state. To understand the rise of Muslim Democracy in Turkey, one must consider the economic-liberalization policies of Prime Minister (later President) Turgut Özal (d. 1993) in the 1980s and the vibrant, independent private sector that they made possible. Similarly, Indonesia's Suharto regime in its later years mixed state support for moderate Islam with engagement in global trade. The same trend was evident in Malaysia, where the UMNO government combined economic globalization with promotion of a nationalist and moderate Muslim political platform that would support those economic policies. While Bangladesh and Pakistan lag behind Turkey, Indonesia, and Malaysia in terms of participation in global trade, they too boast robust private sectors that exert growing political influence. Yet the deeper involvement in the global economy and the greater independence of the Turkish, Indonesian, and Malaysian private sectors seem to correlate with the more Islamically moderate character of Muslim Democracy in those countries as compared to Pakistan or Bangladesh.

In addition to the military dynamic and the economic dynamic, a third motor of Muslim Democracy seems to be the existence of strong competition over votes. With no one party able easily to dominate the process, all parties feel pressed to act pragmatically. The presence of multiple parties with strong organizational structures and political legacies (some dating back earlier than the democratic opening) in turn fosters competition. Despite sustained bouts of military rule or one-party dominance in all these countries, multiparty politics has retained its vitality in each, and parties have bounced back as political processes have opened.

Regular competitive elections have both pushed religious parties toward pragmatism and pulled other parties into more diligent efforts to represent Muslim values. The net effect is to reward moderation. The game is to win the middle. This is the politics of what electoral experts call "the median voter," around whose position on the issue spectrum majorities cluster. Competition over the Muslim electorate means that non-Islamist groups can integrate those who vote based on Muslim values into broader platforms and wider coalitions than Islamists are capable of marshaling. In 1990s Malaysia, for instance, the UMNO successfully competed for the urban and middle-class Muslim vote and thwarted challenges by the Islamist PAS. At about the same time, the PML was doing much the same thing to the JI in Pakistan.

In Muslim-majority countries where the factors listed above do not exist or are weak, the prospects that Muslim Democracy will emerge are much lower. Yet even in such societies, the activities of Muslim Democrats elsewhere may prove relevant to local political discussions. In particular, if and when Muslim Democracy gains coherence, it will become readier for export to countries unable to produce it from scratch. Muslim Democracy can travel. In the 1990s, Pakistan's PML consciously sought to imitate Malaysia's UMNO. More recently, the rise of the Turkish AKP has been noted in Arab circles, secular, official, and Islamist alike. In Egypt, the Islamist Muslim Brotherhood has been keenly watching developments in Turkey, and some within Brotherhood ranks have begun taking measured steps toward the middle. In Algeria, it is the government that has been encouraging the Turkish model by trying to push the Islamic Salvation Front (FIS) to start acting more like the AKP.

The rise of Muslim Democracy suggests that the values of Muslims—which are not to be confused with the demands of Islamists—can interact with practical election strategies to play the main role in shaping political ideas and driving voter behavior.[6] In the end, Muslim Democracy represents the triumph of practice over theory, and perhaps of the political over the Islamic. The future of Muslim politics is likely to belong to those who can speak to Muslim values and ethics, but within the framework of political platforms fit to thrive in democratic settings.

After 1945, Christian Democracy sought to change Catholic attitudes toward democracy in order to channel religious values into mass politics.[7] Christian Democracy drew on Catholic identity, but also related it to social programs and welfare concerns. Christian Democrats provided the means for conservative religious values to find expression in secular politics. The rise of Christian Democracy reflected the desire of Church leaders to provide a voice for Catholic views in democracies, but it was also the result of strategic choices by political actors who saw opportunity in mobilizing religious values to further their political interests.[8]

Similar forces are now at work in some Muslim-majority countries, with ripple effects that will likely be felt throughout the Muslim world. Like the Catholic Church in the last century, Islamic-oriented parties are grasping the need to relate religious values to secular politics. As was also the case in Europe, secular parties and politicians are sensing the benefits of including appeals to religious values in their platforms. Thus Muslim Democracy, like Christian Democracy before it, is emerging as a political tendency that is strongly tied to both the democratic process and the use of direct appeals to the concerns of religious voters.

LIMITS AND POTENTIAL

Considered together, the cases of Pakistan and Turkey point to the limits as well as the potential of Muslim Democracy. They help us to discern what is driving the rise of Muslim Democracy, what it stands for, whom it represents, and what challenges it faces. Ironically, Turkey has moved in a more liberal direction even though its Muslim Democratic party springs from Islamist roots, whereas in Pakistan the push toward Muslim Democracy that the non-Islamist PML began has been cut short by a military takeover. Economic factors figure prominently in both cases, and in both the military has played a large role, albeit with vast differences between one case and the other.

In Pakistan, 1988 saw a period of military rule come to a close with the mysterious midair death of General Zia, whose regime had mixed authoritarianism with Islamization. The main prodemocracy force at the time was the secular-leftist Pakistan People's Party (PPP). To limit PPP gains in the 1988 elections and guard their own interests, the departing generals cobbled together a PML–Islamist coalition called the Islamic Democratic Alliance (IJI).

Between 1988 and 1993, the power struggle between the PPP and the IJI plus the military's continued meddling transformed right-of-center politics into more than a tool for keeping civilian institutions weak. In 1990, the IJI won the elections after the military dismissed the PPP government. As the IJI's several parts, now secure in government, began to pursue their own respective agendas, the coalition frayed. The PML and the Islamists both began to sense a chance to dominate Pakistani politics as never before—under conditions of elected civilian rule. The PML moved first, distancing itself from both the generals and the Islamists (who remained close to each other) to wage the 1993 election campaign on its own with a platform that promised economic growth while placating nationalist and Muslim sensibilities. The latter strategy involved stealing such staples of Islamist rhetoric as the call for the enforcement of *shari'a*—although to please its more secular supporters the PML never did more than gesture at this goal.

Although the PPP wound up winning the October 1993 parliamentary elections, the PML's gambit succeeded at least in part. The party carried the Muslim vote and pushed JI to the margins with a dismal showing. This was the first time in the Muslim world that political maneuvering within a competitive electoral process had put a brake on Islamism. The next election, in 1997, only made the trend more evident as the PML returned to power with almost two-thirds of the seats in the National Assembly while the Islamists found themselves reduced to their smallest parliamentary contingent ever. To achieve this, the PML had cast itself simultaneously as a modern democratic party that was committed to the development of Pakistan and as the standard-bearer of Islamic identity—the latter a claim bolstered by the PML's success in taking over seats once held by avowed Islamists.[9] As is shaping up to be the case in Turkey today, it was the promise of Islamic legislation rather than its fulfillment that proved a sufficiently popular formula.

Between 1993 and 1999, the PML continued to push a mixture of business-friendly economic policies and nationalist-cum-Islamic appeals. Infrastructure development and globalization went hand-in-hand with a nuclear-weapons program, confrontations with India, and rhetorical support for Islamic legislation. Balancing the demands of the various constituencies at which these postures were severally aimed was the PML's challenge. Business interests supported peace with India, for instance, while nationalists and Islamists wanted a tougher stance. As the 1990s wore on, such tensions began to undermine the PML's appeal to its Muslim-minded voter base and gave the military angles to play against the party in advance of the 1999 coup.

It was the PML's very success, however, that set the stage for its fall. The generals began to worry that the party's strategy—which we can now see was a rough-and-ready version of Muslim Democracy—would actually succeed. There followed Musharraf's 1999 coup against Sharif and the systematic dismantling, under military tutelage, of the PML. When Musharraf allowed controlled elections to be held in 2002, Islamists did spectacularly well, rebounding all the way up to a best-ever 20 percent vote share. While Musharraf, especially since 9/11, has postured as Pakistan's sole bulwark against radical Islamist rule, a more accurate statement of the facts would say that the military did full-bore Islamism a huge favor by yanking the PML from power and stopping the country's uncertain yet real progress toward Muslim Democracy.

TURKISH TRAILBLAZERS

In Turkey, the 1990s were a decade of struggle between Islamists and the military. Turkey's powerful military, unlike Pakistan's, did not support Islamist activism, and was restrained in its actions by its own commitment to democracy, economic reform, and European Union (EU) dictates regarding the rule of law.

The end of a bout of direct military rule in the early 1980s had opened the door for Islamists to enter politics. In 1987, Necmettin Erbakan organized the Welfare Party (RP) to marshal Islamist support among the lower and lower-middle classes as well as the booming independent private sector. By 1994, the RP was winning municipal races in Istanbul and Ankara. A year later, it took 22 percent of the vote in national parliamentary elections. In 1996, the RP formed a governing coalition with the secular True Path Party. Erbakan became prime minister of Atatürk's militantly secular Kemalist republic.

The Turkish military, long the fierce keeper of Kemalism's secular-nationalist flame, was not reconciled to an Islamist ascendancy. Beginning in early 1997, the generals launched what Cengiz Çandar has dubbed a "postmodern coup," manipulating the courts and the parliamentary process to upend Erbakan's government.[10] The RP found itself under a formal ban for transgressing the constitution's secularist red lines. Some of the party's activists tried to organize a new formation called the Virtue Party, but in 2001 that too was banned. Right-wing and especially nationalist parties stepped into the resulting gap by including appeals to traditional Muslim values in secular platforms. The lesson was not lost on Islamist politicians.

The military's politico-juridical strike against the Islamists split the Muslim-values bloc. In 2002, a group of younger Islamist politicians under Erdogan—the onetime mayor of Istanbul who had just served a jail term on charges of inflaming religious passions—broke with Erbakan to form the AKP, leaving the Virtue Party's traditional-Islamist rump to rename itself the Felicity Party. The November 2002 elections were an AKP romp, as the party won a clear plurality of the popular vote and a huge majority of the seats in parliament.[11] Felicity won a scant 2.5 percent of the vote nationwide, well short of the 10 percent needed for parliamentary representation.

Many AKP members once belonged to the Welfare and Virtue parties. Yet there are also middle-class and lower-middle-class elements with no history of Islamist ties. In many ways, the AKP is less an extension of Welfare and Virtue than a reconstruction of the center-right, economically liberal Motherland Party (ANAP) of Turgut Özal, the architect of Turkey's bold plunge into democracy and the global economy in the 1980s.

More than two years into its rule, the AKP is still an electoral strategy in search of a governing agenda. It lacks a clear platform, much less a fully thought-out approach to the role of Islam in politics. And yet its experience so far is important in several respects. First, it is a case in which Islamist activists embraced a process of moderation and pragmatic change. Second, it highlights the factors that govern the rise of Muslim Democracy. Third, it gives us the best picture we have so far of what Muslim Democracy might become and what it might stand for. Then too, the AKP's case tells much about the tensions that inhere in the development of Muslim Democracy, the consolidation of its political position, and how it can contribute to the institutionalization of liberal democracy.

The AKP is the brainchild of Virtue Party moderates, led by Erdogan, who concluded that Turkey's military would never allow an overtly Islamist party back into power, and—still more importantly— that the ban on Islamic parties was helping other right-of-center parties such as the Nationalist Action Party, which had come to hold nearly a quarter of the seats in parliament by 1999. Erdogan and his colleagues realized that there was a robust base of Muslim-minded voters, and that the military would never allow an Islamist party to tap that base. Consequently, the AKP presented itself as a center-right party that appealed to Muslim values only indirectly, through the medium of more generically traditional values. By sublimating Muslim-minded politics into a broader appeal to traditional and conservative values in a society where the political center of gravity is on the center-right, the AKP was able to put together the wide support base that became the launching pad for its rocket ride to power in 2002.

Part of this skillfully executed effort involved crafting appeals that traveled across class lines. The AKP is popular in Istanbul and Ankara slums where Islamists have become known for their efficient management of social services such as law enforcement, sewage disposal, and trash pickup. The AKP watchword of "conservative democracy" (the phrase that Erdogan prefers to "Muslim democracy," in part to allay military and EU fears that he might be a theocrat in a necktie[12]) also appeals to the "Anatolian tigers"—the pious and prosperous Muslims of the new private sector, whose "green capitalism" forms the basis of the independent bourgeoisie.[13] To keep those with more traditional Islamist leanings on board, the AKP is often more vociferous on secular matters (such as criticism of Israel) than on their purely religious concerns.

THE BURDENS AND LIMITS OF POWER

The AKP must now master the challenge, common to all democratic parties, of balancing a set of divergent constituent demands within a single winning platform. Power and its responsibilities arguably make this harder. The urban poor like populist economics. The business community wants tightly managed fiscal and monetary policy that meets EU admissions standards.

Many AKP voters expect the party to tackle contentious symbolic issues such as the current ban on women's headscarves. With an eye on their conservative and nationalist supporters who do not necessarily

favor overtly religious politics, AKP leaders shied away from the heads-
carf issue, and instead endorsed a bill that would criminalize adultery,
for the former seems more like a purely "Islamic" issue while the latter
can be called a matter of upholding "traditional values." Yet even here
the AKP has faced problems: When the EU strongly objected to the
adultery bill, the AKP quickly dropped it. The emphasis on "conservative" as distinguished from "Muslim" democracy in AKP parlance is also
meant to help position the party as a potential partner for the Christian
Democratic parties of the EU nations. What the AKP actually stands
for, in short, is being worked out gradually as the limits of the possible
become clearer. This degree of pragmatism sits uneasily with the AKP's
high-minded Islamic idealists (the party's very name in Turkish forms
an acronym for "pure," "unsullied," or "honest"), but Erdogan's personal
popularity and the Islamic credentials of the party's founders have helped
to bridge the gap.

Since taking office, the AKP has shown more interest in strengthening democracy than in delivering on the demands of its most Muslim-
minded supporters. This approach may signal a shift from a state-centered
to a society-centered perspective, from a strategy of struggling to capture
state power on behalf of Islam to one of seeking to foster a civil society
and a deeply rooted democratic order that together will embody Muslim
values and limit state power.

This has meant serving the interests of private business, pursuing
full EU membership, and deemphasizing the most Islamist aspects of
the party's agenda—in other words, promising to create a space within
which Muslim values can express themselves, but not pushing an
Islamist legislative agenda. As it leads Turkey toward the EU, the AKP
is now able credibly to present itself as the country's great champion of
modernization—and as such has entered into a de facto competition with
the military, which has long claimed that title for itself. In keeping with
this, the AKP is increasingly engaging in the de facto promotion of what
social theorists call "differentiation," as the party's actions, omissions,
"body language," and actual language all seem to be recommending a
distinction between the private practice of Islam (encouraged) and its
public expression or imposition (approached shyly and with caution, if
not abjured outright).

A strongly felt need to keep the military at bay no doubt underlies
much of the AKP's strategy. Sensing this, the party's more pious
supporters are giving it latitude as it avoids and postpones dealing with
Islamic issues. The party also tells the faithful that a "soft" approach to
Islam will ensure closer ties between Turkey and Europe. Europe alone
has the capability to build institutional boundaries around the military

and to protect Turkish democracy. Since liberal democracy is far more receptive to religious expression than is Kemalist secularism, Muslim-minded voters can see an interest in not pushing too hard for their favorite policies now, in hopes of strengthening Turkey's ties to Europe and with them Turkish liberal democracy. Although it is quite likely that Europe too will look unfavorably on drives for certain types of Islamic legislation, the EU will also perhaps do so somewhat less strenuously than will the Turkish military. And of course the Anatolian tigers and the rest of the AKP's private-sector base strongly favor closeness to Europe as a key to Turkey's hopes for prosperity.

As we have seen, the AKP currently has rather limited room for strategic choice, stuck as it is between its various groups of supporters, the Kemalist military and state establishment, and the Europeans. And yet that choice is pushing the party to define the middle in Turkish politics in terms of conservative values that embrace broader Islamic values and concerns, but which are not limited to narrow interpretations of Islamic law. Erdogan's refusal to let the AKP be called a "Muslim" party bespeaks a large measure of sincerity as well as a dash of calculation.

Will the AKP's gambit succeed? Will the party prove itself able to establish a coherent definition of Muslim Democracy (with or without the actual name) that can channel a politics of Islamic concerns and aspirations into liberal-democratic channels? The answers will come not from the realm of theory and ideology, but from that of pragmatism and politics. Competitions for power—and the calculations to which these competitions give rise—are promoting continual and far-reaching change, regardless of whatever the AKP's original intentions may have been. In the ironic realm of history, even the winners often build other than they know. The result will be "secularization" as Martin Marty once defined it: "a complex set of radical religious changes, in which people act and think religiously in ways which differ from those of the past."[14] This is also the process that Stathis Kalyvas identifies in the development of European Christian Democracy, wherein unsecular political positions, once subjected to the pressures of competition, gradually adapted to the values and rules of democracy.

Turkey presents perhaps the most developed instance of Muslim Democracy, but the process is in evidence elsewhere as well. Even at this early stage it is clear that the sheer competitive logic inherent in open politics is driving Muslim Democracy forward, especially in places where gradual democratization has ensured the continuation of that competition through repeated elections. Established parties, a robust private sector, and an ongoing democratic process (even a rough and troubled one) are the ingredients that need to be in the mix if Muslim

Democracy is to put down roots and blossom. Muslim Democracy offers the Muslim world the promise of moderation. As Islamists find themselves facing—or caught up in—the Muslim Democratic dynamic, they will find themselves increasingly facing the hard choice of changing or suffering marginalization.

For an example of what such change might look like, consider a recent *fatwa* (religious decree) that the Shi'ite Muslim ayatollah Ali Sistani issued ahead of the 30 January 2005 elections in Iraq. Sistani sought to impress upon women their religious duty to vote even if their husbands forbade them to do so. Sistani is well known as a major backer of a unified Shi'ite-candidates' list. Evidently the imperative of notching a big win in the elections—more than any arguments about religious reform or women's rights—compelled the most senior Shi'ite religious leader in Iraq to advocate not only the enfranchisement of women, but even their right (or as Sistani would probably prefer to put it, their specific duty in this case) to disobey their husbands.[15]

Finally, it is Muslim Democracy—and not the creaky and brittle authoritarianisms by which the Muslim world is so beset—that offers the whole world its best hope for an effective bulwark against radical and violent Islamism.[16] Muslim Democracy provides a model for pragmatic change. That change will in turn be the harbinger, not the follower, of more liberal Islamic thought and practice.

NOTES

1. After the November 2002 Turkish elections, some in the West began extolling the Justice and Development Party of Recep Tayyip Erdogan as a group of "Muslim Democrats" not unlike the Christian Democrats. See, for example, Radwan A. Masmoudi, "A Victory for the Cause of Islamic Democracy: An American Muslim Analyzes the Surprise Election in Turkey," www.beliefnet.com/story/116/story_11673_1.html. While I plainly think that Masmoudi was on to something, I should note that Erdogan himself has taken pains publicly to disown the "Muslim Democrat" label and to embrace the idea of "conservative democracy" instead. See Erdogan's remarks in Vincent Boland, "Eastern Premise," *Financial Times* (London), 3 December 2004.

2. See John L. Esposito and John O. Voll, *Islam and Democracy* (New York: Oxford University Press, 1996); and Larry Diamond, Marc F. Plattner, and Daniel Brumberg, eds., *Islam and Democracy in the Middle East* (Baltimore: Johns Hopkins University Press, 2003).

3. Stathis Kalyvas, "Unsecular Politics and Religious Mobilization," in Thomas Kselman and Joseph Buttigieg, eds., *European Christian Democracy* (Notre Dame: University of Notre Dame Press, 2003), 293–320.

4. Genevieve Abdo, *No God But God: Egypt and the Triumph of Islam* (New York: Oxford University Press, 2000); Hakan Yavuz, *Islamic Political Identity in Turkey* (New York: Oxford University Press, 2003); Bahtiar Effendy, *Islam and the State in Indonesia* (Athens, Ohio: Ohio University Press, 2003); Seyyed Vali Reza Nasr, *Islamic Leviathan: Islam and the Making of State Power* (New York: Oxford University Press, 2001).

5. Vali Nasr, "Military Rule, Islamism, and Democracy in Pakistan," *Middle East Journal* 58 (Spring 2004): 195–209.

6. Saiful Mujani and R. William Liddle "Politics, Islam, and Public Opinion," *Journal of Democracy* 15 (January 2004): 109–23.

7. José Casanova, *Public Religions in the Modern World* (Chicago: University of Chicago Press, 1994), 5–39.

8. Stathis Kalyvas, *The Rise of Christian Democracy in Europe* (Ithaca, N.Y.: Cornell University Press, 1996), 2–4.

9. As Nawaz Sharif once put it, he wanted to be "both the [Turkish Islamist leader Necmettin] Erbakan and the [economically modernizing Malaysian prime minister] Mahatir of Pakistan." Author's interview, Lahore, Pakistan, October 1997.

10. Cengiz Çandar, "Postmodern Darbe" (Postmodern coup), *Sabah* (Istanbul), 28 June 1997. See also Cengiz Çandar, "Redefining Turkey's Political Center," *Journal of Democracy* 10 (October 1999): 129–41.

11. Ziya Önis and Fuat Keyman, "Turkey at the Polls: A New Path Emerges," *Journal of Democracy* 14 (April 2003): 95–107.

12. As Erdogan put it to one interviewer, "[W]e are conservative democrats. . . . our notion of conservative democracy is to attach ourselves to the customs, traditions, and values of our society, which is based on the family. . . . This is a democratic issue, not a religious issue." Vincent Boland, "Eastern Premise," *Financial Times* (London), 3 December 2004.

13. Hakan Yavuz, "Opportunity Spaces, Identity, and Islamic Meaning in Turkey," in Quintan Wiktorowicz, ed., *Islamic Activism: A Social*

Movement Theory Approach (Bloomington: Indiana University Press, 2004), 270–88.

14. Martin Marty, *The Modern Schism: Three Paths to the Secular* (New York: Harper and Row, 1969), 108.

15. This *fatwa*—apparently spoken rather than written—was reported from Baghdad by *Newsweek* correspondent Rod Nordland in a dispatch on the Iraqi elections dated 30 January 2005. Nordland wrote that "Sistani's *fatwa* ordered Shia women to vote, even if their husbands told them not to." See www.msnbc.msn.com/id/6887461/site/newsweek. Nordland and Babak Dehghanpisheh reported in a dispatch dated 14 February 2004 that every third candidate on the Shi'ite list that Sistani helped to create was a woman. See www.msnbc.msn.com/id/6920460/site/newsweek.

16. Alfred Stepan and Aqil Shah, "Pakistan's Real Bulwark," *Washington Post*, 5 May 2004, A29.

Nasr, Seyyed Vali Reza. The Rise of "Muslim Democracy." Journal of Democracy 16:2 (2005), 13–27. © National Endowment for Democracy and The Johns Hopkins University Press. Reprinted with permission of The Johns Hopkins University Press.

K aren Armstrong, in her history of Islam, notes that political activity has always been central to the Muslim experience. Indeed, from the earliest times, "politics was no secondary issue for Muslims . . . it had been the theater of their religious quest."* It is unsurprising, then, that recent decades have seen a resurgence of what is today known as "political Islam." The term describes the phenomenon of Islamic principles being employed as political reference points. Sometimes called Islamism, political Islam represents an effort to bring about reform in the Muslim world through non-Western means. As a genuinely indigenous movement, political Islam is aimed at achieving social and governmental reform in a manner that is consistent with the teachings contained in the Koran. Considering the many and varied interpretations of the Muslim holy book, there are different forms of political Islam in the world today. Most are moderate; some are extreme. A handful of Islamist groups advocate violence, threatening the advances made by their less radical counterparts. For the tiniest minority, political Islam is a springboard into terrorism.

In the essay that follows, Graham Fuller acknowledges all this but contends that political Islam remains the best hope for the success of democratic-style reform in the Muslim Middle East. Fuller warns against measuring political Islam solely by the yardstick of mature Western democracy. He also cautions against accepting definitions of the movement written by either the most radical Islamists or the repressive authoritarian governments who oppose them. Neither of these cares much for the type of peaceful, lasting reform that the Middle East needs. If nurtured carefully, the author concludes, political Islam could be the vehicle for democracy in a complex and often chaotic part of the world.

NOTES
*   Karen Armstrong, *Islam: A Short History* (New York: Random House, 2000), 157.

The Future of Political Islam
GRAHAM E. FULLER

IT'S NOT OVER 'TIL IT'S OVER

Were the attacks of September 11, 2001, the final gasp of Islamic radicalism or the opening salvo of a more violent confrontation between Muslim extremists and the West? And what does the current crisis imply for the future of the Islamic world itself? Will Muslims recoil from the violence and sweeping anti-Westernism unleashed in their name, or will they allow Osama bin Laden and his cohort to shape the character of future relations between Muslims and the West?

The answers to these questions lie partly in the hands of the Bush administration. The war on terrorism has already dealt a major blow to the personnel, infrastructure, and operations of bin Laden's al Qaeda network. Just as important, it has burst the bubble of euphoria and sense of invincibility among radical Islamists that arose from the successful jihad against the Soviet occupation of Afghanistan. But it is not yet clear whether the war will ultimately alleviate or merely exacerbate the current tensions in the Muslim world.

Depending on one's perspective, the attacks on the World Trade Center and the Pentagon can be seen either as a success, evidence that a few activists can deal a grievous blow to a superpower in the name of their cause, or as a failure, since the attackers brought on the demise of their state sponsor and most likely of their own organization while galvanizing nearly global opposition. To help the latter lesson triumph, the United States will have to move beyond the war's first phase, which has punished those directly responsible for the attacks, and address the deeper sources of political violence and terror in the Muslim world today.

THE MANY FACES OF ISLAMISM

President Bush has repeatedly stressed that the war on terrorism is not a war on Islam. But by seeking to separate Islam from politics, the West ignores the reality that the two are intricately intertwined across a broad swath of the globe from northern Africa to Southeast Asia. Transforming the Muslim environment is not merely a matter of rewriting school textbooks or demanding a less anti-Western press. The simple fact is that political Islam, or Islamism—defined broadly as the belief that the Koran and the Hadith (Traditions of the Prophet's life) have something important to say about the way society and governance should be ordered—remains the most powerful ideological force in that part of the world.

The Islamist phenomenon is hardly uniform, however; multiple forms of it are spreading, evolving, and diversifying. Today one encounters Islamists who may be either radical or moderate, political or apolitical, violent or quietist, traditional or modernist, democratic or authoritarian. The oppressive Taliban of Afghanistan and the murderous Algerian Armed Islamic Group (known by its French acronym, GIA) lie at one fanatic point of a compass that also includes Pakistan's peaceful and apolitical preaching-to-the-people movement, the Tablighi Jamaat; Egypt's mainstream conservative parliamentary party, the Muslim Brotherhood; and Turkey's democratic and modernist Fazilet/Ak Party.

Turkey's apolitical Nur movement embraces all aspects of science as compatible with Islam because secular scientific knowledge reinforces the wonder of God's world. Indonesia's syncretic Nahdatul Ulama eschews any Islamic state at all in its quest to further appreciation of God's role in human life. Islamist feminist movements are studying the Koran and Islamic law (the shari'a) in order to interpret the teachings for themselves and distinguish between what their religion clearly stipulates and those traditions arbitrarily devised and enforced by patriarchal leaders (such as mandatory head-to-toe covering or the ban on female driving in Saudi Arabia). These are but a few among the vast array of movements that work in the media, manage Web sites, conduct massive welfare programs, run schools and hospitals, represent flourishing Muslim nongovernmental organizations, and exert a major impact on Muslim life.

Islamism has become, in fact, the primary vehicle and vocabulary of most political discourse throughout the Muslim world. When Westerners talk about political ideals, they naturally hark back to the Magna Carta, the American Revolution, and the French Revolution. Muslims go back to the Koran and the Hadith to derive general principles about good governance (including the ruler's obligation to consult the people) and concepts of social and economic justice. Neither Islam nor Islamism says much about concrete state institutions, and frankly nobody knows exactly what a modern Islamic state should look like—since few have ever existed and none provides a good model. But Islamists today use general Islamic ideals as a touchstone for criticizing, attacking, or even trying to overthrow what are perceived as authoritarian, corrupt, incompetent, and illegitimate regimes.

No other ideology has remotely comparable sway in the Muslim world. The region's nationalist parties are weak and discredited, and nationalism itself has often been absorbed into Islamism; the left is marginalized and in disarray; liberal democrats cannot even muster enough supporters to stage a demonstration in any Muslim capital. Like it or not, therefore, various forms of Islamism will be the dominant intellectual current in the region for some time to come—and the process is still in its infancy. In the end, modern liberal governance is more likely to take root through organically evolving liberal Islamist trends at the grassroots level than from imported Western modules of "instant democracy."

A DYNAMIC PHENOMENON

Most Western observers tend to look at the phenomenon of political Islam as if it were a butterfly in a collection box, captured and skewered for eternity, or as a set of texts unbendingly prescribing a single path. This is why some scholars who examine its core writings proclaim Islam to be incompatible with democracy—as if any religion in its origins was about democracy at all.

Such observers have the question wrong. The real issue is not what Islam is, but what Muslims want. People of all sorts of faiths can rapidly develop interpretations of their religion that justify practically any political quest. This process, moreover, is already underway among Muslims. Contemporary Islam is a dynamic phenomenon. It includes not only bin Laden and the Taliban, but also liberals who are clearly embarking on their own Reformation with potentially powerful long-term consequences. Deeply entrenched traditionalists find these latter stirrings a threat, but many more Muslims, including many Islamists, see such efforts to understand eternal values in contemporary terms as essential to a living faith.

Regrettably, until recently Islam had been living (with striking periodic exceptions) in a state of intellectual stagnation for many hundreds of years. Western colonizers further vitiated and marginalized Islamic thought and institutions, and post-independence leadership has done no better, tending to draw on quasi-fascist Western models of authoritarian control. Only now is Islam emerging into a period of renewed creativity, freedom, and independence. Much of this new activity, ironically, is occurring in the freedom of the West, where dozens of Islamic institutes are developing new ideas and employing modern communications to spur debate and disseminate information.

The process of diversification and evolution within modern Islamism is driven by multiple internal forces, but these developments are always ultimately contingent on the tolerance of local regimes, the nature of local politics, and the reigning pattern of global power. Most regimes see almost any form of political Islam as a threat, since it embodies a major challenge to their unpopular, failing, and illegitimate presidents-for-life or isolated monarchs. How the regime responds to the phenomenon often plays a major role in determining how the local Islamist movement develops.

Does the regime permit elections and free political discussion? How repressive is it, and how violent is the political culture in which it operates? How do existing economic and social conditions affect the political process? The answers to these questions go a long way toward describing how Islamists—like all other political actors—will behave in any particular country. That said, these days nearly all Islamists push hard for democracy, believing that they will benefit from it and flourish within it. They also have discovered the importance of human rights—at least in the political field—precisely because they are usually the primary victims of the absence of rights, filling regional jails in disproportionate numbers.

Some skepticism is due, of course, about the ability of Islamists to run effective and moderate governments, especially when the three Islamic state models to date—Iran, Sudan, and the Taliban's Afghanistan—have all failed dramatically in this area. Only Iran has lately shown signs of exciting evolution within an Islamic framework. But it is worth recalling that all of those regimes came to power by social revolution, military coup, or civil war, virtually guaranteeing continuing despotism regardless of which party was in charge.

The true test of any Islamist party comes when it gains office by the ballot box and must then adhere while in power to the democratic norms it touted in opposition. History unfortunately gives few precedents here. Turkey's brief experience under an elected Islamist-led coalition comes closest, but the government was removed by the military after a year of mixed performance, leaving the experiment unfinished. Secular Turks continue to elect Islamist mayors in major cities across the country, however, including Istanbul and Ankara, because they deliver what constituents want.

Americans brought up to venerate the separation of church and state may wonder whether a movement with an explicit religious vision can ever create a democratic, tolerant, and pluralistic polity. But if Christian Democrats can do it, there is no reason in principle why Islamists cannot. This is what the cleric President Mohammed Khatami is trying to achieve in Iran, in fact, although his efforts are being blocked by a hard-line clerical faction. Non-Muslims should understand that democratic values are latent in Islamic thought if one wants to look for them, and that it would be more natural and organic for the Muslim world to derive contemporary liberal practices from its own sources than to import them wholesale from foreign cultures. The key question is whether it will actually do so.

WHO'S BESIEGING WHOM?

The liberal evolution of political Islam faces some formidable obstacles. The first, as noted, comes from the local political scene, where Islamists are routinely suppressed, jailed, tortured, and executed. Such circumstances encourage the emergence of secret, conspiratorial, and often armed groups rather than liberal ones.

The second obstacle comes from international politics, which often pushes Islamist movements and parties in an unfortunate direction. A familiar phenomenon is the Muslim national liberation movement. In more than a dozen countries, large, oppressed Muslim minorities, who are also ethnically different from their rulers, have sought autonomy or independence—witness the Palestinians, Chechens, Chinese Uighurs, Filipino Moros, and Kashmiris, among others. In these cases, Islam serves to powerfully bolster national liberation struggles by adding a "holy" religious element to an emerging ethnic struggle. These causes have attracted a kind of Muslim "foreign legion" of radicalized, volunteer mujahideen, some of whom have joined al Qaeda.

A third obstacle comes from the Islamists' own long list of grievances against the forces and policies perceived to be holding Muslims back in the contemporary world, many of them associated with liberalism's supposed avatar, the United States. The litany includes U.S. support for authoritarianism in the Muslim world in the name of stability or material interests such as ensuring the flow of oil, routine U.S. backing of Israeli policies, and Washington's failure to press for democratic political processes out of fear that they might bring Islamist groups to power.

Islamists, too, deserve criticism for playing frequently opportunistic political games—like so many other fledgling parties. Where they exist legally, they often adopt radical postures on Islamic issues to embarrass the government. The major Islamist PAS movement in Malaysia, for example—which now governs two of the country's ten states—has called for full implementation of the shari'a and application of traditional Muslim punishments (including amputations and stoning), in part to show up the poor Islamic credentials of the central government. In Egypt and Kuwait, meanwhile, Islamist groups regularly call for more conservative social measures, partly to score political points, and have often inhibited the intellectual freedom on Islamic issues which these societies desperately require. Such posturing tends to bid up the level of Islamic strictness within the country in question in a closed atmosphere of Islamic political correctness. Still, most Islamists have quite concrete domestic agendas related to local politics and social issues that are far removed from the transnational, apocalyptic visions of a bin Laden.

Ironically, even as Westerners feel threatened by Islam, most in the Muslim world feel themselves besieged by the West, a reality only dimly grasped in the United States. They see the international order as dramatically skewed against them and their interests, in a world where force and the potential for force dominate the agenda. They are overwhelmed by feelings of political impotence. Muslim rulers fear offending their protectors in Washington, Muslim publics have little or no influence over policy within their own states, bad leaders cannot be changed, and public expression of dissent is punished, often brutally. This is the "stability" in the Middle East to which the United States seems wedded.

Under such conditions, it should not be surprising that these frustrated populations perceive the current war against terrorism as functionally a war against Islam. Muslim countries are the chief target, they contend, Muslims everywhere are singled out for censure and police attention, and U.S. power works its will across the region with little regard for deeper Muslim concerns. A vicious circle exists: dissatisfaction leads to anti-regime action, which leads to repression, which in turn leads to terrorism, U.S. military intervention, and finally further dissatisfaction. Samuel Huntington's theory of a "clash of civilizations" is seemingly vindicated before the Muslim world's eyes.

THEIR MUSLIM PROBLEM—AND OURS

Several regimes have decided to play the dangerous game of trying to "out-Islam the Islamists," embracing harsh social and intellectual interpretations of Islam themselves so as to bolster their credentials against Islamist opposition. Thus in Egypt, the government-controlled University of al-Azhar, a prestigious voice in interpreting Islam, issues its own brand of intolerant fundamentalist rulings; Pakistan does something similar. The issue here is not the actual Islamist agenda but whose Islamist writ will dominate. Islam is simply the vehicle and coinage of the struggle between the state and its challengers.

In a comparable fashion, Islam and Islamist movements today provide a key source of identity to peoples intent on strengthening their social cohesion against Western cultural assault. Religious observance is visibly growing across the region, often accompanied by the "Arabization" of customs in clothing, food, mosque architecture, and ritual—even in areas such as Africa and East Asia, where no such customs had previously existed and where claims to cultural authenticity or tradition are weak to say the least. Association with the broader umma, the international Muslim community, is attractive because it creates new bonds of solidarity that can be transformed into increased international clout.

Islam and Islamist concepts, finally, are often recruited into existing geopolitical struggles. In the 1980s, for example, the rivalry between Saudi Arabia and Iran, which many Muslims often cloaked as a simple Sunni versus Shi'a competition, was as much political as it was religious. The Saudis hoped that their puritanical and intolerant Wahhabi vision of Islam would prevail over the Iranian revolutionary vision. For better or worse it did, partly because the Saudis could bankroll movements and schools far outside Saudi borders, and partly because many Sunnis considered Iran's Shi'ism anathema. The radical Islamic groups one sees today in the Philippines, Central Asia, the Caucasus, Afghanistan, and Pakistan, among other places, are partly the fruits of this export of Wahhabism, nourished by local conditions, ideological and material needs, and grievances.

Islam has thus become a vehicle and vocabulary for the expression of many different agendas in the Muslim world. The West is not at war with the religion itself, but it is indeed challenged by the radicalism that some groups have embraced. Muslims may too readily blame the West for their own problems, but their frustrations and current grievances are real. Indeed, the objective indicators of living conditions in the Islamic world—whether political, economic, or social—are generally turning down. Cultures and communities under siege naturally tend to opt for essentialism, seeking comfort and commonality in a back-to-basics view of religion, a narrowing and harshening of cultural and nationalist impulses, and a return to traditional community values. Muslims under pressure today are doing just this, retreating back to the solid certainties of essentialist Islam while their societies are in chaos. When Grozny was flattened by Russian troops, the Chechens declared Islamic law—clinging to an unquestioned traditional moral framework for comfort, familiarity, and reassuring moral discipline.

As a result, even as liberalization is occurring within some Islamist movements, much of the Islamic community is heading in the other direction, growing more austere and less tolerant and modernist. The same harsh conditions produce a quest for heroes, strongmen, and potential saviors. One of the saddest commentaries today, in fact, is the

Muslim thirst for heroes who will stand up and defy the dominant U.S.-led order—a quest that has led them to cheer on the Saddam Husseins and bin Ladens of the world.

The Muslim world is therefore in a parlous condition. Some in the West may think that Islam's problem is not their problem, that Muslims just need to face reality and get on with it. But the September 11 attacks showed that in a globalized world, their problems can become our problems. The U.S. tendency to disregard popular Muslim concerns as Washington cooperates with oppressive and insecure regimes fosters an environment in which acts of terrorism become thinkable and, worse, even gratifying in the eyes of the majority. The vast bulk of Muslims, of course, will go no further than to cheer on those who lash out. But such an environment is perhaps the most dangerous of all, because it legitimizes and encourages not the tolerant and liberalizing Islamists and peacemakers, but the negativistic hard-liners and rejectionists.

THE SILENT MUSLIM MAJORITY

Few Muslims around the world want to inflict endless punishment on the United States or go to war with it. Most of them recognize what happened on September 11 as a monstrous crime. But they still hope that the attacks will serve as a "lesson" to the United States to wake up and change its policies toward the Middle East. Most would emphatically reject, however, a key contention of President George W. Bush, that those who sympathize with the attacks are people who "hate freedom." Nearly all Muslims worldwide admire and aspire to the same political freedoms that Americans take for granted. A central complaint of theirs, in fact, is that U.S. policies have helped block the freedoms necessary to develop their personal and national capacities in comparable ways.

Muslim societies may have multiple problems, but hating American political values is not among them. U.S. policymakers would be wise to drop this simplistic, inaccurate, and self-serving description of the problem. They should instead consider what steps the United States can take to spread those political values to areas where they have been noticeable chiefly by their absence.

For Muslims who live in the West, the attacks of September 11 posed a moment of self-definition. However acutely attuned they might have been to the grievances of the broader Muslim world, the vast majority recognized that it was Western values and practices with which they identified most. This reaction suggests there may be a large silent majority in the Islamic world, caught between the powerful forces of harsh and entrenched regimes on the one hand and the inexorable will of an angry superpower on the other. Right now they have few channels of expression between acceptance of a miserable status quo and siding with the world-wreckers' vision of apocalyptic confrontation. How can the United States help mobilize this camp? What can make the members of this silent majority think they are anything but ringside spectators at a patently false clash of civilizations unfolding before their eyes?

Today most moderate Islamists, as well as the few Muslim liberals around, maintain a discouragingly low profile. Although they have condemned the September 11 attacks, they have been reluctant to scrutinize the conditions of their own societies that contribute to these problems. This myopia stems partly from an anxiety about signing on to the sweeping, unpredictable, and open-ended U.S. agenda for its war on terrorism. That said, however, it also stems from a failure of will to preach hard truths when society is under siege.

Given the authoritarian realities of life in the region, what acceptable outlets of expression are available? Islamists and other social leaders should find some way of setting forth a critique of Muslim society that will galvanize a call for change. Even if presidents-for-life cannot be removed, other demands can be made—for better services, more rights, freer economies. It is inexcusable that a Muslim civilization that led the entire world for a thousand years in the arts and sciences today ranks near the bottom of world literacy rates. Although conditions for women vary widely in the Muslim world, overall their levels of education and social engagement are depressingly low—not just a human scandal but also a prime indicator of underdevelopment. When highly traditional or fanatic groups attempt to define Islam in terms of a social order from a distant past, voices should be raised to deny them that monopoly.

The United States, meanwhile, should contribute to this effort by beginning to engage overseas Muslims vigorously, including those Islamic clerics who enjoy great respect and authority as men of uncompromised integrity. Both sides will benefit from a dialogue that initially will reveal deep fissures in thought and approach, but that over time may begin to bridge numerous gaps. Many of these clerics represent undeniably moderate forces within political Islam, but their own understanding of the West, though far from uniformly hostile, is flawed and often initially unsympathetic. They could learn from visits to the United States and dialogue with Americans—if ever they were granted visas.

It is worth noting, however, that this process will be fought hard by elements on both sides. The first group of opponents will be the friendly Muslim tyrants themselves, those regimes that stifle critiques from respected independent clerics and restrict their movements. The second group of opponents will come from the United States and will try to discredit the Muslim travelers by pointing to rash statements about Israel they may have made at one point or another. Given the passions aroused in the Middle East by the Arab-Israeli conflict, very few if any prominent Muslim figures will have the kind of liberal record of interfaith dialogue and tolerance that Americans find natural and appropriate. That should not disqualify them as potential interlocutors, however. Given the importance of the issues involved and the realities of the situation, the initial litmus test for being included in the conversation should be limited to a prohibition on incitement to terrorism and advocacy of war.

TURKISH DELIGHT?

Americans need to be mindful of the extent to which Islam is entwined with politics throughout the Muslim world. This connection may pose problems, but it is a reality that cannot be changed by mere appeals for secularism. The United States should avoid the Manichean formulation adopted by Bush that nations are either "with us or with the terrorists"; that is not what is going on, any more than Islamism is what bin Laden calls "a struggle between Islam and unbelief." The real story is the potential rise of forces in the Muslim world that will change not Islam itself, but rather the human understanding of Islam, laying the groundwork for a Muslim Reformation and the eventual emergence of a politics at once authentically Islamist yet also authentically liberal and democratic. The encouragement of such trends should be an important objective of U.S. policy.

One successful model that merits emulation is Turkey. This is not because Turkey is "secular"; in fact, Turkish "secularism" is actually based on total state control and even repression of religion. Turkey is becoming a model precisely because Turkish democracy is beating back rigid state ideology and slowly and reluctantly permitting the emergence of Islamist movements and parties that reflect tradition, a large segment of public opinion, and the country's developing democratic spirit. Political Islam in Turkey has evolved rapidly out of an initially narrow and nondemocratic understanding of Islam into a relatively responsible force, whether it overlaps entirely with American ideals or not.

Other promising cases to explore include Kuwait, Bahrain, Morocco, Jordan, Yemen, Malaysia, and Indonesia—all of which are at differing stages of political and social liberalization and evolution. All are working to avoid the social explosion that comes with repression of Islamic politics as a vehicle of change. Opening the political process enables people to sort out the effective moderates from the rhetorical radicals and reactionaries. Significantly, citizens of these states have not been prominent among the major terrorist groups of the world, unlike citizens of the U.S. allies Egypt and Saudi Arabia.

Most great religions have elements of both tolerance and intolerance built into them: intolerance because they believe they carry the truth, perhaps the sole truth, and tolerance because they also speak of humanity, the common origins of mankind, concepts of divine justice, and a humane order for all. Violence does not flow from religion alone—even bigoted religion. After all, the greatest horrors and killing machines in history stemmed from the Western, secular ideologies of fascism and communism. Religion is not about to vanish from the face of the earth, even in the most advanced Western nations, and certainly not in the Islamic world. The West will have to deal with this reality and help open up these embittered societies. In the process, the multiple varieties of Islam—the key political realities of today—will either evolve in positive directions with popular support, or else be discredited when they deliver little but venom. Muslim publics will quickly know the difference when offered a choice.

Terrorists must be punished. But will Washington limit itself to a merely punitive agenda to treat only the symptoms of crisis in the Muslim world? A just settlement for the Palestinians and support of regional democratization remain among the key weapons that can fight the growth of terrorism. It will be a disaster for the United States, and another cruel chapter in the history of the Muslim world, if the war on terrorism fails to liberalize these battered societies and, instead, exacerbates those very conditions that contribute to the virulent anti-Americanism of today. If a society and its politics are violent and unhappy, its mode of religious expression is likely to be just the same.

In a sea of autocracies and authoritarian regimes, dotted with islands of anti-modern Muslim fundamentalism, Israel stands out. This tiny nation is the Middle East's only true liberal democracy, modeled after those of Europe. Only Israel can claim to possess a stable representative government characterized by the rule of law, party politics, and free elections. Only Israel guarantees broad civil liberties for its citizens, if not for the Palestinians living under Israel's occupational authority. Only Israel boasts of Western-style economic freedom, social and gender equality, and a vibrant civil society.

Most importantly, unlike its Arab neighbors, Israel has made great advances toward resolving the conflict between religion and politics that bedevils the region. Judaism and democracy have become partners in government in Israel, without initiating a political and social descent into theocracy. Despite periodic conflicts between Jewish extremists and the national leadership, usually over the issue of Jewish settlements in the occupied territories of the West Bank and Gaza, Israel has developed into a state that is both devoutly religious and resolutely modern in its acceptance of secular principles of government. Israelis have coupled religion and the state in a manner that supports both while protecting each from the other. Muslim reformers might be well advised to look at Jewish democracy as a model for Muslim democracy.

How Israelis accomplished this feat is the subject of Gerald Steinberg's essay. In this piece, Steinberg explores the various compromises made by both the religious and political elements in Israeli society in the interest of building a nation that accommodates the demands of God and liberal democracy. Though far from perfect, Israel has proven that compromise is possible between the divine and the democratic.

"Democratic Peace" and the Jewish Political Tradition
GERALD M. STEINBERG

In considering the relationship between democracy and religion in the Middle East in the context of "democratic peace" theories, Israel is clearly a unique case. The political institutions of the modern state of Israel—a "Jewish state" (or a state for the Jews) in a region characterized by states in which Islam is the official religion and dominant culture—

were modeled on the conceptions developed in Europe during the late nineteenth century. As a result, democratic institutions and principles are an integral part of the Israeli political culture, in a manner that is fundamentally different from that of the rest of the region.

The effort to merge the long and complex Jewish tradition with Western liberal democracy created considerable tension in Israeli society. The Jewish population (which constitutes 80 percent of the total and is the main focus of this chapter) is sharply divided between secular and religious communities. The religious or traditional sector, constituting between 20 percent and 60 percent of the population (depending on definitions and issues), is itself split across a number of dimensions (national religious, ultra-orthodox, Sephardic, etc.) but is characterized in general by a major emphasis on Jewish history and tradition. Historically, the acceptance of divine authority is at the core of Jewish practices and beliefs. According to most rabbinical edicts, in clashes between religious requirements and the demands of secular political leaders or institutions, the former must prevail. In recent years, the increasing role of the secular court system in Israeli society has led to major protests and mass demonstrations involving religious opponents and secular supporters.

Following the 1991 Madrid Middle East Peace Conference and the 1993 Declaration of Principles (the "Oslo" agreement), the discourse in Israel has focused increasingly on the intersection and interaction between democracy, the Jewish tradition, and peace negotiations. The changing relationship between these three central aspects of Israeli society, and the tension between them, is reflected in many areas and dimensions. Israeli political and religious leaders, as well as educators and journalists, often address themselves to the relationship between these factors.[1]

The uniqueness of the Israeli case is also the result of the religious tradition that emphasizes the centrality of the Land of Israel. Jewish sovereignty and settlement in this Land, based on the biblical Covenant, beginning with Abraham, and associated religious commandments, are fundamental aspects of the tradition. As a result, changes in the status of the territory and, in particular, the exchange of "land for peace" are very important religious issues to many Israelis.

In this context, the roles of democracy and secular political institutions are sources of intense controversy, both within the religious community and between this sector and secular Israeli society. The 1993 Oslo agreement and subsequent pacts unleashed an intense and often violent debate. While opponents closed highways and sought to prevent implementation of the agreements, proponents accused them of using violent and undemocratic means to obstruct the policies of the government chosen by the majority in a democratic and free election.

In response, critics of the process, both religious and secular, argued that, despite the formal trappings of democracy, the broader concepts of transparency, accountability, free and open debate, and minority rights are not always respected or even recognized by a narrow political elite.

Criticism was exacerbated by a political system that focused power in the hands of a few individuals, elected indirectly. Until 1996, the prime minister was the head of the party that succeeded in building a governing coalition in the Knesset (the Israeli parliament). Because the government has a parliamentary majority in the Knesset, this legislative body does not play an effective role in terms of checks and balances. For some religious Israelis, the narrowly secular government lacked a mandate for the far-reaching changes embodied in the Oslo agreements. (The secrecy of the negotiations and the sudden reversal of long- and strongly held policies that had prohibited any contact with the Palestine Liberation Organization contributed to the intensity of the disaffection among opponents.) Others rejected the authority of the government to make decisions that violated religious precepts regarding the sanctity of the Land.

The assassination of Prime Minister Rabin in November 1995 occurred in the context of these conflicts. This tragedy, in turn, triggered a national re-examination of the different strands and interpretations of the Jewish tradition, the relationship between the Jewish and democratic aspects of Israeli society, and the impact of the peace process. As a result of these events, the roles of pluralism and democracy are increasingly the subjects of discussions and debates within religious society.[2] Interpretations of Jewish tradition and law (*halacha*) that stress the legitimacy of pluralism and secular democratic government are gaining support. In addition, a number of rabbis and religious intellectuals have stressed the need to balance the importance of sovereignty in the Land of Israel with the precepts emphasizing peace and the preservation of human life (*pikuach nefesh*). Indeed, the external events related to the Middle East peace efforts triggered an intense internal debate on the interpretation of the Jewish tradition. The results of this debate, as well as the substance of the negotiation process and the developments toward democracy and pluralism in neighboring Islamic states, will also determine the future policies that are adopted by Israel.

NATIONALISM AND DEMOCRACY IN ISRAELI SOCIETY

As an ethno-national community unified by an ancient religious tradition, and tracing its legitimacy to events that took place over 2,000 years ago, Israel is an exceptional political entity.[3] The foundations of the

Zionist movement and the modern state of Israel are based on a combination of both ancient Jewish and modern Western political traditions. In Jewish history, the concept of a nation-state long predates modern nationalism, which developed in the wake of the French Revolution.[4] Indeed, the principle of national sovereignty in a territorial state with defined borders is inherent in centuries of Jewish history and tradition. According to Jewish commentators, the objective of the biblical narrative from Genesis through the Exodus and the wandering in the desert is to establish the rights of the Jewish people to sovereignty in the Land of Israel.[5] These concepts remained central to Jewish philosophy and practice during 2,000 years of exile following the destruction of Jerusalem and the Roman conquest.

With the modern revival of Jewish nationalism, nineteenth- and twentieth-century Zionism was also strongly influenced by modern democracy and nationalism. Many of Israel's secular "founding fathers," who were responsible for forming its political institutions, came from Eastern Europe, and they incorporated many of the concepts and institutions that were then current. The governmental system is a parliamentary democracy with universal suffrage, and the basic freedoms of speech and of the press are protected under law. Furthermore, the North American and European Jewish Diasporas are strongly committed to democratic norms, and their close links with and strong influence in Israel have reinforced these norms.[6]

However, for over 50 years, during both the pre-state and post-independence periods, most aspects of Israeli society were controlled by a single dominant group, embodied in Mapai (the Israeli Workers' Party). As Yonathan Shapiro has noted, Israeli political processes were characterized by procedural democracy based on majoritarian hegemony, in contrast to pluralistic liberal democracy and the protection of minority rights.[7] The power structure controlled all aspects of public life (the economy, the media, health care, education, and even sports and entertainment), and often furthered its objectives through illegal and less than democratic means.[8] This elite was also militantly secular, substituting socialist Zionism and statism for religious tradition.[9]

The dominance of the Labor Party was broken in 1977 (following the "earthquake" of the 1973 War), but narrow electoral victories in 1992 and 1999 revived the tendency toward formal majoritarian definitions of democracy, in which concepts of minority rights and consensus based on compromise and pluralism are often overwhelmed. On issues of religious tradition in the public sphere, religious Israelis often feel that they have been relegated to the status of a "besieged minority." Similarly, the ultra-orthodox majorities in parts of Jerusalem, Bnai Brak, and other areas are often intolerant with respect to secular and even other religious groups.

The nature of the Israeli population and the lack of experience with democratic institutions have constituted an additional obstacle to the adoption of more pluralistic and tolerant norms. Following the establishment of the state of Israel in 1948, the Israeli population increased tenfold, from 600,000 to over 6 million. During the 1950s and 1960s, many of these immigrants were Jewish refugees from the Middle East (from North Africa to Iraq and Iran); later, the majority of immigrants came from the former Soviet Union. The vast majority had no previous exposure to liberal democracy. Although participation in party politics and elections is very high (often exceeding 90 percent of the eligible voters, excluding those abroad at the time, as Israel has no provisions for absentee voting), the strong emotions regarding the expression of opposing views, and, in some cases, the violence that has characterized election campaigns, may be attributable to the briefness of the democratic tradition.

Immigrants were absorbed into a political culture that used elections and political processes as vehicles for dominance and control over the allocation of public resources. As these groups formed their own parties and developed political power (that is, Shas or Russian parties), they have followed this pattern, seeking to use the process to enhance narrow sectoral interests. As a result, although democratic processes and institutions are firmly entrenched, pluralistic institutions and norms remain relatively weak and vulnerable.

RELIGION AND DEMOCRACY IN ISRAEL

Zionism is rooted deeply in Jewish tradition, and the concept of "Return to the Land of Israel" was nurtured as a central aspect of religious precept and practice during 2,000 years of exile. The conditions required for the Return were heatedly debated throughout this period, with some religious authorities supporting individual *aliya* (literally, "going up") from exile to the Land in a practical sense. Their opponents prohibited this, requiring divine intervention and restoration of the Temple in Jerusalem (which, according to one interpretation, would descend as a complete entity from heaven) prior to the end of exile. However, throughout this period, the concept of the Return remained a central precept of the Jewish religion.[10] As Rabbi Zvi Yehuda Kook wrote, "[t]he quintessential value of the entire Torah, including its commandments that are not dependent on Eretz Israel, lies in the Land of Israel."[11]

With the inception of political Zionism, these approaches were also manifested in the attitudes of religious groups. In 1948, the Declaration of Independence proclaimed Israel as *Medinat HaYehudim*—a Jewish state—founded on the principles of liberty, justice, and peace as conceived by the Prophets of Israel, and guaranteeing the full social and political equality of all its citizens.[12] (Christians, Muslims, Druze, and others are acknowledged as members of minority groups in the predominantly Jewish environment. From the Jewish perspective, the Arab–Israeli conflict is not the result of religious antagonism. Judaism and Jewish tradition view Islam in a positive light, in part because Islam is monotheistic and is based on Jewish precepts and texts,[13] and in part because Jews have been treated relatively well under Islamic rule, despite being relegated to second-class status as *dhimmis*.)

From the beginning of the Zionist movement, Jewish society in Israel has been divided between religious and secular communities, and each group, as well as the numerous subgroups, has held strong ideological and value-oriented views on the future of Israel and the Jewish people. For religious Israelis, the state of Israel was seen as the seed from which the Jewish nation would re-emerge following the decimation of the Jewish people in the twentieth century, culminating in the Holocaust. Indeed, in Jewish tradition, the return to the Land of Israel and an end to the exile were equated with Messianic redemption. In this context, the religious Zionists (Mizrachi) saw the establishment of a sovereign Jewish state as marking the first steps in this redemption.[14] In a manner consistent with this view, the physical return to the Land was seen as requiring and providing the conditions for a religious framework for society. "The religious Zionist sees no justification for a separation between national social life and [Jewish law]."[15]

In the first decades following independence, the tension between the Jewish and secular democratic (majoritarian) emphases was reflected in the difficulties in developing national policies in a number of areas of friction. These included education, personal status (marriage, divorce, burial, etc.), kosher food regulations, and the operation of public services on the Sabbath (transportation, entertainment, etc.).[16] Continuing the Ottoman *millet* system, personal status was regulated according to membership of a particular recognized religious group (Jewish, Catholic, Protestant, Muslim, Druze, etc.), and every citizen was expected to be a member of one of these groups. Separate secular and religious (rabbinical for the majority Jewish population) court systems were established, as was a Chief Rabbinate, all financed by the state. Religious Israeli children attended separate religious schools, whereas secular Israelis attended secular schools. Equal status was an important principle but, in contrast to Western liberal democratic norms, this equality was group based and not individual. Each person was entitled to rights and bound by obligations as a member of a recognized religious group.

During this period, efforts to develop a written constitution failed owing to differences over the official status of the Rabbinate and fundamental principles relating to the nature of a Jewish state and the role of the religious establishment.[17] The "ultra-orthodox" community did not (and does not) recognize the legitimacy of the secular state and, in contrast to the "modern orthodox" approach, linked political salvation, in the form of restored Jewish sovereignty in the Land of Israel, with religious salvation. For some, a secular Jewish state was and is considered an abomination.[18]

In the absence of agreement, the Knesset began to adopt a series of Basic Laws dealing with specific issues and institutions, which formed the constitutional skeleton. In many cases, the drafting and adoption of these Basic Laws were also the result of negotiation and compromise between the religious and secular factions in the Knesset.

In order to avoid internal divisions during the 1948 Arab–Israeli war, which threatened national survival, conflicts in this area were resolved by acceptance of the status quo in areas of disagreement. Thus, for example, the separate school systems that had existed during the Mandate period were continued, and the level of official Sabbath observance with respect to public transportation, which varied from place to place (the buses operated on the Sabbath in Haifa but not in Jerusalem or Tel Aviv), was continued. In a broader sense, the Israeli political system was consociational in nature, incorporating different groups (cleavages) into the government by dividing resources among the groups, while allowing each group a high level of internal autonomy.[19]

Beyond these specific policy differences, the role of democracy and the authority of the secular political system are also points of contention. Commentators note that the Jewish tradition and religion are not, per se, anti-democratic, and the governing concept of a covenant between the people (*edah*) and God is central.[20] Popular acceptance and ratification of rulers, including kings, are an important norm with roots in biblical and Talmudic sources. The tradition and legal framework emphasize popular participation in government,[21] and in later periods many Jewish communities adopted democratic practices.[22]

The Bible and the Talmud (Tractate Sanhedrin) also emphasize the importance of establishing a clear and accepted political authority, and a number of passages suggest that, even during Talmudic times, democratic concepts were important. Jewish sages declared that the legitimacy of different forms of government is based on first securing the consent of the governed.[23] During the Mandate period, Chief Rabbi Avraham Yitzchak Hacohen Kook and other authorities expanded the traditional frameworks to include a democratic state and its president or prime minister.[24]

However, as Schweid notes, "there is a substantial difference between socio-religious democracy, which in the Jewish religion carries a significant portion of its values, and secular democracy, which was adopted recently as the basis for government on the basis of external European origins. . . . Religious democracy is based on the concept of the supremacy of the Torah, whose authority is superhuman (*al enoshi*)." It is up to the human leaders (rabbis, prophets, etc.) to interpret the words of the Torah and to make the legal rulings on this basis, but they receive their authority, or are recognized by the religious institutions, consistent with popular will. "In this sense, democracy is expressed in the requirement that the religious leadership respond to the legitimate demands of the populace, on the one hand, and from the popular desire to obey the rulings of the religious leaders according to Torah principles, on the other."[25] According to Liebman,[26] in principle the differences are sharper, but in most cases "[t]here is no major or peculiar incompatibility between halakah and democracy in practice because Jewish law is subject to interpretation."[27]

As a result of both religious/ideological and political/cultural factors, the consociational model appears to be weakening, and the clash between the secular and religious norms has become particularly pronounced.[28] The expanded authority and scope taken on by the secular court system in the past decade have contributed to the undermining of the status quo. Under the influence of Judge Aharon Barak (Chief Justice of the High Court of Appeal), the courts have entered into areas and assumed powers that had, in the past, been rejected by the secular courts as outside their areas of jurisdiction. The secular courts have ruled on cases pertaining to religious conversion practices, property division in divorce, public allocations to religious institutions, and other areas that had previously been considered "off limits." In response, religious (primarily, but not exclusively, ultra-orthodox) groups organized protest movements, and in 1999 over 100,000 people participated in a major rally in Jerusalem. The ultra-orthodox groups have also sought to use their political power in the Knesset and the government to trim the powers of the secular courts. Thus, the nature of Israeli democracy is still highly dynamic and evolving.

RELIGION, DEMOCRACY, AND THE PEACE PROCESS

In the first two decades of Israeli statehood, foreign and security policy (issues of war and peace) did not play a significant role in the religious–secular debate. The armistice lines resulting from the 1948 War created the territorial boundaries of the state of Israel, and the question of settlement outside these lines was moot.[29] The prospects for formal peace were also remote, given the widespread Arab rejection of the legitimacy of the state of Israel and repeated vows to destroy the Jewish state.[30] In this period, frequent cross-border terror attacks, Israeli military responses, and periodic wars were the dominant elements of the political environment.

This situation changed radically following the 1967 War, in which the Israeli forces took control of East Jerusalem and the West Bank areas that were occupied and then annexed by Jordan in 1948–9. These areas, known to Israelis as Judea and Samaria (based on their biblical names), include many biblical sites, such as Hebron, Bethlehem, Beth El, Shechem (Nablus in Arabic), which had been closed to Jews since 1948.

The return to the ancient Jewish quarter of Jerusalem and the Temple Mount was of great historic and religious importance. This small area contains the remains of Solomon's Temple, the Second Temple, as well as synagogues and other sacred sites. Throughout the 2,000 years of exile, Jews continued to pray daily for the restoration of Jerusalem, and Jewish weddings include a ritual in which a glass is broken to symbolize mourning for Jerusalem. The loss of this area during the 1948 War and the subsequent destruction and desecration of much of the Jewish quarter were and continue to be a source of contention and emotion.[31]

For many members of the religious community in Israel, the outcome of the 1967 War provided a divinely ordained opportunity to re-establish Jewish control over the Sacred City of Jerusalem and all of the Land of Israel, and to observe the religious commandments that pertained to this Land. Settlement in these areas became the primary objective for religious nationalists but not, at the time, for the ultra-orthodox (Haredi) communities—as will be discussed in detail below.

The results of the 1967 War also changed Israeli democracy in a fundamental manner, and altered the approach of the religious sectors of society with respect to issues of security, territory, and borders. Immediately after the 1967 War ended, movements were organized with the goal of building Jewish settlements in the captured areas, including Sinai, the Golan, and the West Bank. These settler movements included many religious Jews, but this was not an exclusively religious cause and also encompassed secular Israelis. However, the religious parties and leaders were prominent, and their role increased over time.

Their political power was enhanced by the stalemate between the two secular political blocs (Labor/Left and Likud/Right). The religious parties, and the National Religious Party (NRP) in particular, used this power to lobby the government to provide incentives for the settlements, and they consistently worked to expand and strengthen Jewish sovereignty and control in these areas. (Initially, the secular community was divided, with some joining forces with the religious settlement movement to form the Greater Land of Israel Movement, while others called for withdrawal from the "Occupied Territories" in the context of a peace treaty.)

Shortly after the 1967 War, Rabbi Zvi Yehuda Kook published a list of biblical quotations and passages to demonstrate that withdrawal from "the eternal land of our forefathers" was prohibited under religious law and unacceptable.[32] Members of the Gush Emunim movement declared that "in the Jewish tradition lies the key to the understanding of the uniqueness and mission of the people and the Land of Israel. . . . Forfeiting Jewish roots puts into question the very value of Israel's survival and their adherence to Eretz Israel."[33]

From this perspective, democratic procedures, particularly with respect to settlement activities, were not central considerations. Settlements were established without the permission of the government, and led to intermittent confrontations with the police and army (for example, Sebastia, 1974; later known as Kadum and Elon Moreh). The settlers were often able to negotiate a compromise, allowing them to maintain a presence on state-owned land nearby, and eventually growing into larger settlements.[34] Although religious objectives were given priority over obedience to the law, the culture of "illegalism," fostered by the secular founders of Zionism and Israel, also contributed to this pattern of behavior.[35]

The tension between democracy and religious hierarchy in the context of Middle East peace negotiations increased during the negotiations between Egypt and Israel following the 1978 Camp David Accords, and the agreement by the Israeli government to dismantle settlements in the Sinai. Although the Yamit settlement and the rest of Sinai are outside the biblical boundary of the Land of Israel, religious Jews and rabbis led the protests and resistance efforts, in large part to demonstrate their commitment to maintaining control over the settlements in Judea and Samaria.

At the time, the Israeli government was headed by Menachem Begin and the Likud Party, and the National Religious Party was a member of the ruling coalition. This government could not be accused of being militantly secular and anti-religious or oblivious to Jewish values and history. Nevertheless, the confrontations with the government (including the army sent to dismantle the settlements) were very intense and often violent. The religious leaders declared that the secular political power structure lacked the authority to violate Jewish law. This group called on soldiers to ignore government orders to dismantle settlements, rather than violate religious edicts.

The confrontations resumed and intensified following the 1993 Oslo agreement, when the territory involved was the heartland of Jewish settlement in Judea and Samaria. The creation of the Palestinian Authority, and the transfer of territory to it, were anathema to the concept of exclusive Jewish sovereignty in the Land of Israel. This situation, combined with the waves of Palestinian suicide bombings and other forms of violence, and the continued rejection of Israeli legitimacy among Palestinians, led to the massive protests that developed in 1994 and 1995. This atmosphere, in turn, provided the background for the assassination of Prime Minister Yitzchak Rabin by a fellow Jew in November 1995.

As the negotiation and implementation of withdrawal agreements proceeded, these issues continued to be highly contentious. However, as will be seen below, the public debate in the Jewish religious community (as distinct from the majority secular and Arab communities in Israel) crystallized into three different approaches.

THREE RELIGIOUS RESPONSES

The Jewish religion is by no means monolithic, and there are many different schools of interpretation. In a broad sense, the confrontation between religious and democratic authority in Israel generated three responses within the religious authority. Each response emphasizes a different central principle in considering the relative importance of the three primary values: (1) sovereign control over the Land, (2) the sanctity of life and the prevention of war, and (3) the role of democracy and avoidance of civil conflict. (There is also a fourth approach, which opposes maintenance of control over inhabited occupied territories, based on the biblical injunction to treat the stranger with dignity, "for you were strangers in the land of Egypt" (Exodus 22: 21). This approach often overlaps with the third group and will be discussed in a further development of this chapter.)

THE PRIMACY OF SOVEREIGNTY OVER THE LAND OF ISRAEL

The centrality of settlement in the Land of Israel became a major focus of religious nationalist ideology after the 1967 War, and the principle was essential to the rise of the Young Guard in the NRP, beginning in 1963.[36] For this group, settlement in the territories and opposition to any withdrawal are a religious requirement that is not open to compromise and bargaining.[37] The commandment is based on the biblical verse: "And you shall take possession of the land and settle in it, for I have given the land to you to possess it" (Numbers 33: 53).

Building on the commandment to settle the Land, this group relies on the religious messianic ideology of Rabbi Zvi Yehuda Kook, in which the state of Israel is viewed as the beginning of the flowering of Jewish redemption. The Israeli military successes are interpreted in terms of miraculous divine intervention, precisely in order to implement the commandment of settlement in the Land of Israel.[38] Major leaders of this movement include former Chief Rabbis of Israel such as Rabbi Avraham Shapira, Rabbi Haim Druckman, who headed the religious youth group Bnei Akiva, and Yitzchak Levy, head of the NRP and cabinet minister from 1996 until 1998. In addition, some ultra-orthodox groups, such as the Lubovitch (Chabad) movement, have taken a similar position.[39]

In the 1973 elections, a substantial portion of religious Zionists who traditionally supported the NRP voted for other parties, in large part as a result of policies that were not sufficiently vigorous on security policy and support for settlements in the territories. In 1977, however, following a change in leadership and a more "Land of Israel" centered platform, support for the NRP increased.[40] Since then, the NRP has emphasized the territorial issue.

Adherents of this group support a policy that gives priority to Jewish sovereignty in the land and they oppose territorial withdrawal. In 1981–2, following the signing of the Egyptian–Israeli peace treaty and prior to the evacuation of Yamit in the Sinai region, a number of rabbis issued an edict forbidding the transfer of any part of the Land of Israel to non-Jewish control.[41] In 1985, the Council of Jewish Settlements in Judea, Samaria, and Gaza declared that any surrender of territory in these areas would "represent a prima facie annulment of the State of Israel . . . whose purpose is to bring Jews to the sovereign Land of Israel."[42]

In December 1993, following the Oslo agreement, the late Rabbi Shlomo Goren, a former Chief Rabbi, published a ruling forbidding Jews to evacuate any settlement in the biblical Land of Israel, which includes Judea, Samaria, and Gaza, and declared that Israeli soldiers should disobey any such evacuation orders: "according to Halacha [Jewish law], a soldier who receives an order that runs contrary to Torah law should uphold the Halacha, and not the secular order. And since settling the land is a commandment, and uprooting the settlements is breaking the commandment, the soldier should not carry out an order to uproot settlements."[43] He was not alone in his opinions, and many other rabbis issued similar statements and rulings.[44]

In April 1994, discussion of possible evacuation of the Jewish residents of Hebron caused a number of rabbis, including Chief Rabbi Avraham Shapira, Rabbi Moshe-Zvi Neria of the Bnei Akiva movement, and Rabbi Shaul Yisraeli, to direct soldiers to reject any order to evacuate Jews from Hebron or other settlements.[45] Citing the religious importance of Hebron to Jews, an NRP member of the Knesset, Hanan Porat, declared that "[t]his would be a palpably illegal order, which I could not carry out, as it goes against my conscience and everything I believe. I would be willing to pay the price by going to jail."[46]

In July 1995, during the intense national debate that took place following the Oslo Declaration of Principles and the Cairo implementation agreements, seven rabbis (eight more joined the ruling later on) belonging to the Council of Religious Zionist Rabbis and headed by former Ashkenazi Chief Rabbi Avraham Shapira issued another religious (halachic) edict. It declared that "there is a Torah prohibition against uprooting [IDF] Israeli Defense Force bases and transferring the sites to Gentiles, since this contravenes a positive [Torah] commandment and also endangers life and the existence of the state."[47]

Subsequently, another decree stated that the peace process would open "the way for [Arabs] to conquer the entire land" and therefore "it is forbidden, under any circumstance, to hand over parts of Eretz Yisrael to Arabs." Rabbi Nachum Rabinovich, head of the Birkat Moshe Yeshiva in Ma'aleh Adumim, and one of the signatories of the ruling, also cited the precept of protecting life. "Wherever the Israeli army pulls out, settlers' lives will be endangered. There is a fundamental moral issue here and the moral law supersedes any government."[48]

These edicts explicitly emphasized the view that rabbinical authority supersedes the secular authority of the government (whether democratic or in any other form). Its authors based their argument on Maimonides (twelfth century, Spain) who wrote that, "even if the king ordered [one] to disobey the Torah, he should not be listened to."[49] From this perception, a secular government has no right to violate Jewish law, which places primacy on control over the Land of Israel.[50] The rabbinical authorities also cited threats to national security resulting from territorial withdrawal, claiming precedence of their analysis over the judgment of the professional military and political leaders. This is an extraordinary development in the context of Jewish religious authority, although consistent with the overall trend toward *daat Torah*—the doctrine that attributes expertise and authority in all public issues to prominent rabbinical figures.[51]

These edicts had a quick and substantive impact. In August 1995, a soldier was sentenced to 28 days in military jail for refusing to evict settlers encamped without permission near Hebron. He stated that he refused the order on ideological grounds and that he did not join the army to fight Jews.[52]

The reactions to these developments were intense and came from all sections of the Israeli population. Secular Israelis generally condemned the rabbinical edicts; among the religious sectors of society, the responses were mixed. As will be seen below, many rabbis criticized the edicts for undermining the military command structure and for paving the way for anarchy and disorder.

The assassination of Prime Minister Rabin in November 1995 shocked some leaders and members of this group, and led them to a fundamental reassessment of philosophy and policy. This process accelerated during the Netanyahu period (1996–9) and contributed to strengthening the support for alternative positions within the religious community, as will be discussed in the following sections.

In the 1999 election campaign, the NRP's more militant supporters of the settlers and opponents of concessions in the peace process, such as Hanan Porat, lost power and were replaced by more dovish members of the party.[53] (Porat then joined a new party, The National Union, which placed territorial issues at the forefront. This party did quite poorly in the elections, and Porat resigned his Knesset seat. However, at a later stage, the NRP leadership asked Rabbi Haim Druckman, whose positions on territorial issues are similar to those of Porat, to take the second position on the Knesset list.) At the same time, two alternative approaches based on Jewish law and tradition were developed and gained strength.

THE PRIMACY OF HUMAN LIFE AND PREVENTION OF WAR OVER SOVEREIGNTY IN THE LAND OF ISRAEL

From the beginning of the Oslo process, some prominent rabbis and religious leaders ruled that, although settling the Land of Israel is an important commandment, negotiating peace is of even greater importance, citing the importance placed on *pikuach nefesh*, the preservation of human life, in the Torah. They based this ruling on the Biblical verse: "I have put before you life and death, blessing and curse. Choose life— if you and your offspring would live—by loving the Lord your God" (Deuteronomy 30: 19).

This approach was articulated by the late Rabbi Yosef Dov Soloveichik, who lived in the United States and was regarded by many modern orthodox Jews, including Israelis, as the leading authority of his generation. Opposing the rabbinical rulings that gave exclusive emphasis to sovereignty in the Land of Israel, and noting the centrality of *pikuach nefesh*, his view was that policy decisions on these issues are best left to the professional military and political authorities.[54]

Rabbi Ovadia Yosef, the former Sephardic Chief Rabbi of Israel and founder of the Shas political party, adopted a similar position. (Poll data suggest that Shas supporters have tended to be more hawkish than its leadership, but in most cases the voters are willing to accept the religious and political authority of the rabbinical leadership. Shas was a member of the Netanyahu coalition government, but often attempted to exert a moderating influence on policies related to the peace process.) In Rabbi Yosef's opinion, the positive commandment to settle the land is overridden by the commandment to avoid unnecessary loss of life. Thus, he has declared that, "[i]f the heads of the army with the members of the government, declare that lives will be endangered unless territories in the Land of Israel are relinquished, and there is the danger of an immediate declaration of war by the neighboring Arab [states], . . . and if territories are relinquished, the danger of war will be removed, and that there are realistic chances of lasting peace, then it appears, according to all the opinions, that it is permissible to relinquish territories of the Land of Israel . . . [according to the principle of] *pikuach nefesh*."[55] In the same discourse, however, Rabbi Yosef noted that military officers, government officials, and security experts are divided and some have concluded that returning territories could increase the dangers to Israel, and that these views should also be considered.

During this period, Rabbi Yosef was also active in meeting with Arab leaders. In July 1989, Rabbi Yosef met with Egyptian President Hosni Mubarak, and in May 1997 a Palestinian official said Yasser Arafat would welcome Rabbi Yosef's help in renewing the stalled peace talks and getting the process back on track.[56]

The members of the Meimad religious group, founded by Rabbi Yehuda Amital, share this position. The Meimad movement began in protest against the 1982 Lebanon war and its aftermath, and some of its members were associated with Netivot Shalom, a small religious group parallel to the secular Peace Now movement, which provided an alternative to groups such as Gush Emunim and the NRP. Meimad became a political party in 1988 but, after a poor showing in the elections, was transformed into an ideological movement in 1992; it was reconstituted as a party in 1999. Its founders included rabbis, academics, and other professionals who were disaffected with the religious establishment. For this group, policy decisions on issues of war and peace made by a democratic government take precedence over edicts of the religious leadership (see the detailed discussion of this position below).

For members of Meimad, religious law does not require opposition to the "land for peace" formula. In contrast to the messianic interpretation, Rabbi Amital declared that the "miracle of the [1967] Six Day War" was not primarily the conquest of the biblical Land of Israel. "People at the time were concerned about another holocaust, they were receiving letters pleading with them to send their children abroad. So when we won the war, it was a feeling of great relief, a feeling that God saved us from destruction. That was the miracle. It had nothing to do with Judea and Samaria."[57]

Based on this perspective, in 1993–4, Meimad supported the Oslo process, and in the 1996 elections its leaders endorsed the Labor Party and Shimon Peres. Similarly, in 1999 the leadership endorsed Ehud Barak for the office of prime minister, and entered the "One Israel" list (based on the Labor Party). As a result, Meimad placed one member in the Knesset, and joined the governing coalition, and Rabbi Michael Melchoir also became a government minister responsible for religious–secular relations. This process reflected the gradual increase in the relative strength of the approach that places the principle of *pikuach nefesh* (preservation of life) above that of sovereign control over the Land of Israel.

In 2001, following the collapse of the Oslo process, the outbreak of large-scale violence, and the collapse of the Barak government, which led to the election of Ariel Sharon as prime minister, Meimad remained in the government (following the lead of the Labor Party) and Melchior became deputy foreign minister. Although increasingly angry regarding the perceived betrayal of the Palestinian partners in the peace process, Meimad members and leaders continued to be active in seeking ways of restoring the shattered fabric of this relationship.

THE PRIMACY OF THE DEMOCRATIC PROCESS AND THE AVOIDANCE OF CIVIL CONFLICT

As noted, the Jewish religious tradition also includes interpretations that give primacy to the decisions of the secular government, even when these decisions may be seen to violate other religious principles.

As tension increased in Israeli society, along both the secular–religious and the left–right dimensions, a growing number of rabbis began to emphasize the need for authoritative decision-making based on the primacy of the democratically elected government. The emphasis on the legitimacy of secular political institutions and policies was voiced in 1982 during the confrontation over the evacuation of the Yamit settlement in the Sinai. Religious leaders and rabbis warned that "[t]here is a danger that, in an atmosphere of violence, soldiers may be killed, God forbid. Such a war would stain the people of Israel to the extent that will not be wiped out."[58]

This approach has also been emphasized by Meimad, whose platform opposes coercive religious legislation, emphasizes democratic practices in the Jewish state, and actively supports education regarding democratic values in both the religious and secular school systems.[59]

These themes were underscored and became primary issues in November 1995, following the assassination of Prime Minister Yitzchak Rabin. Many religious leaders, including those previously associated with the more "nationalist" and "hawkish" approaches and parties, expressed concerns regarding the impact of internal divisions, violence, and civil conflict on the future of the Jewish people. Examples from history, and, in particular, the internal divisions and senseless hatred (*sinat chinam*) that commentators have cited as the main cause of the destruction of the Second Temple and the long period of exile, were repeated as warnings of future catastrophe. Rabbis from many different groups stressed the theme of national unity and political stability based on the accepted democratic norms and institutions.

The assassination followed months of intense and often violent demonstrations against the policies of the Rabin government (particularly in the wake of terrorism and suicide bombings).[60] In this period, nationalist rabbis issued edicts declaring the prime minister and the government to be in violation of Jewish law (according to their interpretations) by endangering lives through their policies of territorial withdrawal.

In this environment, the assassination, and the perception that some elements in the religious sectors of Israeli society provided justification for this act, led to a fundamental change among many rabbis and religious leaders. Some, such as Rabbi Yoel Ben Nun, who had been a major leader of the territorialist Gush Emunim approach, renounced their earlier views and emphasized the importance of national unity and democracy. In the curricula of the national religious school system (although not in the ultra-orthodox system), programs to emphasize democracy as a core Jewish value have been introduced.

Despite the catastrophic end of the Oslo process, beginning in September 2000, these programs have continued in the religious school systems and in other societal frameworks. Participation in various religious–secular dialogues continued to increase and, in terms of the formal political framework, the establishment and maintenance of a wide government following the election of Ariel Sharon in 2001 had broad backing. These developments indicated that, among the religious population, support for this approach emphasizing national unity based on democratic processes is likely to increase in the future.

"DEMOCRATIC PEACE"?

Before examining the Israeli case in the light of "democratic peace" theories, the nature and limitations of these models should be considered. Universal theories that attempt to explain war and peace in relations among nations in terms of their respective levels of democracy are problematic, at best.[61] Critics have argued convincingly that shared cultural backgrounds and norms, rather than democratic political institutions and practices, seem to account for the absence of military conflict between Western liberal democracies.[62] In regions where democracy is formalistic and procedural and where intense ethno-national conflicts continue, such as South Asia or the former Yugoslavia, democratic peace theories lose much of their explanatory power.

In the Middle East, some political leaders, particularly in Israel, support the view that democratization in the Arab and Islamic states would promote peace agreements.[63] However, even if these societies were to evolve toward greater acceptance of democratic procedures and processes, there is also evidence that democratization, at least in the short term, could increase the salience of the ideological and religious aspects of the conflict with Israel, rather than leading to greater support for negotiated solutions. Even in relatively progressive states such as Jordan, the peace agreement with Israel is widely considered to be the result of external pressure and expediency ("the King's peace"), lacking wide popular support. Some analysts warn that Arab democracies would likely be more virulent in their opposition to Israel, at least until an agreement was reached and a new generation could be raised in the spirit of intercultural tolerance and understanding.[64]

In the Israeli case, the attempt to evaluate the validity of democratic peace theories is complicated by the heterogeneous nature of Israeli society, particularly along the religious–secular dimension, and the close link between the Jewish religion, Zionism (as the expression of Jewish nationalism), the territorial boundaries, and the question of sovereignty. In the few publications that attempt to examine the application of "democratic peace" theories to Israel, these dimensions have largely been overlooked.[65] However, as has been demonstrated in this chapter, for a significant segment of Israeli society, the mix of attitudes toward the religious significance of the Land of Israel, democracy as the basis for national unity, and other religious issues, such as the commandment to preserve life, are determining factors.

In this sense, it is important to recognize the dynamic nature of the situation. Although democratic institutions and processes in Israel are firmly established, the tensions between the secular political structure and the traditions and legal norms of the Jewish tradition can be expected to remain and perhaps intensify. Although the majority of Jewish Israelis define themselves as secular, rather than religious, identification with Jewish norms and practices has been growing in the past two decades. (Poll data show that close to half of the population maintains traditional Jewish practices such as lighting candles on the Sabbath or kosher dietary rules.[66]) Religious parties, such as Shas, led by Rabbi Ovadia Yosef, have grown in strength in the past decade. (Shas is also an ethnic party, encompassing Sephardi Jews, but members of this group, in general, are far less likely to be secular compared with the Ashkenazi Jewish population.) As the narrow and short-lived support for the post-Zionist ideology demonstrated, Israel will continue to be a Jewish state, in a cultural, social, and political sense, and the debate over the meaning and substantive impact of this framework will also continue.

However, the presence or growth of religious influence in Israeli politics does not mean that inherent religious/ideological opposition to the "land for peace" formula will also increase. As noted, the Shas leadership, the Meimad movement, and many prominent ultra-orthodox rabbis and leaders subscribe to the school that gives priority to the preservation of human life (*pikuach nefesh*) ahead of maintaining total sovereignty in the Land of Israel.

This change is also reflected in support for major changes in Israeli policy with respect to the peace process. Public opinion polls and recent election results show that the majority of Jewish Israelis, including significant portions of the religious population, are now willing to accept a Palestinian state in the context of a permanent status agreement and an end to the threat of violence. In addition, although support for Jewish sovereignty in the Land of Israel, based on religious commandments, is still quite strong, the possibility of dismantling some settlements and of consolidating others in settlement blocs gradually gained support in this community during the period of optimism following the Oslo agreement.[67] This optimism was reflected in the result of the 1999 elections, in which Netanyahu was defeated by Ehud Barak, on a platform emphasizing accelerated negotiations toward full peace agreements with both Syria and the Palestinians. It was clear that such agreements would require major Israeli territorial withdrawals, essentially to the 1948 armistice lines (with the exception of Jerusalem). Nevertheless, a significant portion of religious voters (although by no means a majority) seemed willing to accept this framework.[68] The Shas party, under the "spiritual guidance" of Rabbi Ovadia Yosef, became the third largest in the Knesset, with 17 seats (out of 120), and joined Barak's government. In addition, the representative of Meimad, Rabbi Michael Melchior, became a cabinet member.

However, the failure of the Camp David summit in July 2000, which was designed to complete the Oslo process with the promised "permanent status agreement," and the massive violence that began at the end of September led to fundamental changes in Israeli perceptions of the Palestinians. Within a few months, as casualties mounted and cease-fire efforts failed, the Barak administration lost public support and a number of parties, including Shas, withdrew from the government. Barak lost his parliamentary majority and, in special elections held in February 2001, opposition leader Ariel Sharon was selected as prime minister by an overwhelming and unprecedented majority. This outcome was a clear signal of a major shift in Israeli public opinion, across the political spectrum, in which the negotiation process with the Palestinians was widely seen to have ended in failure. Instead, in the wake of continued violence and high casualties, including numerous suicide bombings, the focus shifted to security. Religious leaders and voters supported Sharon, and their views were largely indistinguishable from the broad national consensus on these issues.

If and when peace and permanent status negotiations between Israel and the Palestinians resume, this period of intense violence is likely to influence public attitudes toward the "land for peace" formula, the question of a Palestinian state, and related issues. Like other sectors in Israeli society, the leaders of the religious parties and their supporters have become embittered and disillusioned with the failed promises of peace. The more hard-line positions, emphasizing the sacredness of the Land of Israel and the centrality of Jewish sovereignty in Jerusalem, regained some support in this period of violence. However, an end to terrorism and a fundamental change in relations with the Palestinians and neighboring Arab states could lead to a recovery in support for compromise. Within the religious sectors, the emphasis on national unity has continued to increase, and in the future, should a government be elected that adopts policies involving major territorial concessions, it is likely to receive support in order to prevent internal division.

In more general terms, although the tension between the religious and democratic secular authority will also continue and perhaps intensify, the situation is dynamic. The religious tradition and leadership provide a wide range of options, and the support for these different approaches, particularly with respect to possible agreements with the Arab states, is variable. The relative impact of these views on Israeli policy with respect to the peace process will depend on a combination of internal and external factors, including the perceived benefits and risks of agreements and the success in implementing them in ways that clearly demonstrate the understanding of and sensitivity to Jewish history and tradition.

NOTES

This chapter is dedicated to the memory of Professor Daniel Elazar, whose pioneering work on the Jewish political tradition provided the foundation for academic analysis of this important topic.

1. Arye Carmon, "Political Education in the Midst of a National Identity Crisis: The Compatibility of Judaism and Democracy as a Pedagogical Theme," in Ehud Sprinzak and Larry Diamond, eds., *Israeli Democracy under Stress*, Boulder, CO: Lynne Rienner, 1993, pp. 293–308.

2. See, for example, *The State of Israel as a Jewish and Democratic State* (*Medinah Israel K'medinah Yehudit V'Demokratit*): *Proceedings of the 21st World Congress of Jewish Studies* (in Hebrew), Jerusalem: World Union Jewish Studies, 1997.

3. Bernard Susser and Eliezer Don-Yehiya, "Democracy versus Nationalism: Israel as an Exceptional Case" (in Hebrew: *Tarbut Demokratit*), Ramat Gan: Bar Ilan University, vol. 1, 1999, p. 18. For an English version, see Bernard Susser and Eliezer Don-Yehiya, "Israel and the Decline of the Nation-State in the West," *Modern Judaism*, May 1994, pp. 187–202.

4. Susser and Don-Yehiya, "Democracy versus Nationalism," p. 19; Yosef Salmon, "Tradition and Nationalism," in Jehuda Reinharz and Anita Shapira, eds., Essential Papers on Zionism, New York: New York University Press, 1996, p. 98.

5. Rashi (Rabbi Shlomo Yitzchaki), eleventh-century Jewish commentator, in his commentary on the book of Genesis.

6. Susser and Don-Yehiya, "Democracy versus Nationalism," citing Jacob Katz, *Emancipation and Assimilation*, Westmead, Farnborough: Gregg International, 1972, p. 131.

7. Yonathan Shapiro, "The Historical Origins of Israeli Democracy," in Sprinzak and Diamond, eds., *Israeli Democracy under Stress*, pp. 65–82.

8. Ehud Sprinzak, *Ha'Ish Hayashar B'enav: Illegalizm BeChevrah HaYisraelit* [*Illegalism in Israeli Society*], Tel Aviv: Sifriyat Poalim, 1986.

9. Eliezer Don-Yehiya, "Religion, Social Cleavages, and Political Behavior: The Religious Parties and the Elections," in Daniel J. Elazar and Shmuel Sandler, eds., *Who's the Boss: Israel at the Polls, 1988–90*, Detroit, MI: Wayne State University Press, 1992, p. 91.

10. See, for example, Moshe Hallamish and Aviezer Ravitzky, *The Land of Israel in Medieval Jewish Thought* (in Hebrew), Jerusalem: Yad Izhak Ben-Zvi, 1991.

11. Zvi Yehuda Kook, "Ha-Torah Ve'Ha-aretz [The Torah and the Land]," *Yuval HaMizrachi*, Jerusalem, 1952, cited by Salmon, "Tradition and Nationalism," p. 97.

12. *Palestine Post*, 16 May 1948, pp. 1–2, reprinted in Itamar Rabinovich and Jehuda Reinharz, eds., *Israel in the Middle East*, New York: Oxford University Press, 1984, p. 12.

13. This position was taken by Maimonides, the Jewish scholar and legal authority who lived in the twelfth century.

14. This theme was emphasized in the writings of the proto-Zionists who preceded Herzl, such as Alkalai, Kalischer, and Friedland. See Arthur Hertzberg, *The Zionist Idea*, New York: Atheneum, 1959; Salmon, "Tradition and Nationalism," pp. 94–116; Aviezer Ravitzky, *Messianism, Zionism, and Jewish Religious Radicalism*, Chicago: University of Chicago Press, 1996, pp. 1–2.

15. Salmon, "Tradition and Nationalism," p. 99.

16. Charles Liebman and Eliezer Don-Yehiya, *Religion and Politics in Israel*, Bloomington, IN: Indiana University Press, 1984; Norman L. Zucker, *The Coming Crisis in Israel*, Cambridge, MA: MIT Press, 1973; Eliezer Don-Yehiya, *Conflict and Consensus in Jewish Political Life*, Ramat Gan: Bar-Ilan University Press, 1986.

17. Emanuel Rackman, *Israel's Emerging Constitution 1948–1951*, New York: Columbia University Press, 1955. These issues also arose in 1948 with regard to the wording of the Declaration of Independence. "For the secularist, anti-religious left . . . any mention of Divine providence was anathema. For religious Jews . . . the proclamation of the reestablishment of the Jewish state could not appear without such a reference." The compromise was to use the phrase "Rock of Israel" to allude to, but not specifically mention, God. See Daniel

J. Elazar, *The Constitution of Israel*, Jerusalem: Jerusalem Center for Public Affairs, 1996, p. 2.

18. See, for example, Menachem Friedman, "The Ultra-Orthodox and Israeli Society," in Keith Kyle and Joel Peters, eds., *Whither Israel: The Domestic Challenges*, London: Royal Institute of International Affairs, 1994.

19. Liebman and Don-Yehiya, *Religion and Politics in Israel*.

20. Daniel J. Elazar and Stuart A. Cohen, *The Jewish Polity: Jewish Political Organizations from Biblical Times to the Present*, Bloomington, IN: Indiana University Press, 1985.

21. Ibid., p. 6.

22. There is a vast literature on Judaism and democracy, reflecting the centrality of this issue in Israel and the Jewish community. See, for example, *Jewish Political Studies Review*, vol. 12, nos. 3 & 4, 2000 (special issue on Communal Democracy and Liberal Democracy in the Jewish Political Tradition); and vol. 5, nos. 1 & 2, 1993 (special issue on Israel as a Jewish State); Eliezer Schweid, *Democracy and Halakhah*, Lanham, MD: University Press of America, 1994; Shlomo Dov Goitein, "Political Conflict and the Use of Power in the World of the Geniza," in Daniel J. Elazar, ed., *Kinship and Consent: The Jewish Political Tradition and Its Contemporary Uses*, Ramat Gan: Transaction Publishers, 1997, pp. 281–3; Eli Clark, "After the Majority Shall You Incline': Democratic Theory and Voting Rights in Jewish Law," *Torah U-Madda Journal*, New York: Yeshiva University Press, 1999, pp. 97–133; Charles Liebman, *Religion, Democracy and Israeli Society*, Reading: Harwood Academic Publishers, 1997.

23. See Daniel J. Elazar, "Judaism and Democracy: The Reality," *Jerusalem Letter*, no. 48, 17 March 1986, Jerusalem: Jerusalem Center for Public Affairs.

24. Amnon Bazak, "'And You Shall Live by Them'—A Test of Principles: An In Depth Look at the Question of the Sanctity of Life and the Completeness of the Land" (in Hebrew), *Meimad Journal*, Issue 3, April 1995, p. 17.

25. Schweid, *Democracy and Halakhah*, p. 182; see also Eliezer Schweid, "The Jewish State and Democracy," *Jerusalem Letter*, no. 298, 15 July 1994, Jerusalem: Jerusalem Center for Public Affairs.

26. Charles S. Liebman, "Religion and Democracy in Israel," in Sprinzak and Diamond, eds., *Israeli Democracy under Stress*, p. 274.

27. Indeed, from the perspective of Jewish tradition, it is not only democracy but, more broadly, the concept of the modern sovereign state that lacks legitimacy. As Elazar and Cohen note, "the Jewish political tradition does not recognize state sovereignty in the modern sense of absolute independence. No state—a human creation—can be sovereign. Classically, only God is sovereign and He entrusts the exercise of His sovereign powers to the people as a whole, mediated through His Torah-as-constitution as provided through His covenant with Israel." Elazar and Cohen, *The Jewish Polity*, p. 5.

28. For a development of this thesis, see Asher Cohen and Bernard Susser, "From Accommodation to Decision: Transformations in Israel's Religio-Political Life," *Journal of Church and State*, vol. 38, Autumn 1996. For a contrasting view, see Eliezer Don-Yehiya, *The Politics of Accommodation: Settling Conflicts of State and Religion in Israel* (in Hebrew), Jerusalem: Floersheimer Institute for Policy Studies, 1997.

29. Liebman and Don-Yehiya, *Religion and Politics in Israel*.

30. Given the long history of anti-Semitism, culminating in the Holocaust, religious Jews were and remain particularly suspicious of the intentions of the outside world. This historical memory contributes to general skepticism regarding the possibilities for peace. As Amos Oz has written, "Perhaps it was a lunatic proposition; to transform, in two or three generations, a mass of persecuted, intimidated Jews, consumed with love-hate toward their countries of origin, into a nation serving as a shining example to the Arab surroundings, a model for the entire world." *Po Ve-sham Be-eretz Yisrael* [*Here and There in the Land of Israel*], Tel Aviv: Am Oved, 1983, p. 189.

31. In the late 1930s and during the 1940s, religious Zionist leaders "reluctantly" accepted partition, and accepted the policy of restraint in response to Arab terror attacks. See Itamar Wahrhaftig, "The Position of the Rabbis in the Controversy over Partition (1939)" (in Hebrew), *Tehumin*, vol. 9, 1988, pp. 269–301, cited by Stuart A. Cohen, *The Scroll or the Sword? Dilemmas of Religion and Military Service in Israel*, London: Harwood Academic Publishers, 1997, p. 28.

32. Zvi Yehuda Kook, Lemaan Daat and Lo Taguro, cited by Yael Yishai, *Land or Peace: Whither Israel?* Stanford, CA: Hoover Institution Press, 1987, p. 130.

33. Shlomo Aviner, "A Double Crisis," *Nekuda*, vol. 14, 15 May 1980, cited by Yishai, *Land or Peace*, p. 131.

34. Yishai, *Land or Peace*, pp. 116–19.

35. Sprinzak, *Ha'Ish Hayashar B'enav: Illegalizm BeChevrah HaYisraelit.*

36. Don-Yehiya, "Religion, Social Cleavages, and Political Behavior," p. 91.

37. See, for example, Yaakov Filber, *Ayelet HaShachar* [*Sunrise*], Jerusalem: Hamachon LeCheker Mishnat Hara'ayah, 1991.

38. Zvi Yehuda Kook, *Or Lenitavati* [*A Light to My Pathway*], Jerusalem: Hamachon Al Shem Rav Zvi Yehuda Hacohen Kook, 1989.

39. Menachem Friedman, "The First Non-Zionist Right Wing," *Meimad Journal* (in Hebrew), Issue 7, May–June 1996, p. 14.

40. Don-Yehiya, "Religion, Social Cleavages, and Political Behavior," p. 9.

41. See Cohen, *The Scroll or the Sword?*, p. 27.

42. Davar (Tel Aviv), 4 November 1985, cited by Liebman, "Religion and Democracy in Israel," p. 276.

43. Herb Keinon, "Goren Tells Troops: Disobey Orders," *Jerusalem Post*, 20 December 1993.

44. Cohen, *The Scroll or the Sword?*, p. 31.

45. Sarah Honig, "NRP: IDF Commands Should Be Obeyed 'Unless They Are Illegal,'" *Jerusalem Post*, 1 April 1994; Liat Collins, "Rabbinate Defers Decision on Soldiers' Disobeying Orders to Evacuate Jews," *Jerusalem Post*, 5 April 1994.

46. Honig, "NRP."

47. Herb Keinon, Batsheva Tsur, and Evelyn Gordon, "Rabbis: Soldiers Must Stay in Areas. Rabin Asks A-G to Probe if Decree Is Seditious," *Jerusalem Post*, 13 July 1995.

48. Hillel Halkin, "Israel, Rabbis Battle for Soul of Their Army," *Forward*, 21 July 1995.

49. Keinon et al., "Rabbis." A detailed discussion of this issue is presented by Yaakov Blidstein, "And Even if They Tell You Right Is Left: The Strength of Institutional Authority in Halacha and Its Boundaries," in Avi Sagi and Zeev Safrai, eds., *Between Authority and Autonomy in Jewish Tradition* (in Hebrew), Tel Aviv: Hakibbutz Hameuchad, 1997.

50. Eliezer Don-Yehiya, "Jewish Messianism, Religious Zionism, and Israeli Politics: The Origins and Impact of Gush Emunim," *Middle Eastern Studies*, vol. 23, April 1987, pp. 214–23.

51. Gershon Bacon, "Daat Torah v'chevli Hamashiach: LeSheyalat Ha'ideologiya Shel 'Agudat Yisrael' BiPolin," in Sagi and Safrai, eds., *Between Authority and Autonomy in Jewish Tradition*, reprinted from *Tarbiz*, vol. 52, no. 5743, 1983, pp. 497–508; see also Lawrence Kaplan, "'Daas Torah': A Modern Conception of Rabbinic Authority," in Moshe Sokol, ed., *Rabbinic Authority and Personal Autonomy*, Northvale, NJ: Aronson, 1992.

52. Alon Pinkas, "Soldier Jailed for Refusing to Evict Settlers," *Jerusalem Post*, 17 August 1995.

53. Gerald M. Steinberg, "Foreign Policy and Security Issues in the 1999 Elections," in Daniel Elazar and Ben Mollov, eds., *Israel at the Polls 1999*, London: Frank Cass, 2000.

54. Cited by Adam Doron, *Medinat Yisrael V'Eretz Yisrael* [*The State of Israel and the Land of Israel*], Tel Aviv: Beit Berel, 1988.

55. Ovadia Yosef, "Hachzarat Shtachim Me'eretz Yisrael Bimkom Pikuach Nefesh [Ceding Territory in the Land of Israel vs. the Sanctity of Life]," in Yitzchak Rafael, ed., *Lectures Presented at the 21st National Conference on Torah She'baal Peh*, Jerusalem: Mosad Harav Kook, 1980, p. 14; see also Ovadia Yosef, "Me'sirat Shtachim Me'eretz Yisrael Bimkom Pikuach Nefesh [Giving Territories of the Land of Israel vs. the Sanctity of Life]," in Yitzchak Rafael, ed., *Lectures Presented at the 31st National Conference on Torah She'baal Peh*, Jerusalem: Mosad Harav Kook, 1990. These analyses generated an exchange of articles, religious edicts, and responses in this and other publications, which are beyond the scope of this paper.

56. Michal Yudelman and Sarah Honig, "Arafat Wants to Meet Yosef," *Jerusalem Post*, 30 May 1997.

57. Herb Keinon, "Extraordinary Events," *Jerusalem Post*, 25 November 1994.

58. Itamar Warhaftig, "The Soul Should Not be Granted," *Nekuda*, no. 41, 19 March 1982, cited by Yishai, *Land or Peace*, p. 241.

59. *Meimad Journal* (in Hebrew), Issue 14, September 1998, back page.

60. Gerald M. Steinberg, "Peace, Security and Terror in the 1996 Elections," in Daniel J. Elazar and Shmuel Sandler, eds., *Israel at the Polls 1996*, London: Frank Cass, 1997.

61. See, for example, Jack S. Levy, "Domestic Politics and War," *Journal of Interdisciplinary History*, vol. 18, no. 4, Spring 1988, pp. 653–73. For a critical review of this literature, see James Lee Ray, "The Future of International War," in David Garnham and Mark Tessler, eds., *Democracy, War and Peace in the Middle East*, Bloomington, IN: Indiana University Press, 1995, pp. 3–33.

62. Errol Anthony Henderson, "The Democratic Peace Through the Lens of Culture, 1820–1989," *International Studies Quarterly*, vol. 42, no. 3, September 1998, pp. 461–84.

63. Garnham and Tessler, *Democracy, War and Peace in the Middle East*, Introduction, pp. xvii–xviii.

64. Jo-Ann Hart, "Democracy and Deterrence," in Garnham and Tessler, eds., *Democracy, War and Peace in the Middle East*, p. 37.

65. This omission can be found in Gabriel Sheffer, "Israel and the Liberalization of Arab Regimes," in Garnham and Tessler, eds., *Democracy, War and Peace in the Middle East*, pp. 268–88; and Gad Barzilai, *Democracy at War: Argument and Consensus in Israel* (in Hebrew), Tel Aviv: Sifriyat Poalim, 1992.

66. Shlomit Levy, Hanna Levinson, and Elihu Katz, "Observances and Social Interaction Among Israeli Jews," Jerusalem: Louis Guttman Israel Institute of Applied Social Research, 1993.

67. In the wake of the Oslo agreement (the "Declaration of Principles") in 1993, support was widespread and opposition was too limited to affect public policy. However, following waves of terrorism and the continued hostile rhetoric from Palestinians, including Yasser Arafat, protest grew. These factors led to the defeat of the Labor Party and Shimon Peres in the 1996 elections. See Gerald M. Steinberg, "Peace, Security and Terror in the 1996 Elections," *Israel Affairs*, vol. 4, no. 1, Autumn 1997 (special issue on Israel at the Polls 1996).

68. Gerald M. Steinberg, "Foreign Policy in the 1999 Israeli Elections," *Israel Affairs*, vol. 7, nos. 2&3, Winter/Spring 2001, pp. 174–98 (special issue on Israel at the Polls 1999).

Women represent half of any given society in the world. Their needs and demands, therefore, cannot be ignored if a nation hopes to remain vibrant, dynamic, and democratic. Indeed, the extent to which civil rights and equal opportunities are available to women is a key indicator of democracy's fortunes within a particular society and culture. As Nikki R. Keddie, the author of the following article, puts it, a country cannot be "truly democratic if it treats half its population as second-class citizens without full and equal rights." Women, in other words, cannot be safely excluded from the promise of democracy.

But that is precisely the case across much of the Middle East. Despite the strenuous efforts made by Western and Middle Eastern reformers, women in many Muslim countries are straitjacketed by narrow interpretations of Islam and centuries-old traditions of male domination. Noticeable improvements can be seen here and there in places such as Iran and Syria, but, by and large, women continue to struggle under restrictions put into place by men resistant to changes in the social hierarchy.

More than a problem of equity, the exclusion of women from political society makes progress toward democracy virtually impossible. Democracy cannot flourish in an environment of compulsory inequality. Resistance to women's rights, in essence, erects an impenetrable barrier to genuine liberalization and reform. At some point, democracy in the Middle East collides with that barrier and is repulsed. This explains why small democratic steps forward in the Muslim Middle East are so often followed by substantial authoritarian leaps backward. Traditional fears and anxieties check the progress of both women and democracy. Thus, as the next author makes clear, until women are given a better place in the social and political orders of the Middle East, democracy will remain a distant and perhaps unattainable goal.

A Woman's Place: Democratization in the Middle East
NIKKI R. KEDDIE

The awarding of the 2003 Nobel Peace Prize in October to Iranian activist attorney Shirin Ebadi highlights the struggle of Middle Eastern women for human and women's rights. It also highlights a vital though complex connection between the status of women and the prospects for democracy. Despite attempts by some Muslims to reinterpret Islam as compatible with gender equality, resistance to improving women's status has generally been greater in the Muslim world than elsewhere. No society can be truly democratic if it treats half its population as second-class citizens without full and equal rights. But not all paths to reform are created equal. The introduction of electoral systems without strong constitutional protections could empower fundamentalists who want to enforce strict versions of Islamic law, while democratization efforts undertaken by outside military intervention could provoke an anti-Western reaction. Either development could set back women's rights as well as political reform in the region.

It is wrong to view most Muslim countries, Iran included, as monolithic autocracies in which women are primarily victims rather than people working to carve out a more autonomous and democratic existence. Women's struggles, along with the forces of modernization, have increased the public roles open to women in the Muslim world despite the growing power of Islamism, and this expansion of women's roles constitutes in itself a force for democratization.

ISLAMISTS AND SECULARISTS

The word democracy has several meanings. In the United States the tendency has been to focus on voting and parliamentary government. By these criteria, only Turkey among Middle Eastern Muslim countries has a largely democratic system. Yet a number of other Middle Eastern countries have been increasing the role of free elections and parliamentary or consultative bodies. The problem encountered lately is that free voting may favor Islamists who refuse to extend, and often limit, women's rights. In many Muslim countries, the main lines of division regarding women's rights have been between secular nationalists who promote an extension of women's rights—whether because they are women's advocates or because they have an interest in modernizing values and achievements—and Islamists, whose programs are nearly always regressive regarding the role of women when seen from the viewpoint of modern universalist values. There are also gender-egalitarian Islamists, but they have not yet been able to change seriously the trend of Islamists' influencing governments in ways that create less egalitarian conditions for women.

In the recent history of the Muslim world, it has been mainly the Westernized bourgeoisie and upper classes that have favored the extension of women's rights, while the urban and rural popular classes and the small bourgeoisie tied to the traditional economy and to local clerics have not. Islamist movements, which today, despite contrary impressions in the West, are predominantly gradualist rather than militant, have grown in most Muslim countries for a variety of reasons. Among these are the rapid urbanization of non-Westernized rural populations, which are often helped in cities not by their governments but by clerical or Islamist groups; economic and social crises to which Islamists promise solutions where secular governments have failed; and resentment of Western and especially U.S. and Israeli actions in the Middle East. Like American fundamentalists, Islamists tend to support a strict reading of selected parts of scripture and religious tradition, many of which endorse a subordinate role for women and a dominant role for men.

Secular rulers in the Middle East have often taken the lead in recognizing that increased women's rights and labor-force participation are essential to the creation of modern nations and societies, whether democratic, authoritarian, or something in between. Pioneering women primarily of middle- and upper-class background, supported by male reformist politicians and writers, organized and fought for women's rights in most Middle Eastern countries from the early twentieth century on, and these struggles sometimes influenced the rulers who introduced major reforms. Notable examples of reforms were Ataturk's abolition of Islamic law and introduction of a family code based on Swiss law in Turkey in the 1920s and the extension of voting rights to women in 1934; Habib Bourguiba's abolition of polygamy, with Islamic justifications, in Tunisia's personal status code in 1956; Mohammad Reza Shah's approval of feminist-inspired family protection laws in Iran in 1967 and 1975; and Anwar Sadat's promotion of a more egalitarian family law in Egypt.

Most recently, in October 2003, King Mohammad VI presented the Moroccan parliament with a proposed act, quite similar to Iran's family protection law, that raises the marriage age, gives women new property rights in marriage, opens divorce to women, requires a judge's approval for all divorces, and makes polygamy permissible only with a judge's authorization and the consent of the previous wife or wives. Like most Muslim rulers other than Ataturk, the Moroccan king claimed, with apposite quotations, that the reforms were truly Islamic. In Morocco's case, women's movements influenced the new legislation and a large number of elected progressives in parliament contributed important backing to the king's reform efforts.

Contemporary governments that make a strong point of being Islamic either have not reformed Islamic laws regarding women, as in Saudi Arabia, or have turned back reforms that they considered un-Islamic, as with Ayatollah Ruhollah Khomeini's abolition of the family protection law in Iran. In Pakistan, the "Islamic" military dictatorship of Zia ul-Haqq (1977–1988) reintroduced Islamic laws regarding women that were followed by even stricter measures imposed by the current Islamist provincial governments in Pakistan's Baluchistan and Northwest Frontier. Afghanistan suffered under the extreme measures of the Taliban. These laws have, however, mobilized more women to fight for their rights than ever before.

REINTERPRETING ISLAM

Recently the Muslim world has witnessed renewed intellectual and political debate over what constitutes true Islam. Those labeled fundamentalist have stressed certain elements of Islam, particularly aspects of law and custom that differentiate Islamic from modern Western practices. These include laws that limit women and favor men, such as polygamy, easy divorce for men but not for women, presumptive granting of child custody to the father or his family after divorce, requirements that a woman obtain a husband's or male guardian's permission to work or travel, and generalized control over women and girls by male family members.

While fundamentalists favor such limits and laws, a growing group of Muslim reformers finds the true spirit of Islam in verses of the Koran that treat men and women equally as believers. Some reformers argue that verses emphasizing inequality between the sexes were not intended for all time; others point to different interpretations of these verses. Notably, the chapter of the Koran that allows polygamy does so specifically in the context of protecting widows and orphans (who were numerous because of wars), and says that a man should take more than one wife only if he can treat all equally. Later in the same chapter of the Koran it is said that no man can treat all wives equally—implying, according to reformers, that polygamy is not licit. Modernist Islamic arguments were used to justify the abolition of polygamy in Tunisia under Habib Bourguiba in 1956 and to endorse its limitation in several Islamic countries. Only Tunisia and Turkey have outlawed polygamy, and they are the two Muslim countries with legal systems most respectful of gender equality.

History shows that inegalitarian laws and customs were found in all premodern societies. Islam took over many such customs either from pre-Islamic tribal societies or, as with veiling, from pre-Islamic Near Eastern empires, particularly the Byzantine and Persian empires. Polygamy was once universally permitted, though usually rare in practice (as it is in the Muslim world). Changes in the roles of women—not always immediately positive but ultimately leading to greater equality—

came with the rise of capitalism and representative government. Women have had to struggle for their rights in government and in the public sphere and workplace in the West, but this struggle's trajectory has been mainly positive for women. Much of the non-Muslim world has seen greater progress in women's equality than the Muslim world, though one should not exaggerate this difference—the rise in dowry murders in India is in some ways worse, resulting in far more deaths, than anything experienced in the Muslim world.

OBSTACLES TO WOMEN'S RIGHTS

In general, resistance to improving women's legal status has been greater in the Muslim world than elsewhere, and the denial of full and equal rights to half their populations has proved an obstacle to the democratization of Muslim societies. Part of the problem is that the struggle for women's rights in the Muslim world, as in other non-Western regions, has often been attacked as a Western colonialist phenomenon, even by those who accept other Western ideas, such as Marxism or nationalism.

Associating women's rights struggles with subservience to the West makes these struggles more difficult. It also helps account for intellectual efforts in the Muslim world and elsewhere to demonstrate that Islam and the local culture were originally and fundamentally egalitarian, and have been distorted by later patriarchal thinkers and rulers. In Islam there is some basis for this; the Koran and gender relations in Mohammad's time were more egalitarian than dominant interpretations of Islam became later.

Strong correlations can be found between a woman's status in a society and that society's likelihood of being politically democratic. On nearly all indices of women's status—education levels, labor force participation, health, political status and rights—most Muslim countries rank lower than non-Muslim countries with comparable incomes. Muslim countries also rank very low in democratic institutions and in per capita income and rates of development. Some scholars have convincingly tied political and economic underdevelopment to their showing on status-of-women indices.

A number of reasons may be adduced for the low relative status of many (though far from all) women in the Muslim world, and the tendency to ascribe this to Islam does not begin to explain the phenomenon. Islam can be and has been interpreted in many different ways, as have been the equally scriptural monotheistic religions, Judaism and Christianity. The status of women in the Bible is subordinate, as it is in Roman Catholic and fundamentalist Protestant doctrine, yet most believers in developed countries do not accept the traditional Christian view of women's subordination to men. Many believing Muslims similarly do not accept traditional views regarding women, but the factors that have increased fundamentalism in the Muslim world have similarly worked to increase male-dominant religious views.

Promoting the tradition of male dominance, too, is a long history of strongly patriarchal tribes and extended families in the Muslim world, favored in the Middle East by the aridity that encouraged nomadic tribalism. In addition, widespread frustration over Western-backed autocratic and often secular governments—and their failure to produce sufficient social and economic progress—has made a number of people idealize the past and see present problems as a result of deviation from Islamic ideals. The continued Israeli occupation of Arab lands has encouraged a kind of pan-Islamic nationalism that finds solace and support in restating Islamic doctrines. The failures of both secular nationalism and international socialism also have contributed to the search for a different doctrine of worldly salvation.

DEMOCRACY BY INVASION

While the success of democratization in the Middle East requires a greater role for women in the public sphere, this cannot be achieved by outside intervention if history is any guide. The two countries in the Middle East that have most dramatically legislated in ways favorable to women—Turkey and Tunisia—did so only after freeing themselves of foreign control and intervention. No amount of constitutional tinkering inspired by an occupying power appears likely to improve substantially the role of women in Afghanistan or Iraq, even though a minimum requirement of any U.S. intervention should be a guarantee of women's safety and rights. The signs to date in Afghanistan and Iraq regarding such minimum guarantees are not encouraging. In Afghanistan there has been a recrudescence of patriarchal warlord power and warfare and also of the Taliban. Outside of Kabul very few women unveil, and even though women can work and (some) girls can attend school, many Taliban-like limits on their actions and behavior still prevail.

The constitution recently proposed by Afghan President Hamid Karzai includes a few protections for women. The proposed strong presidential system has provisions guaranteeing that a certain number of women be elected to the lower house of parliament and selected by the president for the upper house. Afghanistan is, however, to be an Islamic Republic, with Islam the official religion, and statements about human rights are very general and without specifics regarding women. The place of Islamic courts and law appears ambiguous. The state is to administer justice in accordance with legislation and the constitution, but where relevant provisions do not exist decisions are to be made within constitutional limits "in accordance with [Islamic] jurisprudence and in a way to serve justice in the best possible manner."

There is no guarantee that the constitution's provisions will be carried out, or that ambiguous legal provisions will not be interpreted to leave personal status law largely unreformed and unfavorable to women. A group of Afghan female legists and professionals has recommended a large number of changes in the constitution to guarantee more seats for women nationwide, more workplace protection, an end to trafficking in women, equality in marriage and the family, and equal treatment in all aspects of life. Amin Tarzi, a regional analyst for Afghanistan and Iraq at Radio Free Europe/Radio Liberty, notes that although the draft constitution includes general statements against discrimination, the lack of specific protections and the references to Islamic law may, as they have in the past, provide excuses for dominant males to continue to undermine or ignore women's rights.

In Iraq, women and girls remain unsafe, especially in much of the so-called Sunni Triangle area, including Baghdad. Many are afraid to leave their homes unaccompanied by a man, and some girls are kept from school for fear of kidnapping and rape. As noted by Nicholas Kristof in the November 19, 2003, *New York Times*, women and girls are "arguably worse off now than under Saddam. . . . A new report by the UN Population Fund offers a devastating portrait of the plight of Iraqi women since the war." In addition to other problems, many women have lost access to medical care, even for serious illnesses. Also, a number of Islamists, especially among the majority Shiites, are calling for an Islamic state (among the Shiites, on the Iranian model) and for the imposition of Islamic laws regarding women. Reestablishment of security remains a top priority for the women and girls of Iraq, even more than for the men, and an almost equal priority for both is the creation of jobs and a functioning Iraqi economy and infrastructure. Published interviews with Iraqi girls and women show that these, rather than the details of a new constitution, are their main concerns.

If these basic security and economic issues are met, then women and democratic men presumably will show more interest in a constitution, but they also will realize that a constitution is only one element of a democratic society. I do not believe it is an outsider's role to say what specifics a constitution should include beyond guarantees for equal human rights for both sexes. Whether this is to be encouraged by gender quotas in parliament and in government office is something for local democrats to decide.

My concerns are rather that the entire enterprise of creating democracy by invasion and writing a constitution while under occupation is likely to be tainted, and in many ways abortive, and will hurt women even more than men. The numerous and currently glaring faults of the occupation and the other problems facing Iraq already are being blamed on the United States, both in Iraq and elsewhere, and this has encouraged more people to turn to nondemocratic, including strict Islamist, solutions. Already the occupation forces are making compromises with formerly powerful men and groups to restore order, and these men and groups often promote a greater degree of gender inequality than existed under Saddam Hussein. This is true of even some of the more moderate and less militant Shiite leaders. As already seen in Afghanistan, Palestine, and Chechnya, foreign occupation often strengthens Islamism among those who resist it, and if this trend continues to grow in Iraq, it will likely lead to greater restrictions on women.

INTERNAL FORCES FOR REFORM

The history of British and French colonial policy in the Middle East indicates that the presence of foreign forces increased the veiling, seclusion, and unequal treatment of women as a reaction against Western rule and Western ways. Women who fought for and attained greater equality were often considered subordinate to the West, and some still are. The best way to counteract this has been for indigenous women and concerned men to struggle in their own way for women's rights. This has been dramatically shown in Iran since 1979. Both religious and secular women in increasing numbers have taken advantage of educational opportunities offered by the state and have been highly creative in carving out professional lives for themselves and in everyday resistance to government restrictions. Western groups can help publicize and fund these struggles, but it is far better if these are nongovernmental groups not so easily suspected of possessing ulterior motives.

A few Arab countries have recently taken small steps toward greater democracy and, in some cases, women's rights. Insofar as these developments have international causes, they are not primarily the result of U.S. pressure. More often they derive from a desire to join global trading and investment networks. Countries can more easily join these networks if they establish some democratic legal and electoral norms that much of the world community demands. Also, many Arab leaders now believe that the only way to avoid civil unrest is to encourage alternatives to Islamists, who today often dominate the opposition, partly because only mosque-related oppositional activities escape suppression. Bahrain held parliamentary elections last year with women candidates. Kuwait has held legislative elections and promises enfranchisement of women, though its parliament has expressed disapproval. King Abdullah of Jordan has proposed an expansion of representative government. Other countries have taken similar small steps. Even Saudi Arabia is promising local elective councils in the future, though doubts remain about the seriousness of the proposal and whether it will include women. Overall, past Saudi financing of mosques and schools worldwide that promote their peculiar version of Islam has been seriously restrictive for Muslim women.

Morocco is the most hopeful Arab case. The 2003 legislative changes proposed by King Mohammad VI, unlike earlier legislation in Turkey, Tunisia, and pre-revolution Iran, are not simply a case of reform from above. In Morocco, a sympathetic monarch acceded to pressures from progressives and women's rights advocates. External factors also provided incentives. The king wished to burnish the image of Morocco as a progressive Arab state in the eyes of Western governments at a time when the discourse of democratization in the Middle East has become prevalent. The king repeatedly referred to the sharia (Islamic law) in presenting the reforms. And they do not go as far as the 1956 Tunisian reforms, since polygamy is permitted if the first wife accepts it whereas it is banned in Tunisia.

The reforms that have occurred in the Arab world suggest that generalized Western pressures can have some influence, although the current unpopularity of the U.S. government makes it the least likely source for a lasting effect on popular views of gender questions.

THE CASE OF IRAN

Iran illustrates the problems of simply promulgating egalitarian laws from above without the context of an overall democracy, as the shah did, and also the problems and possibilities for women that are appearing as several other countries shift from a more secular/egalitarian government to one more influenced by Islamists. The relatively egalitarian family protection law of 1967 (and its improved version of 1975), which was largely influenced by women's rights activists, gave Iranian women essentially equal rights in marriage, divorce, and child custody, and allowed a second marriage only with the approval of the first wife and a court. Ayatollah Ruhollah Khomeini from his exile called the law and any marriages and divorces attained under it void, and one of his first acts when his revolutionary government came to power in February 1979 was to annul this reform and return to sharia law. This was more important for reducing women's rights than were the steps, more publicized worldwide, to require Islamic dress for women.

In the years following the Iranian revolution, many women, including some who had been mobilized during the revolution, helped reverse a number of the restrictions put on women. Women were originally excluded from a number of university specialties and professions. Many responded by entering new professions and businesses, where they contributed to ending the university and professional restrictions. In a recent interview Shirin Ebadi said that there are now two women judges with full capacity and that they are women who, like herself, had been removed from their positions right after the revolution.

Changes in health, education, and social mores in Iran have helped create a new generation of women and men eager to create a more democratic government and with many of the skills needed to run it. Women have benefited especially from the health and education measures initiated by the government. The revolutionary state from the first emphasized rural and lower-class urban health services. In 1989 it reversed its formerly hostile position regarding birth control and launched what has become probably the world's most successful national birth control program. Clerical endorsement and the enlistment of trusted local health workers have made birth control acceptable. All newly married couples must attend sex and birth control education classes, and birth control is free and publicized. Since 1989, Iran has shifted from having one of the highest birthrates in the world to a replacement level of just over two births per couple. This is one factor in the greater attention given to the education and cultural development of children. It also has made it easier for mothers to work. Women now live on average to the age of 72, two years longer than men, and life expectancy is still rising and infant mortality falling.

The results of Iran's push for education at all levels are equally impressive. In the 15- to 24-year-old age group, 97 percent of young women are now literate, a huge increase over pre-revolution literacy, even though education was expanding during the shah's reign. Educational institutions have expanded at all levels, including adult education and outside classes in the arts and other skills. Women now account for over 62 percent of entering university students, based on their higher test results. Women also pursue sports more than ever before. Although many exceptions and inconsistencies can be found, the government has entered into a kind of informal agreement with the Iranian people—in essence, the state will permit social change but not political demonstrations. In the large cities boys and girls mix, often in specially designated areas, and even hold hands. Headscarves are pushed back, and coats are short. Also, young people have a greater say in marriage partners, sometimes even marrying against their parents' wishes.

Women still face many problems, however. Even though Iran's GNP has recently been rising rapidly, the economy is not generating enough jobs to absorb educated women or men. The most recent available figures, from 1999, show that only 10 percent of women were part of the workforce, although the real figure is higher because of considerable female employment in the informal economy and in unreported work in rural areas. Although unemployment is high across the board, it is higher among women than men. Senior positions in the civil service are still overwhelmingly a man's preserve.

Most important, in Iran as in many Middle Eastern countries, Islamic law has remained resistant to gender equality, though some reforms have occurred. With a few exceptions legislated during the Iran–Iraq War, child custody still goes to fathers after a very young age, and immediately if the divorced woman remarries. Although a reform provision requires that a court approve all divorces, male petitions are almost never rejected, while a woman can divorce only for a limited number of reasons. An important reform inserted a number of conditions similar to those in the family protection law into each marriage contract, but now the bride and groom must sign them. There are no figures on how many contracts are not signed, although apparently most are. Adulterers still may be stoned to death (a penalty not in the Koran but which entered Islamic law from surrounding areas), though this has become very rare. Fathers possess complete legal rights over their children, who are given almost no legal protection by Islamic law. Male guardians can control or veto a woman's right to work or travel, but women students may now go abroad alone.

WOMEN AND DEMOCRACY

Iran, like much of the Middle East, presents a contradictory picture of a struggle between the forces of reaction or tradition that take Islamic law, including inequality for women, as their main ideological basis, and those who fight for democracy and women's and human rights. The picture is complicated by reformers who are reinterpreting Islamic law in egalitarian directions. These reinterpretations thus far have had a major impact only when rulers have adopted them, as in Morocco, and even then the result has not been completely egalitarian with respect to gender. The question remains whether such reinterpretations can achieve true gender equality, which is a concomitant of true democracy. Reinterpretations of Islam can in any case contribute to the eventual achievement of gender equality, which may ultimately require a large dose of secular separation of mosque from state and new law codes that break radically with past codes.

The Arab countries overall are similar to Iran insofar as many aspects of Arab women's lives have improved, although women have not achieved legal or actual gender equality. Measured in literacy and education, life expectancy, average marriage ages and birthrates, and labor force participation, Arab women are better off than before, but they are still hindered by unequal laws, persistent inegalitarian customs and ideas, and a lack of democratic freedoms. In the Middle East further progress for women will create both an impetus and a precondition for democracy, although the establishment of democracy will demand other difficult changes, including an end to foreign occupations.

Political scientist Samuel P. Huntington recently set out the theory that the current dispute between radical Islam and the West represents one aspect of a global "clash of civilizations." Huntington imagines a historic battle between multiple opposing world orders. In the Middle East, it essentially boils down to two: one thoroughly modern and democratic, the other anti-modern and bound by value systems that negate most of democracy's key elements. Indeed, Huntington states that it is Islamic ideas and practices that slow the advance of democracy in the Middle East. "Islamic culture," he writes, "explains in large part the failure of democracy to emerge in much of the Muslim world."[*]

Pippa Norris and Ronald Inglehart accept the broad outlines of Huntington's interpretive model, but they quarrel with its overly broad focus. They would sharpen it considerably. Islam and the West are indeed clashing, Norris and Inglehart contend, but the contest is over issues almost solely relating to sexuality and gender roles. The authors claim that, in matters not touching upon those two subjects, there is a remarkable amount of agreement between Muslims and non-Muslims. Even in terms of democracy, Muslims as a group welcome political reform and expanded liberties. Responsive governments and open societies appeal as much to Muslims as to their counterparts in Europe and North America. True, many Muslims reject democracy, but that is due to its association with Western imperialism; it has little to do with the essence of the democratic impulse.

The conversation, however, ends abruptly when it comes to such topics as marriage, divorce, family structures, gay rights, and gender equality. Norris and Inglehart argue that therein lies the impediment to democracy and modernization in the Middle East. The Muslim consensus regarding a woman's place in the social order and the nearly unanimous condemnation of Western views concerning sexual identity and family practices stands as the true point of contention between Islam and the West. It is here, according to the authors of the next article, that one finds the true clash of civilizations.

NOTES
[*]   Samuel P. Huntington, *The Clash of Civilizations and the Remaking of World Order* (New York: Touchstone, 1996), 29.

The True Clash of Civilizations
PIPPA NORRIS AND RONALD INGLEHART

Samuel Huntington was only half right. The cultural fault line that divides the West and the Muslim world is not about democracy but sex. According to a new survey, Muslims and their Western counterparts want democracy, yet they are worlds apart when it comes to attitudes toward divorce, abortion, gender equality, and gay rights—which may not bode well for democracy's future in the Middle East.

Democracy promotion in Islamic countries is now one of the Bush administration's most popular talking points. "We reject the condescending notion that freedom will not grow in the Middle East," Secretary of State Colin Powell declared last December as he unveiled the White House's new Middle East Partnership Initiative to encourage political and economic reform in Arab countries. Likewise, Condoleezza Rice, President George W. Bush's national security advisor, promised last September that the United States is committed to "the march of freedom in the Muslim world."

But does the Muslim world march to the beat of a different drummer? Despite Bush's optimistic pronouncement that there is "no clash of civilizations" when it comes to "the common rights and needs of men and women," others are not so sure. Samuel Huntington's controversial 1993 thesis—that the cultural division between "Western Christianity" and "Orthodox Christianity and Islam" is the new fault line for conflict—resonates more loudly than ever since September 11. Echoing Huntington, columnist Polly Toynbee argued in the British Guardian last November, "What binds together a globalized force of some extremists from many continents is a united hatred of Western values that seems to them to spring from Judeo-Christianity." Meanwhile, on the other side of the Atlantic, Democratic Rep. Christopher Shays of Connecticut, after sitting through hours of testimony on U.S.–Islamic relations on Capitol Hill last October, testily blurted, "Why doesn't democracy grab hold in the Middle East? What is there about the culture and the people and so on where democracy just doesn't seem to be something they strive for and work for?"

Huntington's response would be that the Muslim world lacks the core political values that gave birth to representative democracy in Western civilization: separation of religious and secular authority, rule of law and social pluralism, parliamentary institutions of representative government, and protection of individual rights and civil liberties as the buffer between citizens and the power of the state. This claim seems all too plausible given the failure of electoral democracy to take root throughout the Middle East and North Africa. According to the latest Freedom House rankings, almost two thirds of the 192 countries around the world are now electoral democracies. But among the 47 countries with a Muslim majority, only one fourth are electoral democracies—and none of the core Arabic-speaking societies falls into this category.

Yet this circumstantial evidence does little to prove Huntington correct, since it reveals nothing about the underlying beliefs of Muslim publics. Indeed, there has been scant empirical evidence whether Western and Muslim societies exhibit deeply divergent values—that is, until now. The cumulative results of the two most recent waves of the World Values Survey (WVS), conducted in 1995–96 and 2000–2002, provide an extensive body of relevant evidence. Based on questionnaires that explore values and beliefs in more than 70 countries, the WVS is an investigation of sociocultural and political change that encompasses over 80 percent of the world's population.

A comparison of the data yielded by these surveys in Muslim and non-Muslim societies around the globe confirms the first claim in Huntington's thesis: Culture does matter—indeed, it matters a lot. Historical religious traditions have left an enduring imprint on contemporary values. However, Huntington is mistaken in assuming that the core clash between the West and Islam is over political values. At this point in history, societies throughout the world (Muslim and Judeo-Christian alike) see democracy as the best form of government. Instead, the real fault line between the West and Islam, which Huntington's theory completely overlooks, concerns gender equality and sexual liberalization. In other words, the values separating the two cultures have much more to do with eros than demos. As younger generations in the West have gradually become more liberal on these issues, Muslim nations have remained the most traditional societies in the world.

This gap in values mirrors the widening economic divide between the West and the Muslim world. Commenting on the disenfranchisement of women throughout the Middle East, the United Nations Development Programme observed last summer that "no society can achieve the desired state of well-being and human development, or compete in a globalizing world, if half its people remain marginalized and disempowered." But this "sexual clash of civilizations" taps into far deeper issues than how Muslim countries treat women. A society's commitment to gender equality and sexual liberalization proves time and again to be the most reliable indicator of how strongly that society supports principles of tolerance and egalitarianism. Thus, the people of the Muslim world overwhelmingly want democracy, but democracy may not be sustainable in their societies.

TESTING HUNTINGTON

Huntington argues that "ideas of individualism, liberalism, constitutionalism, human rights, equality, liberty, the rule of law, democracy, free markets, [and] the separation of church and state" often have little resonance outside the West. Moreover, he holds that Western efforts to promote these ideas provoke a violent backlash against "human rights imperialism." To test these propositions, we categorized the countries included in the WVS according to the nine major contemporary civilizations, based largely on the historical religious legacy of each society. The survey includes 22 countries representing Western Christianity (a West European culture that also encompasses North America, Australia, and New Zealand), 10 Central European nations (sharing a Western Christian heritage, but which also lived under Communist rule), 11 societies with a Muslim majority (Albania, Algeria, Azerbaijan, Bangladesh, Egypt, Indonesia, Iran, Jordan, Morocco, Pakistan, and Turkey), 12 traditionally Orthodox societies (such as Russia and Greece), 11 predominately Catholic Latin American countries, 4 East Asian societies shaped by Sino-Confucian values, 5 sub-Saharan Africa countries, plus Japan and India.

Despite Huntington's claim of a clash of civilizations between the West and the rest, the WVS reveals that, at this point in history, democracy has an overwhelmingly positive image throughout the world. In country after country, a clear majority of the population describes "having a democratic political system" as either "good" or "very good." These results represent a dramatic change from the 1930s and 1940s, when fascist regimes won overwhelming mass approval in many societies; and for many decades, Communist regimes had widespread support. But in the last decade, democracy became virtually the only political model with global appeal, no matter what the culture. With the exception of Pakistan, most of the Muslim countries surveyed think highly of democracy: In Albania, Egypt, Bangladesh, Azerbaijan, Indonesia, Morocco, and Turkey, 92 to 99 percent of the public endorsed democratic institutions—a higher proportion than in the United States (89 percent).

Yet, as heartening as these results may be, paying lip service to democracy does not necessarily prove that people genuinely support basic democratic norms—or that their leaders will allow them to have democratic institutions. Although constitutions of authoritarian states such as China profess to embrace democratic ideals such as freedom of

religion, the rulers deny it in practice. In Iran's 2000 elections, reformist candidates captured nearly three quarters of the seats in parliament,
but a theocratic elite still holds the reins of power. Certainly, it's a step
in the right direction if most people in a country endorse the idea of
democracy. But this sentiment needs to be complemented by deeper
underlying attitudes such as interpersonal trust and tolerance of unpopular groups—and these values must ultimately be accepted by those who
control the army and secret police.

The WVS reveals that, even after taking into account differences in
economic and political development, support for democratic institutions
is just as strong among those living in Muslim societies as in Western (or
other) societies. For instance, a solid majority of people living in Western
and Muslim countries gives democracy high marks as the most efficient
form of government, with 68 percent disagreeing with assertions that
"democracies are indecisive" and "democracies aren't good at maintaining
order." (All other cultural regions and countries, except East Asia and
Japan, are far more critical.) And an equal number of respondents on both
sides of the civilizational divide (61 percent) firmly reject authoritarian
governance, expressing disapproval of "strong leaders" who do not "bother
with parliament and elections." Muslim societies display greater support
for religious authorities playing an active societal role than do Western
societies. Yet this preference for religious authorities is less a cultural
division between the West and Islam than it is a gap between the West
and many other less secular societies around the globe, especially in sub-
Saharan Africa and Latin America. For instance, citizens in some Muslim
societies agree overwhelmingly with the statement that "politicians who
do not believe in God are unfit for public office" (88 percent in Egypt,
83 percent in Iran, and 71 percent in Bangladesh), but this statement
also garners strong support in the Philippines (71 percent), Uganda (60
percent), and Venezuela (52 percent). Even in the United States, about
two fifths of the public believes that atheists are unfit for public office.

However, when it comes to attitudes toward gender equality and
sexual liberalization, the cultural gap between Islam and the West wid-
ens into a chasm. On the matter of equal rights and opportunities for
women—measured by such questions as whether men make better
political leaders than women or whether university education is more
important for boys than for girls—Western and Muslim countries score
82 percent and 55 percent, respectively. Muslim societies are also distinctively less permissive toward homosexuality, abortion, and divorce.

These issues are part of a broader syndrome of tolerance, trust,
political activism, and emphasis on individual autonomy that constitutes
"self-expression values." The extent to which a society emphasizes these

self-expression values has a surprisingly strong bearing on the emergence and survival of democratic institutions. Among all the countries included in the WVS, support for gender equality—a key indicator of tolerance and personal freedom—is closely linked with a society's level of democracy.

In every stable democracy, a majority of the public disagrees with the statement that "men make better political leaders than women." None of the societies in which less than 30 percent of the public rejects this statement (such as Jordan, Nigeria, and Belarus) is a true democracy. In China, one of the world's least democratic countries, a majority of the public agrees that men make better political leaders than women, despite a party line that has long emphasized gender equality (Mao Zedong once declared, "women hold up half the sky"). In practice, Chinese women occupy few positions of real power and face widespread discrimination in the workplace. India is a borderline case. The country is a long-standing parliamentary democracy with an independent judiciary and civilian control of the armed forces, yet it is also marred by a weak rule of law, arbitrary arrests, and extrajudicial killings. The status of Indian women reflects this duality. Women's rights are guaranteed in the constitution, and Indira Gandhi led the nation for 15 years. Yet domestic violence and forced prostitution remain prevalent throughout the country, and, according to the WVS, almost 50 percent of the Indian populace believes only men should run the government.

The way a society views homosexuality constitutes another good litmus test of its commitment to equality. Tolerance of well-liked groups is never a problem. But if someone wants to gauge how tolerant a nation really is, find out which group is the most disliked, and then ask whether members of that group should be allowed to hold public meetings, teach in schools, and work in government. Today, relatively few people express overt hostility toward other classes, races, or religions, but rejection of homosexuals is widespread. In response to a WVS question about whether homosexuality is justifiable, about half of the world's population say "never." But, as is the case with gender equality, this attitude is directly proportional to a country's level of democracy. Among authoritarian and quasi-democratic states, rejection of homosexuality is deeply entrenched: 99 percent in both Egypt and Bangladesh, 94 percent in Iran, 92 percent in China, and 71 percent in India. By contrast, these figures are much lower among respondents in stable democracies: 32 percent in the United States, 26 percent in Canada, 25 percent in Britain, and 19 percent in Germany.

Muslim societies are neither uniquely nor monolithically low on tolerance toward sexual orientation and gender equality. Many of the

Soviet successor states rank as low as most Muslim societies. However, on the whole, Muslim countries not only lag behind the West but behind all other societies as well. Perhaps more significant, the figures reveal the gap between the West and Islam is even wider among younger age groups. This pattern suggests that the younger generations in Western societies have become progressively more egalitarian than their elders, but the younger generations in Muslim societies have remained almost as traditional as their parents and grandparents, producing an expanding cultural gap.

CLASH OF CONCLUSIONS

"The peoples of the Islamic nations want and deserve the same freedoms and opportunities as people in every nation," President Bush declared in a commencement speech at West Point last summer. He's right. Any claim of a "clash of civilizations" based on fundamentally different political goals held by Western and Muslim societies represents an oversimplification of the evidence. Support for the goal of democracy is surprisingly widespread among Muslim publics, even among those living in authoritarian societies. Yet Huntington is correct when he argues that cultural differences have taken on a new importance, forming the fault lines for future conflict. Although nearly the entire world pays lip service to democracy, there is still no global consensus on the self-expression values—such as social tolerance, gender equality, freedom of speech, and interpersonal trust—that are crucial to democracy. Today, these divergent values constitute the real clash between Muslim societies and the West.

But economic development generates changed attitudes in virtually any society. In particular, modernization compels systematic, predictable changes in gender roles: Industrialization brings women into the paid work force and dramatically reduces fertility rates. Women become literate and begin to participate in representative government but still have far less power than men. Then, the post-industrial phase brings a shift toward greater gender equality as women move into higher-status economic roles in management and gain political influence within elected and appointed bodies. Thus, relatively industrialized Muslim societies such as Turkey share the same views on gender equality and sexual liberalization as other new democracies.

Even in established democracies, changes in cultural attitudes—and eventually, attitudes toward democracy—seem to be closely linked with modernization. Women did not attain the right to vote in most historically Protestant societies until about 1920, and in much of Roman

Catholic Europe until after World War II. In 1945, only 3 percent of the members of parliaments around the world were women. In 1965 the figure rose to 8 percent, in 1985 to 12 percent, and in 2002 to 15 percent.

The United States cannot expect to foster democracy in the Muslim world simply by getting countries to adopt the trappings of democratic governance, such as holding elections and having a parliament. Nor is it realistic to expect that nascent democracies in the Middle East will inspire a wave of reforms reminiscent of the velvet revolutions that swept Eastern Europe in the final days of the Cold War. A real commitment to democratic reform will be measured by the willingness to commit the resources necessary to foster human development in the Muslim world. Culture has a lasting impact on how societies evolve. But culture does not have to be destiny.

SECTION THREE

Democracy
and Extremism

Autocratic states are breeding grounds for discontent and hopelessness, both of which contribute to the rise of terrorism. Democracies, on the other hand, channel popular unrest and anxiety toward the electoral process, thus defusing tensions that otherwise might be resolved violently. Democratic reform in the Middle East, therefore, can be considered a crucial part of the so-called "war on terror." As President George W. Bush noted in a speech on democracy in the region, fighting terror means an end to "sixty years of Western nations excusing and accommodating the lack of freedom in the Middle East."* Autocracy, in other words, can no longer be indirectly tolerated. Long-term global stability and U.S. national security, in the end, are tightly bound up with the fate of democracy in the Middle East.

There is a problem, though. Democratic societies are not well situated for fighting terrorism. Their concerns for freedom, due process, and the rule of law leave them vulnerable to terrorist exploitation. Terrorists often enjoy a certain degree of impunity or at least a lower risk of detection in a democratic setting, because of the safeguards put into place to protect the citizenry. The nearly sacred status of personal liberty and limited government authority can help terrorists avoid apprehension and plot their crimes with less fear of being discovered. Autocratic states, by comparison, are much more effective at rooting out terrorist networks and combating extremist violence. Minimal regard for civil rights, seemingly omnipresent security services, and broad government powers over the daily lives of the citizenry allow autocratic regimes to pursue militant organizations relentlessly. The more undemocratic a government is, especially in the Middle East, the more effective and efficient it is at neutralizing terrorist threats, at least in the short run.

This presents the West with a dilemma. Which takes precedence: promoting democracy or fighting terror? In the following essay, Thomas Carothers examines this problem of balancing the desire for democracy with the necessity of security. Taking a global perspective, the author claims that a middle ground exists, which the Western democracies need to occupy. The United States, in particular, he says, has little choice but to continue to engage regimes that only grudgingly implement political and social reforms; these governments too often prove quite successful at countering terror. The leverage gained by continued support, however, must be used to push for change. Security is crucial, Carothers argues, but the promise of democracy must be realized if that security is to have any enduring meaning and purpose.

NOTES
* Phyllis Bennis, "Bush on Middle East 'Democracy' & 'Ending Occupation' in Iraq." Available online at http://www.ips-dc.org/comment/Bennis/demendoc.htm. Accessed November 27, 2006.

Promoting Democracy and Fighting Terror
THOMAS CAROTHERS

SPLIT PERSONALITY

When George W. Bush took office two years ago, few observers expected that promoting democracy around the world would become a major issue in his presidency. During the 2000 presidential campaign Bush and his advisers had made it clear that they favored great-power realism over idealistic notions such as nation building or democracy promotion. And as expected, the incoming Bush team quickly busied itself with casting aside many policies closely associated with President Bill Clinton. Some analysts feared democracy promotion would also get the ax. But September 11 fundamentally altered this picture. Whether, where, and how the United States should promote democracy around the world have become central questions in U.S. policy debates with regard to a host of countries including Egypt, Iran, Iraq, Kyrgyzstan, Pakistan, Russia, Saudi Arabia, Uzbekistan, and many others.

Although the war on terrorism has greatly raised the profile of democracy as a policy matter, it has hardly clarified the issue. The United States faces two contradictory imperatives: on the one hand, the fight against al Qaeda tempts Washington to put aside its democratic scruples and seek closer ties with autocracies throughout the Middle East and Asia. On the other hand, U.S. officials and policy experts have increasingly come to believe that it is precisely the lack of democracy in many of these countries that helps breed Islamic extremism.

Resolving this tension will be no easy task. So far, Bush and his foreign policy team have shown an incipient, albeit unsurprising, case of split personality: "Bush the realist" actively cultivates warm relations with "friendly tyrants" in many parts of the world, while "Bush the neo-Reaganite" makes ringing calls for a vigorous new democracy campaign in the Middle East. How the administration resolves this uncomfortable dualism is central not only to the future of the war on terrorism but also to the shape and character of Bush's foreign policy as a whole.

FRIENDS IN LOW PLACES

It is on and around the front lines of the campaign against al Qaeda that the tensions between America's pressing new security concerns and its democracy interests are most strongly felt. The most glaring case is Pakistan. The cold shoulder that Washington turned toward General Pervez Musharraf after he seized power in 1999 has been replaced by a bear hug. In recognition of the Pakistani leader's critical supporting role in the war on terrorism, the Bush administration has showered Musharraf with praise and attention, waived various economic sanctions, assembled a handsome aid package that exceeded $600 million in 2002, and restarted U.S.-Pakistan military cooperation.

Bush officials insist that they combine their embrace with frequent private messages to Musharraf about the importance of returning to democracy. But during the past year the Pakistani president has steadily consolidated his authoritarian grip, a process punctuated by a clumsy referendum last spring and a sweeping series of antidemocratic constitutional amendments in the summer. Bush and his aides have reacted only halfheartedly to this process, publicly repeating tepid calls for democracy but exerting no real pressure.

This soft line is a mistake and should be revised, yet the complexities of the situation must also be acknowledged. Pakistan's cooperation in the campaign against al Qaeda is not a nice extra—it is vital. In addition, a return to democracy in Pakistan is not simply a matter of getting an authoritarian leader to step aside. The two main civilian political parties have failed the country several times, and during the 1990s discredited themselves in many Pakistanis' eyes with patterns of corruption, ineffectiveness, and authoritarian behavior. Democratization will require a profound, multifaceted process of change in which Pakistan's military will have to not only give up formal leadership of the country but pull out of politics altogether. Meanwhile, the civilian politicians will have to remake themselves thoroughly and dedicate themselves to rebuilding public confidence in the political system. Rather than erring on the side of deference to Musharraf, Washington should articulate such a long-term vision for Pakistan and pressure all relevant actors there to work toward it.

Central Asia, meanwhile, presents a mosaic of dilemmas relating to the trade-off between democracy and security in U.S. foreign policy. The U.S. need for military bases and other forms of security cooperation in the region has moved Washington much closer to the autocratic leaders of Uzbekistan, Kazakhstan, and Kyrgyzstan. Even Saparmurat Niyazov, the totalitarian megalomaniac running Turkmenistan, received a friendly visit from Defense Secretary Donald Rumsfeld in April 2002. At the same time, U.S. officials are pushing for reform in the region, emphasizing to their local counterparts that this is a once-in-a-lifetime opportunity for the region's states to obtain significant outside support for the full set of economic, political, and social reforms necessary to join the modern world.

Surprisingly, it is in Uzbekistan, one of the region's harshest dictatorships, where this dual approach may pay at least modest dividends. President Islam Karimov has undoubtedly received a boost at home from the new diplomatic attention, economic aid, and military partnership with the United States. Yet for the first time since Uzbekistan became independent, U.S. officials are also meeting regularly with a wide range of Uzbek officials and conveying strongly worded messages about the need for change. And there are signs of nascent political and economic reforms, albeit small, tentative ones. Karimov is still very much a dictator with little understanding of or interest in either democracy or market economics. But he also seems to realize that some positive moves are necessary to ensure his own political future and that the increased external support post–September 11 is a real opportunity.

Unfortunately, in Kazakhstan the U.S. approach appears less promising. President Nursultan Nazarbayev displays no interest in meeting the United States even partway. Instead, he is using the new context to tighten his dictatorial hold on the country and is openly spurning U.S. reform efforts. Given Kazakhstan's sizable oil and gas reserves, and Nazarbayev's cooperation on both security and economic measures, he appears to have calculated correctly that the Bush administration is unlikely to step up its mild pressure for reform. If the United States is serious about trying to steer Kazakhstan away from potentially disastrous authoritarian decay, however, Washington will have to become more forceful.

Kyrgyzstan is a more ambiguous but still discouraging case. President Askar Akayev is less dictatorial than Karimov or Nazarbayev but has also slid toward authoritarianism in recent years. The Bush administration has made some effort to steer him away from this unfortunate path. But it has not taken full advantage of the Kyrgyz elite's obvious eagerness for a close security relationship with the United States to push hard on key issues such as freeing political prisoners or curbing corruption.

Running throughout all of the new U.S. security relationships in South and Central Asia is an institutional divide that weakens the administration's ability to balance security and democracy. The State Department has shown some real commitment to raising human rights and democracy issues with these countries. The Pentagon, on the other hand, often focuses more on the immediate goal of securing military access or cooperation and less on the politics of the relevant host government. Given the importance that foreign leaders place on the U.S. military, they may sometimes assume that friendly words from the Pentagon mean they can ignore other messages they are receiving. Ensuring a consistent U.S. front on democracy and human rights, therefore, is a prerequisite for a coherent approach.

Afghanistan is perhaps the most telling example of this challenge. The initial post–September 11 action by the United States in that country was of course not a downgrading of democracy concerns but a sudden step forward, through the ouster of the fundamentalist Taliban regime. But the conduct of U.S. military operations there has since undermined the administration's promises of a lasting, deep commitment to democratic reconstruction. The Pentagon initially relied on Afghan warlords as proxy fighters against al Qaeda, arming them and thus helping them consolidate their regional power. This assistance helped entrench the centrifugal politics that threaten Afghanistan's weak new government. Ironically, the strategy seems also to have been a partial military miscalculation, leading to the escape of a significant number of al Qaeda fighters at Tora Bora.

At the same time, administration opposition to the use of either U.S. or un peacekeeping troops outside of Kabul, and significant shortfalls in the delivery of promised aid, make it impossible for the Karzai government to guarantee security, gain meaningful control beyond the capital, or achieve legitimacy by delivering peace to its citizens. Ethnic rivalries, the opium trade, and newly empowered local strongmen make a return to state failure and civil war a very real possibility. Despite the insistence of many U.S. officials in the immediate aftermath of September 11 on the connection between failed states and vital U.S. security interests, the Bush team's aversion to nation building has not really changed.

No easy solutions to Afghanistan's profound political problems are in sight. At a minimum, however, the administration must strengthen its commitment to making reconstruction work. This means not only delivering more fully on aid, but exerting real pressure on regional power brokers to accept the Kabul government's authority and working harder to establish an Afghan national army. No matter how pressing are the other fronts of the war against al Qaeda (such as the increasingly worrisome situation in northern Pakistan), the United States must fulfill the responsibilities for reconstruction that came with its invasion of Afghanistan.

RIPPLE EFFECTS

The tensions posed by the war on terrorism for U.S. support of democracy abroad have quickly spread out beyond the immediate front lines. Southeast Asia is one affected region. Indonesia has become an important theater in the U.S. antiterrorist campaign, because of U.S. fears that al Qaeda leaders are taking refuge there and that the country's numerous Islamist groups are connecting with extremist networks. The White House continues to support Indonesia's shaky, somewhat democratic government. But in a setback on human rights policy, the administration has proposed restarting aid to the Indonesian military. That aid was progressively reduced during the 1990s in response to the Indonesian forces' atrocious human rights record and was finally terminated in 1999, when Indonesian troops participated in massacres in East Timor. Administration officials have downplayed this decision to renew military aid, stressing that most of the proposed $50 million package is directed at the police rather than the military. But the willingness of the U.S. government to enter into a partnership with a security force that just a few years ago was involved in a horrendous campaign of slaughter and destruction against civilians sends a powerful negative message throughout the region and beyond. Some officials argue that the new training programs will give U.S. military personnel a chance to instruct their Indonesian counterparts in human rights. But U.S. officials repeatedly made the same argument in defense of these programs in previous decades, right up to when the Indonesian military committed the human rights abuses that sank the relationship.

Malaysia's leader, Prime Minister Mahathir Mohamad, is another beneficiary of a changed U.S. foreign policy. Mahathir has made himself useful to Washington by arresting Islamic militants, sharing intelligence, and cooperating in other ways with an antiterrorist campaign that neatly dovetails with his authoritarian domestic agenda. And in response, Washington's previous critical stance toward the Malaysian leader— highlighted in Vice President Al Gore's much-publicized call for *reformasi* during his visit to Kuala Lumpur in 1998—has been reversed.

Top U.S. officials now laud Mahathir as "a force for regional stability" and "a model of economic development that has demonstrated tolerance," and President Bush praised him at an amicable joint press conference after Mahathir's visit to the White House in May 2002.

An emphasis on democracy and human rights is also in question in U.S. policy toward Russia and China. Russia's new role as a U.S. ally in the war on terrorism has progressed less smoothly than some initially hoped, with significant continuing differences over Iraq, Iran, Georgia, and other places. Nevertheless, President Bush regards President Vladimir Putin very favorably and has not pressed the Russian leader about his shortcomings on democracy and human rights, such as in Chechnya or with regard to maintaining a free press. Somewhat similarly, the Chinese government has been able to leverage the new security context to solidify a much friendlier U.S.-China relationship than seemed likely in the early months of 2001, when the Bush administration appeared to view China as threat number one.

In both cases, however, the change is more of degree than kind. Bush's surprisingly personal and warm embrace of Putin started before September 11, with Bush getting "a sense of [Putin's] soul" during their meeting in Slovenia in June 2001. And at no time prior to September 11, whether under Bush or Clinton before him, was the Russian government subjected to any significant U.S. government criticism for Chechnya or any of its other democratic flaws. With respect to China, it is true that September 11 did block movement toward a new hard-line policy from Washington that some administration hawks may have wanted. But the current relatively positive state of relations, with mild U.S. pressure on human rights greatly outweighed by an ample, mutually beneficial economic relationship, is not especially different from the overall pattern of the past decade or more.

One can look even further afield and identify possible slippage in U.S. democracy policies resulting from the war on terrorism, such as insufficient attention to the growing crisis of democracy in South America or inadequate pressure on oil-rich Nigeria's flailing president, Olusegun Obasanjo, to turn around his increasingly poor governance of Africa's most populous nation. Ironically, and also sadly, however, the greatest source of negative ripple effects has come from the administration's pursuit of the war on terrorism at home. The heightened terrorist threat has inevitably put pressure on U.S. civil liberties. But the administration failed to strike the right balance early on, unnecessarily abridging or abusing rights through the large-scale detention of immigrants, closed deportation hearings, and the declaration of some U.S. citizens as "enemy combatants" with no right to counsel or even to contest the designation. The Justice Department's harsh approach sent a powerful negative signal around the world, emboldening governments as diverse as those of Belarus, Cuba, and India to curtail domestic liberties, supposedly in aid of their own struggles against terrorism. In the United States, an independent judiciary and powerful Congress ensure that the appropriate balance between security and rights is gradually being achieved. In many countries, however, the rule of law is weak and copycat restrictions on rights resound much more harmfully.

REAGAN REBORN?

Whereas "Bush the realist" holds sway on most fronts in the war on terrorism, a neo-Reaganite Bush may be emerging in the Middle East. In the initial period after September 11, the administration turned to its traditional autocratic allies in the Arab world, especially Egypt and Saudi Arabia, for help against al Qaeda. This move did not sacrifice any U.S. commitment to democracy; for decades, the United States had already suppressed any such concerns in the region, valuing autocratic stability for the sake of various economic and security interests. Over the course of the last year, however, a growing chorus of voices within and around the administration has begun questioning the value of America's "friendly tyrants" in the Middle East. These individuals highlight the fact that whereas the autocratic allies once seemed to be effective bulwarks against Islamic extremism, the national origins of the September 11 attackers make clear that these nations are in fact breeders, and in the case of Saudi Arabia, financiers, of extremism. Invoking what they believe to be the true spirit of President Ronald Reagan's foreign policy, they call for a change toward promoting freedom in U.S. Middle East policy. The core idea of the new approach is to undercut the roots of Islamic extremism by getting serious about promoting democracy in the Arab world, not just in a slow, gradual way, but with fervor and force.

President Bush is clearly attracted by this idea. Last summer his declarations on the Middle East shifted noticeably in tone and content, setting out a vision of democratic change there. According to this vision, the United States will first promote democracy in the Palestinian territories by linking U.S. support for a Palestinian state with the achievement of new, more democratic Palestinian leadership. Second, the United States will effect regime change in Iraq and help transform that country into a democracy. The establishment of two successful models of Arab democracy will have a powerful demonstration effect, "inspiring reforms throughout the Muslim world," as Bush declared at the United Nations in September. As the policies toward Iraq and Palestine unfold, the administration may also step up pressure on recalcitrant autocratic allies and give greater support to those Arab states undertaking at least some political reforms, such as some of the smaller Persian Gulf states. The decision last August to postpone a possible aid increase to Egypt as a response to the Egyptian government's continued persecution of human rights activist Saad Eddin Ibrahim was a small step in this direction.

It is not yet clear how sharply Bush will shift U.S. Middle East policy toward promoting democracy. Certainly it is time to change the long-standing practice of reflexively relying on and actually bolstering autocracy in the Arab world. But the expansive vision of a sudden, U.S.-led democratization of the Middle East rests on questionable assumptions. To start with, the appealing idea that by toppling Saddam Hussein the United States can transform Iraq into a democratic model for the region is dangerously misleading. The United States can certainly oust the Iraqi leader and install a less repressive and more pro-Western regime. This would not be the same, however, as creating democracy in Iraq.

The experience of other countries where in recent decades the United States has forcibly removed dictatorial regimes—Grenada, Panama, Haiti, and most recently Afghanistan—indicates that post-invasion political life usually takes on the approximate character of the political life that existed in the country before the ousted regime came to power. After the 1982 U.S. military intervention in Grenada, for example, that country was able to recover the tradition of moderate pluralism it had enjoyed before the 1979 takeover by Maurice Bishop and his gang. Haiti, after the 1994 U.S. invasion, has unfortunately slipped back into many of the pathologies that marked its political life before the military junta took over in 1991. Iraqi politics prior to Saddam Hussein were violent, divisive, and oppressive. And the underlying conditions in Iraq—not just the lack of significant previous experience with pluralism but also sharp ethnic and religious differences and an oil-dependent economy—will inevitably make democratization there very slow and difficult. Even under the most optimistic scenarios, the United States would have to commit itself to a massive, expensive, demanding, and long-lasting reconstruction effort. The administration's inadequate commitment to Afghanistan's reconstruction undercuts assurances by administration officials that they will stay the course in a post-Saddam Iraq.

Furthermore, the notion that regime change in Iraq, combined with democratic progress in the Palestinian territories, would produce domino democratization around the region is far-fetched. A U.S. invasion of Iraq would likely trigger a surge in the already prevalent anti-Americanism in the Middle East, strengthening the hand of hard-line Islamist groups and provoking many Arab governments to tighten their grip, rather than experiment more boldly with political liberalization. Throughout the region, the underlying economic, political, and social conditions are unfavorable for a wave of democratic breakthroughs. This does not mean the Arab world will never democratize. But it does mean that democracy will be decades in the making and entail a great deal of uncertainty, reversal, and turmoil. The United States can and should actively support such democratic change through an expanded, sharpened set of democracy aid programs and real pressure and support for reforms. But as experience in other parts of the world has repeatedly demonstrated, the future of the region will be determined primarily by its own inhabitants.

Aggressive democracy promotion in the Arab world is a new article of faith among neoconservatives inside and outside the administration. However, it combines both the strengths and the dangers typical of neo-Reaganite policy as applied to any region. Perhaps the most important strength is the high importance attached to the president's using his bully pulpit to articulate a democratic vision and to attach his personal prestige to the democracy-building endeavor.

But two dangers are also manifest. One is the instrumentalization of prodemocracy policies—wrapping security goals in the language of democracy promotion and then confusing democracy promotion with the search for particular political outcomes that enhance those security goals. This was often a problem with the Reagan administration's attempts to spread democracy in the 1980s. To take just one example, for the presidential elections in El Salvador in 1984, the Reagan administration labored mightily to establish the technical structures necessary for a credible election. The administration then covertly funneled large amounts of money to the campaign of its preferred candidate, José Napoleón Duarte, to make sure he won the race. This same tension between democracy as an end versus a means has surfaced in the administration's press for democracy in the Palestinian territories. Bush has urged Palestinians to reform, especially through elections, yet at the same time administration officials have made clear that certain outcomes, such as the reelection of Yasir Arafat, are unacceptable to the United States. A post-invasion process of installing a new "democratic" regime in Iraq would likely exhibit similar contradictions between stated principle and political reality.

The administration demonstrated worrisome signs of the same tendency last April during the short-lived coup against Venezuela's problematic populist president, Hugo Chávez. Washington appeared willing or even eager to accept a coup against the leader of an oil-rich state who is despised by many in the U.S. government for his anti-American posturing and dubious economic and political policies. But given that it came in a region that has started to work together to oppose coups, and that other regional governments condemned Chavez's ouster, the administration's approach undermined the United States' credibility as a supporter of democracy. If democracy promotion is reduced to an instrumental strategy for producing political outcomes favorable to U.S. interests, the value and legitimacy of the concept will be lost.

The second danger is overestimating America's ability to export democracy. U.S. neoconservatives habitually overstate the effect of America's role in the global wave of democratic openings that occurred in the 1980s and early 1990s. For example, they often argue that the Reagan administration brought democracy to Latin America through its forceful anticommunism in the 1980s. Yet the most significant democratization that occurred in Argentina, Brazil, and various other parts of South America took place in the early 1980s, when Reagan was still trying to embrace the fading right-wing dictators that Jimmy Carter had shunned on human rights grounds. Excessive optimism about U.S. ability to remake the Middle East, a region far from ripe for a wave of democratization, is therefore a recipe for trouble—especially given the administration's proven disinclination to commit itself deeply to the nation building that inevitably follows serious political disruption.

A FINE BALANCE

The clashing imperatives of the war on terrorism with respect to U.S. democracy promotion have led to a split presidential personality and contradictory policies—decreasing interest in democracy in some countries and suddenly increasing interest in one region, the Middle East. The decreases are widespread and probably still multiplying, given the expanding character of the antiterrorism campaign. Yet they are not fatal to the overall role of the United States as a force for democracy in the world. Some of them are relatively minor modifications of policies that for years imperfectly fused already conflicting security and political concerns. And in at least some countries where it has decided warmer relations with autocrats are necessary, the Bush administration is trying to balance new security ties with proreform pressures. More broadly, in many countries outside the direct ambit of the war on terrorism, the Bush administration is trying to bolster fledgling democratic governments and pressure nondemocratic leaders for change, as have the past several U.S. administrations. Sometimes diplomatic pressure is used, as with Belarus, Zimbabwe, and Burma. In other cases, Washington relies on less visible means such as economic and political support as well as extensive democracy aid programs, as with many countries in sub-Saharan Africa, southeastern Europe, the former Soviet Union, Central America, and elsewhere. Quietly and steadily during the last 20 years, democracy promotion has become institutionalized in the U.S. foreign policy and foreign aid bureaucracies. Although not an automatically overriding priority, it is almost always one part of the foreign policy picture. Partly to address "the roots of terrorism," moreover, the administration has also proposed a very large new aid fund, the $5 billion Millennium Challenge Account. By signaling that good governance should be a core criterion for disbursing aid from this fund, President Bush has positioned it as a potentially major tool for bolstering democracies in the developing world.

Although the new trade-offs prompted by the war on terrorism are unfortunate, and in some cases overdone, the fact that U.S. democracy concerns are limited by security needs is hardly a shocking new problem. Democracy promotion has indeed become gradually entrenched in U.S. policy, but both during and after the Cold War it has been limited and often greatly weakened by other U.S. interests. President Clinton made liberal use of pro-democracy rhetoric and did support democracy in many places, but throughout his presidency, U.S. security and economic interests—whether in China, Egypt, Jordan, Kazakhstan, Saudi Arabia, Vietnam, or various other countries—frequently trumped an interest in democracy. The same was true in the George H.W. Bush administration and certainly also under Ronald Reagan, whose outspoken support for freedom in the communist world was accompanied by close U.S. relations with various authoritarian regimes useful to the United States, such as those led by Suharto in Indonesia, Mobutu Sese Seko in Zaire, the generals of Nigeria, and the Institutional Revolutionary Party of Mexico.

George W. Bush is thus scarcely the first U.S. president to evidence a split personality on democracy promotion. But the suddenness and prominence of his condition, as a result of the war on terrorism, makes it especially costly. It is simply hard for most Arabs, or many other people around the world, to take seriously the president's eloquent vision of a democratic Middle East when he or his top aides casually brush away the authoritarian maneuverings of Musharraf in Pakistan, offer warm words of support for Nazarbayev in Kazakhstan, or praise Mahathir in Malaysia. The war on terrorism has laid bare the deeper fault line that has lurked below the surface of George W. Bush's foreign policy from the day he took office—the struggle between the realist philosophy of his father and the competing pull of neo-Reaganism.

There is no magic solution to this division, which is rooted in a decades-old struggle for the foreign policy soul of the Republican Party and will undoubtedly persist in various forms throughout this administration and beyond. For an effective democracy-promotion strategy, however, the Bush team must labor harder to limit the trade-offs caused by the new security imperatives and also not go overboard with the grandiose idea of trying to unleash a democratic tsunami in the Middle East. This means, for example, engaging more deeply in Pakistan to urge military leaders and civilian politicians to work toward a common vision of democratic renovation, adding teeth to the reform messages being delivered to Central Asia's autocrats, ensuring that the Pentagon reinforces proreform messages to new U.S. security partners, not cutting Putin slack on his democratic deficits, going easy on the praise for newly friendly tyrants, more effectively balancing civil rights and security at home, and openly criticizing other governments that abuse the U.S. example. In the Middle East, it means developing a serious, well-funded effort to promote democracy that reflects the difficult political realities of the region but does not fall back on an underlying acceptance of only cosmetic changes. This will entail exerting sustained pressure on autocratic Arab allies to take concrete steps to open up political space and undertake real institutional reforms, bolstering democracy aid programs in the region, and finding ways to engage moderate Islamist groups and encourage Arab states to bring them into political reform processes.

Such an approach is defined by incremental gains, long-term commitment, and willingness to keep the post–September 11 security imperatives in perspective. As such it has neither the hard-edged appeal of old-style realism nor the tantalizing promise of the neoconservative visions. Yet in the long run it is the best way to ensure that the war on terrorism complements rather than contradicts worldwide democracy and that the strengthening of democracy abroad is a fundamental element of U.S. foreign policy in the years ahead.

Terrorism is not, according to Ladan and Roya Boroumand, some twisted outgrowth of Islam. Acts of monumental violence and destruction are not examples of Muslim religious fervor spun out of control, or sectarian ardor turned murderous. In reality, the authors claim, terrorism is an ideological and ultimately political challenge to liberal democracy; it is anything but an expression of Islamic beliefs or principles. In fact, the extremist violence that emanates from the Middle East today is closer in character to the totalitarian movements of twentieth-century Europe—fascism, Nazism, and Communism—with which it shares radical philosophical roots.

The Boroumands argue that the rhetoric of terror (talk of bloody overthrow, historical struggles, apocalyptic clashes between good and evil, and the like) is drawn not from Islam, but rather from European radicalism. Terrorism as an ideology, therefore, merely camouflages itself with Koranic verse and then masquerades as an authentic Islamic product. Its goals, however, are thoroughly political rather than religious, and thus they represent a political response to the West's social and cultural influence in the Middle East. No matter that the terrorists label themselves and their organizations as Muslim, the Boroumands would contend that they are essentially Western-style militant groups resisting Western power using Western ideas and methods.

In making this claim, the authors run against the grain of prevailing wisdom, which holds that extreme Islamism has its origins in long-standing historical–cultural antagonisms between the European and Muslim worlds. As far as this model is concerned, determining where terrorism came from and where it is going entails a close study of Islam, Arab culture, and the history of Western conflict with the peoples and traditions of the Middle East. The focus is kept precisely there, on the assumption that understanding the place called the Middle East will lead to a better grasp of the phenomenon called terrorism. The Boroumands ask their readers to search elsewhere, geographically and philosophically, for answers. Specifically, they contend that people need to view Middle Eastern radicalism as a cultural import, influenced as it is by European thinking, which Muslims would do well to discard. Once free from such a destructive foreign influence, the authors maintain, the quest for healthy and peaceful ideological alternatives can begin. That, so the thinking goes, would lead eventually to an embracing of democracy.

Terror, Islam, and Democracy
LADAN BOROUMAND AND ROYA BOROUMAND

"Why?" That is the question that people in the West have been asking ever since the terrible events of September 11. What are the attitudes, beliefs, and motives of the terrorists and the movement from which they sprang? What makes young men from Muslim countries willing, even eager, to turn themselves into suicide bombers? How did these men come to harbor such violent hatred of the West, and especially of the United States? What are the roots—moral, intellectual, political, and spiritual—of the murderous fanaticism we witnessed that day?

As Western experts and commentators have wrestled with these questions, their intellectual disarray and bafflement in the face of radical Islamist (notice we do not say "Islamic") terrorism have become painfully clear. This is worrisome, for however necessary an armed response might seem in the near term, it is undeniable that a successful long-term strategy for battling Islamism and its terrorists will require a clearer understanding of who these foes are, what they think, and how they understand their own motives. For terrorism is first and foremost an ideological and moral challenge to liberal democracy. The sooner the defenders of democracy realize this and grasp its implications, the sooner democracy can prepare itself to win the long-simmering war of ideas and values that exploded into full fury last September 11.

The puzzlement of liberal democracies in the face of Islamist terrorism seems odd. After all, since 1793, when the word "terror" first came into use in its modern political sense with the so-called Terror of the French Revolution, nearly every country in the West has had some experience with a terrorist movement or regime. Why then does such a phenomenon, which no less than liberal democracy itself is a product of the modern age, appear in this instance so opaque to Western analysts?

Islamist terror first burst onto the world scene with the 1979 Iranian Revolution and the seizure of the U.S. embassy in Tehran in November of that year. Since then, Islamism has spread, and the ideological and political tools that have helped to curb terrorism throughout much of the West have proven mostly ineffective at stopping it. Its presence is global, and its influence is felt not only in the lands of the vast Islamic crescent that extends from Morocco and Nigeria in the west to Malaysia and Mindanao in the east but also in many corners of Europe, India, the former Soviet world, the Americas, and even parts of western China.

Before the Iranian Revolution, terrorism was typically seen as a straightforward outgrowth of modern ideologies. Islamist terrorists, however, claim to fight on theological grounds: A few verses from the Koran and a few references to the *sunna* ("deeds of the Prophet") put an Islamic seal on each operation. The whole ideological fabric appears to be woven from appeals to tradition, ethnicity, and historical grievances both old and new, along with a powerful set of religious-sounding references to "infidels," "idolaters," "crusaders," "martyrs," "holy wars," "sacred soil," "enemies of Islam," "the party of God," and "the great Satan."

But this religious vocabulary hides violent Islamism's true nature as a modern totalitarian challenge to both traditional Islam and modern democracy. If terrorism is truly as close to the core of Islamic belief as both the Islamists and many of their enemies claim, why does international Islamist terrorism date only to 1979? This question finds a powerful echo in the statements of the many eminent Islamic scholars and theologians who have consistently condemned the actions of the Islamist networks.

This is not to say that Islamic jurisprudence and philosophy propound a democratic vision of society or easily accommodate the principles of democracy and human rights. But it does expose the fraudulence of the terrorists' references to Islamic precepts. There is in the history of Islam no precedent for the utterly unrestrained violence of al-Qaeda or the Hezbollah. Even the Shi'ite Ismaili sect known as the Assassins, though it used men who were ready to die to murder its enemies, never descended to anything like the random mass slaughter in which the Hezbollah, Osama bin Laden, and his minions glory.[1] To kill oneself while wantonly murdering women, children, and people of all religions and descriptions—let us not forget that Muslims too worked at the World Trade Center—has nothing to do with Islam, and one does not have to be a learned theologian to see this. The truth is that contemporary Islamist terror is an eminently modern practice thoroughly at odds with Islamic traditions and ethics.[2]

A striking illustration of the tension between Islam and terrorism was offered by an exchange that took place between two Muslims in the French courtroom where Fouad Ali Saleh was being tried for his role in a wave of bombings that shook Paris in 1985–86. One of his victims, a man badly burned in one of these attacks, said to Saleh: "I am a practicing Muslim. . . . Did God tell you to bomb babies and pregnant women?" Saleh responded, "You are an Algerian. Remember what [the French] did to your fathers."[3] Challenged regarding the religious grounds of his actions, the terrorist replied not with Koranic verses but with secular nationalist grievances.

The record of Saleh's trial makes fascinating reading. He was a Sunni Muslim, originally from Tunisia, who spent the early 1980s "studying" at Qom, the Shi'ite theological center in Iran. He received weapons training in Libya and Algeria, and got his explosives from the pro-Iranian militants of Hezbollah. In his defense, he invoked not only the Koran and the Ayatollah Khomeini but also Joan of Arc—who is, among other things, a heroine of the French far right—as an example of someone who "defended her country against the aggressor." After this he read out long passages from *Revolt Against the Modern World* by Julius Evola (1898–1974), an Italian author often cited by European extreme rightists. This strange ideological brew suggests the importance of exploring the intellectual roots of Islamist terrorism.[4]

THE GENEALOGY OF ISLAMISM

The idea of a "pan-Islamic"[5] movement appeared in the late nineteenth and early twentieth centuries concomitantly with the rapid transformation of traditional Muslim polities into nation-states. The man who did more than any other to lend an Islamic cast to totalitarian ideology was an Egyptian schoolteacher named Hassan al-Banna (1906–49). Banna was not a theologian by training. Deeply influenced by Egyptian nationalism, he founded the Muslim Brotherhood in 1928 with the express goal of counteracting Western influences.[6]

By the late 1930s, Nazi Germany had established contacts with revolutionary junior officers in the Egyptian army, including many who were close to the Muslim Brothers. Before long the Brothers, who had begun by pursuing charitable, associational, and cultural activities, also had a youth wing, a creed of unconditional loyalty to the leader, and a paramilitary organization whose slogan "action, obedience, silence" echoed the "believe, obey, fight" motto of the Italian Fascists. Banna's ideas were at odds with those of the traditional *ulema* (theologians), and he warned his followers as early as 1943 to expect "the severest opposition" from the traditional religious establishment.[7]

From the Fascists—and behind them, from the European tradition of putatively "transformative" or "purifying" revolutionary violence that began with the Jacobins—Banna also borrowed the idea of heroic death as a political art form. Although few in the West may remember it today, it is difficult to overstate the degree to which the aestheticization of death, the glorification of armed force, the worship of martyrdom, and faith in "the propaganda of the deed" shaped the antiliberal ethos of both the far right and elements of the far left earlier in the twentieth century. Following Banna, today's Islamist militants embrace a terrorist cult of martyrdom that has more to do with Georges Sorel's *Réflexions sur la violence* than with anything in either Sunni or Shi'ite Islam.[8]

After the Allied victory in World War II, Banna's assassination in early 1949, and the Egyptian Revolution of 1952–54, the Muslim

Brothers found themselves facing the hostility of a secularizing military government and sharp ideological competition from Egyptian communists. Sayyid Qutb (1906–66), the Brothers' chief spokesman and also their liaison with the communists, framed an ideological response that would lay the groundwork for the Islamism of today.

Qutb was a follower not only of Banna but of the Pakistani writer and activist Sayyid Abu'l-A'la Mawdudi (1903–79), who in 1941 founded the Jamaat-e-Islami-e-Pakistan (Pakistan Islamic Assembly), which remains an important political force in Pakistan, though it cannot claim notable electoral support.[9] Mawdudi's rejection of nationalism, which he had earlier embraced, led to his interest in the political role of Islam. He denounced all nationalism, labeling it as *kufr* (unbelief). Using Marxist terminology, he advocated a struggle by an Islamic "revolutionary vanguard" against both the West and traditional Islam, attaching the adjectives "Islamic" to such distinctively Western terms as "revolution," "state," and "ideology." Though strongly opposed by the Muslim religious authorities, his ideas influenced a whole generation of "modern" Islamists.

Like both of his preceptors, Qutb lacked traditional theological training. A graduate of the state teacher's college, in 1948 he went to study education in the United States. Once an Egyptian nationalist, he joined the Muslim Brothers soon after returning home in 1950. Qutb's brand of Islamism was informed by his knowledge of both the Marxist and fascist critiques of modern capitalism and representative democracy.[10] He called for a monolithic state ruled by a single party of Islamic rebirth. Like Mawdudi and various Western totalitarians, he identified his own society (in his case, contemporary Muslim polities) as among the enemies that a virtuous, ideologically self-conscious, vanguard minority would have to fight by any means necessary, including violent revolution, so that a new and perfectly just society might arise. His ideal society was a classless one where the "selfish individual" of liberal democracies would be banished and the "exploitation of man by man" would be abolished. God alone would govern it through the implementation of Islamic law (*shari'a*). This was Leninism in Islamist dress.

When the authoritarian regime of President Gamel Abdel Nasser suppressed the Muslim Brothers in 1954 (it would eventually get around to hanging Qutb in 1966), many went into exile in Algeria, Saudi Arabia,[11] Iraq, Syria, and Morocco. From there, they spread their revolutionary Islamist ideas—including the organizational and ideological tools borrowed from European totalitarianism—by means of a network that reached into numerous religious schools and universities. Most young Islamist cadres today are the direct intellectual and spiritual heirs of the Qutbist wing of the Muslim Brotherhood.

THE IRANIAN CONNECTION

Banna and the Brotherhood advocated the creation of a solidarity network that would reach across the various schools of Islam.[12] Perhaps in part because of this ecumenism, we can detect the Brothers' influence as early as 1945 in Iran, the homeland of most of the world's Shi'ites.

Returning home from Iraq that year, a young Iranian cleric named Navab Safavi started a terrorist group that assassinated a number of secular Iranian intellectuals and politicians. In 1953, Safavi visited Egypt at the Brothers' invitation and presumably met with Qutb. Although Safavi's group was crushed and he was executed after a failed attempt on the life of the prime minister in 1955, several of its former members would become prominent among those who lined up with the Ayatollah Khomeini (1900–89) to mastermind the Islamic Revolution of 1979.

Khomeini himself first took a political stand in 1962, joining other ayatollahs to oppose the shah's plans for land reform and female suffrage. At this point, Khomeini was not a revolutionary but a traditionalist alarmed by modernization and anxious to defend the privileges of his clerical caste. When his followers staged an urban uprising in June 1963, he was arrested and subsequently exiled, first to Turkey, then to Iraq. The turning point came in 1970, when Khomeini, still in Iraq, became one of the very few Shi'ite religious authorities to switch from traditionalism to totalitarianism. Much like Mawdudi,[13] he called for a revolution to create an Islamic state, and inspired by Qutb, he condemned all non-theocratic regimes as idolatrous. His followers in Iran were active in Islamist cultural associations that spread, among others, the ideas of Qutb and Mawdudi. Qutb's ideology was used by Khomeini's students to recapture for the Islamist movement a whole generation influenced by the world's predominant revolutionary culture—Marxism-Leninism.

Khomeini became a major figure in the history of Islamist terrorism because he was the first truly eminent religious figure to lend it his authority. For despite all its influence on the young, Islamism before the Iranian Revolution was a marginal heterodoxy. Qutb and Mawdudi were theological dabblers whom Sunni scholars had refuted and dismissed. Even the Muslim Brothers had officially rejected Qutb's ideas. As an established clerical scholar, Khomeini gave modern Islamist totalitarianism a religious respectability that it had sorely lacked.

Once in power, the onetime opponent of land reform and women's suffrage became a "progressivist," launching a massive program of nationalization and expropriation and recruiting women for campaigns of revolutionary propaganda and mobilization. The Leninist characteristics of his rule—his policy of terror, his revolutionary tribunals and militias, his administrative purges, his cultural revolution, and his accommodating attitude toward the USSR—alienated the majority of his fellow clerics but also gained him the active support of the Moscow-aligned Iranian Communist Party, which from 1979 to 1983 put itself at the service of the new theocracy.

Khomeini's revolution was not an exclusively Shi'ite phenomenon. Not accidentally, one of the first foreign visitors who showed up to congratulate him was the Sunni Islamist Mawdudi; before long, Qutb's face was on an Iranian postage stamp. Khomeini's successor, Ali Khamenei, translated Qutb into Persian.[14] Khomeini's own interest in creating an "Islamist International"—it would later be known by the hijacked Koranic term Hezbollah ("party of God")—was apparent as early as August 1979.

THE ISLAMIST "COMINTERN"

As these ties suggest, Islamism is a self-consciously pan-Muslim phenomenon. It is a waste of time and effort to try to distinguish Islamist terror groups from one another according to their alleged differences along a series of traditional religious, ethnic, or political divides (Shi'ite versus Sunni, Persian versus Arab, and so on). The reason is simple: *In the eyes of the Islamist groups themselves, their common effort to strike at the West while seizing control of the Muslim world is immeasurably more important than whatever might be seen as "dividing" them from one another.*

The Lebanese-based, Iranian-supported Hezbollah is a case in point. Its Iranian founder was a hardcore Khomeini aide who drew his inspiration from a young Egyptian Islamist—an engineer by training, not a theologian—who was the first to politicize what had been a purely religious term. A closer look at the organization reveals the strong influence of Marxism-Leninism on the ideology of its founders and leadership. The group's current leader, Mohammad Hosein Fadlallah, influenced by Marx's and Nietzsche's theories on violence,[15] has openly advocated terrorist methods and tactical alliances with leftist organizations.[16] Hezbollah is a successful creation of the Islamist "Comintern." "We must," says Sheikh Fadlallah, "swear allegiance to the leader of the [Iranian] revolution and to the revolutionaries as to God himself," because "this revolution is the will of God."[17] One indication of the extent of this allegiance is the fact that all the negotiations over the fate of the hostages held in Lebanon ended up being carried out by Tehran. Similarly, the head of Iran's Revolutionary Guards boasted about having sponsored the attack against French and American peacekeeping forces in Lebanon.[18] Hezbollah's chief military planner, Imad Mughaniyyah, is an Arab who operates from Iran. Western intelligence agencies suspect that Hezbollah has been working with bin Laden on international operations since the early 1990s.[19] Hezbollah's terrorist network in Lebanon contains both Shi'ite and Sunni groups, and there is also a Saudi Arabian wing that was involved in the Khobar Towers bombing, which killed 19 U.S. troops in 1996.

Also inspired by the Iranian Revolution was the independent Sunni terrorist network that later became the basis of al-Qaeda. The Tehran regime began forming propaganda organs to sway opinion among Sunni religious authorities as early as 1982.[20] Among the supranational institutions created was the World Congress of Friday Sermons Imams, which at one time had a presence in no fewer than 40 countries. The overarching goal of these efforts has been to mobilize the "Islam of the people" against the "reactionary Islam of the establishment."[21] For a variety of reasons this network has remained loosely organized, but all of its branches spring from and are fed by the same ideological taproot.

The influence of Iran's Islamist revolution was also cited by the members of Egyptian Islamic Jihad who gunned down President Anwar Sadat in October 1981. Their theoretician was an engineer, Abdessalam Faraj, who was also fond of quoting Qutb to justify terror.[22] The conspirators—including the junior army officers who did the actual shooting—were inspired by the Iranian model, and expected the death of Sadat to trigger a mass uprising that would replay in Cairo the same sort of events which had taken place two years earlier in Tehran[23] (where the Iranian authorities would subsequently name a street after Sadat's killer). Among those imprisoned in connection with the plot was a Cairo physician named Ayman al-Zawahiri. He became Egyptian Islamic Jihad's leader after serving his three-year prison term, met bin Laden in 1985, and then joined him in Sudan in the early 1990s. Zawahiri, who would become al-Qaeda's top operational planner, is reported to have said publicly that Osama is "the new Che Guevara."[24]

The Islamization of the Palestinian question is also partly due to Khomeini's influence on the Palestinian branch of Islamic Jihad. Its founder was another physician, this one named Fathi Shqaqi. His 1979 encomium *Khomeini: The Islamic Alternative* was dedicated to both the Iranian ruler and Hassan al-Banna ("the two men of this century"). The first press run of 10,000 sold out in a few days.[25] Shqaqi, who was of course a Sunni, had nonetheless traveled to Tehran to share the Friday sermon podium with Ali Khomeini, denouncing the Mideast peace process and accusing Yasser Arafat of treason.[26]

DISTORTING ISLAM'S HISTORY AND TEACHINGS

As these examples show, such distinctions as may exist among these terrorist groups are overshadowed by their readiness to coalesce and collab-
orate according to a common set of ideological beliefs. These beliefs are
properly called "Islamist" rather than "Islamic" because they are actually
in conflict with Islam—a conflict that we must not allow to be obscured
by the terrorists' habit of commandeering Islamic religious terminology and injecting it with their own distorted content. One illustration
is the Islamists' interpretation of the *hijra*—Mohammed's journey, in
September 622 C.E., from Mecca to Medina to found the first fully realized and autonomous Islamic community (*umma*). Despite a wealth of
historical and doctrinal evidence to the contrary, half-educated Islamists
insist on portraying this journey as a revolutionary rupture with existing society that licenses their desire to excommunicate contemporary
Muslim societies in favor of their own radically utopian vision.

The Islamic Republic of Iran also rests on heterodoxy, in this case
Khomeini's novel and even idiosyncratic theory of the absolute power of
the single, supreme Islamic jurisprudent (*faqih*). It was not a coincidence
that one of the first uprisings against Khomeini's regime took place
under the inspiration of a leading ayatollah, Shariat Madari.[27] Officials
of the regime have admitted that most Iranian clerics have always taken
a wary view of Khomeinism. It is important to realize that the religious
references which Khomeini used to justify his rule were literally the same
as those invoked a century earlier by an eminent ayatollah who was arguing for the legitimacy of parliamentarism and popular sovereignty on
Islamic grounds.[28] Koranic verses lend themselves to many different and
even contradictory interpretations. It is thus to something other than
Islamic religious sources that we must look if we want to understand
Islamism and the war that it wages on its own society, a war in which
international terrorism is only one front.

In a brief article on bin Laden's 1998 declaration of *jihad* against
the United States, Bernard Lewis showed brilliantly how bin Laden
travestied matters not only of fact (for instance, by labeling the invited
U.S. military presence in Saudi Arabia a "crusader" invasion) but also of
Islamic doctrine, by calling for the indiscriminate butchery of any and all
U.S. citizens, wherever they can be found in the world. Reminding his
readers that Islamic law (*shari'a*) holds *jihad* to be nothing but a regular
war and subject to the rules that limit such conflicts, Lewis concluded,
"At no point do the basic texts of Islam enjoin terrorism and murder.
At no point do they even consider the random slaughter of uninvolved
bystanders."[29]

What gives force to the terrorist notion of *jihad* invented by the Iranians and later embraced by bin Laden is not its Koranic roots—there are none—but rather the brute success of terrorist acts. Bin Laden has spoken with particular admiration of the Iranian-sponsored suicide truck bombing that killed 241 U.S. Marines and others in Beirut on 23 October 1983, precipitating the U.S. withdrawal from Lebanon.[30] Bin Laden was also not the first to think of setting up training camps for international terrorists—the Tehran authorities were there before him.[31]

A Friday sermon given in 1989 by one of these authorities, Ali-Akbar Hashemi Rafsanjani, then president of the Islamic Parliament, reveals better than any other the logic of Islamist terrorism. Attacking the existence of Israel as another front in the pervasive war of unbelief (*kufr*) against Islam, Rafsanjani added:

> If for each Palestinian killed today in Palestine five Americans, English, or French were executed, they would not commit such acts anymore. . . . [T]here are Americans everywhere in the world. . . . [They] protect Israel. Does their blood have any value? Scare them outside Palestine, so that they don't feel safe. . . . There are a hundred thousand Palestinians in a country. They are educated, and they work. . . . [T]he factories that serve the enemies of Palestine function thanks to the work of the Palestinians. Blow up the factory. Where you work, you can take action. . . . Let them call you terrorists. . . . They [the "imperialism of information and propaganda"] commit crimes and call it human rights. We call it the defense of rights and of an oppressed people. . . . They *will* say the president of the Parliament officially incites to terror. . . . [L]et them say it.[32]

There is no reference here to religion; Rafsanjani's appeal is purely political. The West's offense he calls human rights; against it he urges Muslims to wield terror as the best weapon for defending the rights of an oppressed people. Rafsanjani, moreover, proudly commends "terror" by name, using the English word and not a Persian or Arabic equivalent. Thus he employs the very term that Lenin had borrowed from *la Terreur* of the French Revolution. The line from the guillotine and the Cheka to the suicide bomber is clear.

With this in mind, let us look for a moment at the French Revolution, where the modern concept of political terror was invented, to find the explanation that the Islamic tradition cannot give. When it announced its policy of terror in September 1793, the "virtuous minority" which then ran the revolutionary government of France was declaring war on its own society. At the heart of this war was a clash between two understandings of "the people" in whose name this government claimed to rule. One was a group of 25 million actually existing individuals, each endowed with inherent rights. The other was an essentially ideological construct, an abstraction, an indivisible and mystical body, its power absolute. The Terror of the French Revolution was neither a mistake nor an unfortunate accident; it was meant to purify this mystical body of what the terrorist elite regarded as corrupting influences, among which they numbered the notion that individual human beings had unalienable rights.[33]

The spokesmen of the Islamist revolution echo the terrorists of Jacobin France. The denigration of human rights marks the spot where the internal war on Muslim society meets the terrorist war against the West. Suffice it to hear bin Laden's comments on the destruction of the World Trade Center: "Those awesome symbolic towers that speak of liberty, human rights, and humanity have been destroyed. They have gone up in smoke."[34] Every Islamist terror campaign against Westerners during the last 20 years has had as its cognate an Islamist effort to tyrannize over a Muslim population somewhere in the world. Think of the ordeal to which the Taliban and al-Qaeda subjected the people of Afghanistan, or of what ordinary Algerians suffered during the savage Islamist civil wars of the 1990s. Or think of the state terror that daily labors to strangle any hope for recognition of human rights in Iran. To explore fully this correlation between terror against the West and tyranny against Muslims would take a separate essay. Yet we can get an idea of its nature by considering the first instance of Islamist terrorism against the United States, the 1979 hostage-taking in Tehran.

HOLDING DEMOCRACY HOSTAGE TO TERROR

As they released the hostages in January 1981, the Tehran authorities crowed over their victory, which Prime Minster Mohammad Ali Rajai called "the greatest political gain in the social history of the world" and an act that "had forced the greatest satanic power to its knees." At first glance this claim might seem foolish, for the United States had said no to the revolutionary government's demands to hand over the shah and unfreeze Iranian assets. But a closer look shows that the Iranian Islamists had in fact scored a big political and ideological victory over both the United States and their domestic opponents, and thus had ample cause for jubilation.

The seizure of the U.S. embassy took place at a time when Khomeini and his allies had not yet consolidated their tyrannical regime. An Assembly of Experts was drafting the constitution of the Islamic

Republic. Opposition was gaining strength daily in religious as well as in moderate secular circles. The Marxist-Leninist left, angered by a ban on its press, was growing restive. Open rebellions were breaking out in sensitive border regions populated by ethnic Kurds and Azeris. By sending in its cadres of radical students to take over the U.S. embassy and hold its staff hostage, the regime cut through the Gordian knot of these challenges at a single blow and even put itself in a position to ram through its widely criticized Constitution. Rafsanjani's assessment of what the act meant is instructive:

> In the first months of the revolution, the Washington White House decided in favor of a coup d'état in Iran. The idea was to infiltrate Iranian groups and launch a movement to annihilate the revolution. But the occupation of the embassy and the people's assault against the U.S.A. neutralized this plan, pushing the U.S. into a defensive stand.[35]

One could describe this version of the facts as a parody: The U.S. government in 1979 clearly had neither the will nor the ability to stage a coup against the Islamic Republic. But totalitarians typically speak an esoteric language of their own devising. Those who administered the Terror in revolutionary France painted some of their country's best-known republicans with the label "monarchist" before sending them off to be guillotined. The Bolsheviks called striking workers and the sailors of Kronstadt "bandits" and "counterrevolutionaries" before slaughtering them. In 1979, promoting human rights was a prominent aspect of how the United States described its foreign policy. By Rafsanjani's logic, therefore, any Iranian group that spoke of human rights was thereby revealing itself as a tool of the United States.

And indeed, as muddled negotiations over the hostages dragged on, the administration of President Jimmy Carter dropped any talk of supporting democracy in Iran[36]—the very cause for which Carter had taken the risk of ending U.S. support for the shah. Meanwhile, the revolutionary regime began using the Stalinist tactic of claiming that anyone who spoke in favor of a more representative government was really a U.S. agent.[37] With the hostage crisis, the Islamist regime was able to make anti-Americanism such a leading theme that Iranian Marxists rallied to its support, while Moscow extended its tacit protection to the new theocracy.

After the failure of the U.S. military's "Desert One" rescue attempt on 25 April 1980 and eight more months of negotiations, the United States at last succeeded in obtaining the release of the hostages. To do so, it had to agree to recognize the legitimacy of the Iranian revolutionary regime, and it had to promise not to file any complaints against Iran before international authorities, despite the gross violations of human rights and international law that had occurred. Though these concessions may have appeared necessary at the time, in retrospect we can see that they emboldened the Islamists to sink to new levels of hatred and contempt for the West and its talk of human rights. For had not the revolutionary students and clerics in Tehran forced the Great Satan to abandon its principles and brought it to its knees?

The terrorists accurately assessed the extent of their victory and drew conclusions from it. They used terror to achieve their goal, and upon the continued use of terror their survival depends. "[America] is on the defensive. If tomorrow it feels safe, then it will think to implement its imperialistic projects."[38] Among these projects are human rights, which a representative of the Islamic Republic denounced before the UN Human Rights Committee as an "imperialist myth."[39]

From the taking of the hostages in Tehran in 1979 until the terrorist attacks of last September, Western policy makers too often implicitly downgraded the claims of justice and shirked their duty both to their own citizens and to the cause of human rights by refusing to pursue the terrorists with any real determination. Considerations of "pragmatism" and "prudence" were put forward to justify a sellout of justice which, in one of the cruelest ironies revealed by the harsh light of September 11, proved not to have been prudent at all.

Since the impunity granted to the hostage-takers of Tehran, terrorist outrages have increased both in frequency and in scale. In addition to all the questions raised about security measures, intelligence failures, accountability in foreign-policy decision making, and the like, the atrocity of September 11 also forces citizens of democratic countries to ask themselves how strongly they are committed to democratic values. Their enemies may believe in a chimera, but it is one for which they have shown themselves all too ready to die. In the mirror of the terrorists' sacrifice, the citizens of the free world are called to examine their consciences; they must reevaluate the nature of their loyalty to fragile and imperfect democracy. In particular, the strongly solidaristic networks that the Islamist totalitarians have created should make citizens in democratic societies ask how much they and their governments have done to help pro-democracy activists who have been persecuted for years in Iran, in Algeria, in Afghanistan, in Sudan, and elsewhere. Unarmed, they stand on the front lines of the struggle against terror and tyranny, and they deserve support. Here is a moral, political, and even philosophical challenge upon which the minds and hearts of the West should focus.

WHITHER THE MUSLIM WORLD?

Islamist terror poses a different but no less grave problem for those of us (including the authors of this essay) who come from Islamic countries, and it carries a special challenge for Muslim intellectuals. Public opinion in the Muslim world has largely—if perhaps too quietly—condemned the massacres of September 11. In Iran, young people poured spontaneously into the streets, braving arrest and police violence in order to hold candlelight vigils for the victims. But there were also outbursts of celebration in some Muslim countries, and sizeable anti-American demonstrations in Pakistan. Perhaps more disturbing still have been the persistent and widespread rumors going around Muslim societies that somehow an Israeli conspiracy was behind the attack. The force and pervasiveness of this rumor are symptoms of a collective flight from an uncontrollable reality. It is true that the Palestinian question is a painful and complicated one that requires an equitable solution. But it is equally true that reaching for foreign conspiracies has become an easy way of evading responsibility for too many of us from Muslim countries.

For the last several centuries, the Islamic world has been undergoing a traumatizing encounter with the West. Since this encounter began, our history has been a story of irreversible modernization, but also of utter domination on the one side, and humiliation and resentment on the other. To Muslim minds the West and its ways have become a powerful myth—evil, impenetrable, and incomprehensible. Whatever the Western world's unfairness toward Muslims, it remains true that Western scholars have at least made the effort to learn about and understand the Islamic world. But sadly, the great and brilliant works of the West's "Orientalists" have found no echo in a Muslim school of "Occidentalism."

We have been lacking the ability or the will to open up to others. We have opted for an easy solution, that of disguising in the clothes of Islam imported Western intellectual categories and concepts. In doing so we have not only failed to grasp the opportunity to understand the West, we have also lost the keys to our own culture. Otherwise, how could a degenerate Leninism aspire today to pass itself off as the true expression of a great monotheistic religion? The Islamists see themselves as bold warriors against modernity and the West, but in fact it is they who have imported and then dressed up in Islamic-sounding verbiage some of the most dubious ideas that ever came out of the modern West, ideas which now—after much death and suffering—the West itself has generally rejected. Had we not become so alien to our own cultural heritage, our theologians and intellectuals might have done a better job of exposing the antinomy between what the Islamists say and what Islam actually teaches. They might have more effectively undercut the terrorists' claim to be the exclusive and immediate representatives of God on earth, even while they preach a doctrine that does nothing but restore human sacrifice, as if God had never sent the angel to stop Abraham from slaying his son.

Our incapacity to apprehend reality lies at the root of our paranoia. If we were to take a clear and careful look at the West, we would see that it draws its strength from its capacity for introspection and its intransigent self-criticism. We would know that Western culture has never stopped calling on us, on the figure of the stranger, to help it understand itself and fight its vices. When it could not find the other, it invented it: Thomas More imagined a faraway island called Utopia to mirror the social problems of his time; Michel de Montaigne couched his criticisms of French politics in the form of a conversation with an Indian chief from Brazil; and Montesquieu invented letters from a Persian tourist to denounce the vices of Europe.

Had we had our own eminent experts on Western civilization, we might know that the West is a diverse, plural, and complex entity. Its political culture has produced horrors but also institutions that protect human dignity. One of these horrors was the imperialism imposed on Muslim and other lands, but even that did as much harm to the Europeans themselves as it did to us, as anyone familiar with the casualty figures from the First World War will know. Our experts might have helped us understand that Qutb and Khomeini's denunciations of human rights were remarkably similar to Pope Pius VI's denunciation of the French Declaration of the Rights of Man of 1789. We might have grasped that, not long ago, Westerners faced the same obstacles that we face today on the road to democracy. Citizens in the West fought for their freedoms; in this fight they lost neither their souls nor their religion. We too must roll up our sleeves to fight for freedom, remembering that we are first and foremost free and responsible human beings whom God has endowed with dignity.

NOTES

We would like to thank Hormoz Hekmat for his useful comments and critiques and Laith Kubba for providing some useful information.

1. Bernard Lewis, *The Assassins: A Radical Sect in Islam* (New York: Oxford University Press, 1987), 133–34.

2. On the heterodoxy of the Islamists' references to Muslim jurisprudent Ibn Taymiyya (1263–1328), see Olivier Carré, *Mystique et politique: Lecture révolutionnaire du Coran par Sayyid Qutb, Frère musulman radical* (Paris: Cerf, 1984), 16–17. On Ibn Taymiyya's theology and life, see Henri Laoust, *Pluralisme dans l'Islam* (Paris: Librairie Orientaliste Paul Geuthner, 1983).

3. This account of the Saleh case is based on reports in *Le Monde* (Paris), 8 and 10 April 1992.

4. For an overview of the career of Islamist terror networks, see Xavier Raufer, *La Nebuleuse: Le terrorisme du Moyen-Orient* (Paris: Fayard, 1987); Roland Jacquard, *Au nom d'Oussama Ben Laden: Dossier secret sur le terroriste le plus recherché du monde* (Paris: Jean Picollec, 2001); Yossef Bodansky, *Bin Laden: The Man Who Declared War on America* (Rocklin, Calif.: Prima, 1999); Gilles Kepel, *Jihad: Expansion et déclin de l'islamisme* (Paris: Gallimard, 2000); and Yonah Alexander and Michael S. Swetnam, *Usama Bin Laden's al-Qaida: Profile of a Terrorist Network* (New York: Transnational Publishers, 2001).

5. To confront Western colonialism, Muslim intellectuals and religious scholars such as Sayyid Jamal al-Din 'al-Afghani of Iran and Muhammad Abduh of Egypt concluded that a reformation and a new interpretation of Islam were needed in Muslim societies. The reforms that they advocated were aimed at reconciling Islam and modernity. They sought to promote individual freedom, social justice, and political liberalism. After the First World War, however, this movement was succeeded by one that was hostile to political liberalism. On Afghani, see Nikki K. Keddie, *An Islamic Response to Imperialism: Political and Religious Writings of Sayyid Jamal al-Din 'al-Afghani* (Berkeley: University of California Press, 1983). On Abduh, see Yvonne Haddad, "Muhammad Abduh: Pioneer of Islamic Reform," in Ali Rahnema, ed., *Pioneers of Islamic Revival* (London: Zed, 1994), 31–63.

6. This section draws on David Dean Commins, "Hassan al-Banna (1906–49)," in Ali Rahnema, ed., *Pioneers of Islamic Revival*, 146–47; as well as Richard P. Mitchell, *The Society of the Muslim Brothers* (London: Oxford University Press, 1969). See also Gilles Kepel, *Muslim Extremism in Egypt* (Berkeley: University of California Press, 1993).

7. Richard P. Mitchell, *The Society of the Muslim Brothers*, 29.

8. The widespread but mistaken impression that a Shi'ite cult of martyrdom serves as a religious inspiration for suicide attacks is one of the illusions about themselves that the terrorists skillfully

cultivate. It is true that Shi'ites revere Hussein (d. 680 C.E.), the third Imam and a grandson of the Prophet, as a holy martyr. Yet Shi'ite teaching also enjoins the avoidance of martyrdom, even recommending *taqieh* ("hiding one's faith") as a way of saving one's life from murderous persecutors. Moreover, Sunnis are not noted for devotion to Hussein, and yet when it comes to suicide attacks, there is little difference between the Sunnis of al-Qaeda and the mostly Shi'ite cadres of Hezbollah. There are striking similarities between the Islamist justification for violence and martyrdom and the discourse of German and Italian Marxist terrorists from the 1970s. On this subject see Philippe Raynaud, "Les origines intellectuelles du terrorisme," in François Furet et al., eds., *Terrorisme et démocratie* (Paris: Fayard, 1985), 65ff.

9. On Mawdudi, see Seyyed Vali Reza Nasr, *The Vanguard of the Islamic Revolution: The Jama'at-i Islami of Pakistan* (Berkeley: University of California Press, 1994); and Seyyed Vali Reza Nasr, *Mawdudi and the Making of Islamic Revivalism* (New York: Oxford University Press, 1996).

10. Olivier Carré, *Mystique et politique*, 206–7.

11. Muhammad Qutb, Sayyid Qutb's brother, was among the Muslim Brothers who were welcomed in Saudi Arabia. He was allowed to supervise the publication and distribution of his brother's works, and became ideologically influential in his own right: The official justification for the Saudi penal code uses his definition of secular and liberal societies as a "new era of ignorance." Exiled Muslim Brothers became influential in Saudi Arabia. Wahabism, the intolerant and fanatical brand of Islam that prevails in Saudi Arabia, was not in its origins a modern totalitarian ideology, but it provides fertile ground for the dissemination of terrorist ideology and facilitates the attraction of young Saudis to terrorist groups. See Olivier Carré, *L'utopie islamique dans l'Orient arabe* (Paris: Presses de la Fondation Nationale des Sciences politiques, 1991), 112–14; and Gilles Kepel, *Jihad*, 72–75.

12. Banna's followers recalled that he often said, "Each of the four schools [of Islam] is respectable," and urged, "Let us cooperate in those things on which we can agree and be lenient in those on which we cannot." Richard P. Mitchell, *The Society of the Muslim Brothers*, 217.

13. Mawdudi, *The Process of Islamic Revolution* (Lahore, 1955).

14. See Baqer Moin, *Khomeini: Life of the Ayatollah* (London: I.B. Tauris, 1999), 246.

15. Cited in Olivier Carré, *L'utopie islamique dans l'Orient arabe*, 197.

16. Cited in Olivier Carré, *L'utopie islamique dans l'Orient arabe*, 231–32.

17. Olivier Carré, *L'utopie islamique dans l'Orient arabe*, 232.

18. The then-head of the Iranian Revolutionary Guards, Mohsen Rafiqdoust, said that "both the TNT and the ideology which in one blast sent to hell 400 officers, NCOs, and soldiers at the Marine headquarters have been provided by Iran." *Resalat* (Tehran), 20 July 1987.

19. On 22 March 1998, the *Times of London* reported that bin Laden and the Iranian Revolutionary Guards had signed a pact the previous February 16 to consolidate their operations in Albania and Kosovo. Roland Jacquard adds that in September 1999, the Turkish intelligence services learned of an Islamist group financed by bin Laden in the Iranian city of Tabriz. See Roland Jacquard, *Au nom d'Oussama Ben Laden*, 287–88.

20. The first conference on the unification of Islamist movements was organized under Iranian auspices in January 1982. See the speeches of Khamenei and Mohammad Khatami (who is now the elected president of the Islamic Republic) in *Etela'at* (Tehran), 9 January 1982.

21. Xavier Rauffer, *La Nebuleuse*, 175.

22. Charles Tripp, "Sayyid Qutb: The Political Vision," in Ali Rahnema, ed., *Pioneers of Islamic Revival*, 178–79.

23. Gilles Kepel, *Jihad*, 122–23.

24. Roland Jacquard, *Au nom d'Oussama Ben Laden*, 76.

25. Gilles Kepel, *Jihad*, 187 and 579.

26. As reported in *Jomhouri-e Islami* (Tehran), 5 March 1994 (14 esfand 1372), 14 and 2.

27. Reported in the daily *Khalq-e Mosalman*, 4 and 9 December 1979.

28. M.H. Nad'ni, *Tanbih al-Omma va Tanzih al-mella*, 5th ed. (Tehran, 1979), 75–85.

29. Bernard Lewis, "License to Kill: Usama bin Ladin's Declaration of Jihad," *Foreign Affairs* 77 (November–December 1998): 19. Bin Laden's declaration of *jihad* mentions Ibn Taymiyya's authority and yet clearly contradicts the latter's ideas on *jihad*. Ibn Taymiyya explicitly forbids the murder of civilians and submits *jihad* to strict rules and regulations. See Henri Laoust, *Le traite de droit public d'Ibn*

Taimiya (annotated translation of *Siyasa shar'iya*) (Beirut, 1948), 122–35.

30. See "Declaration of war against the Americans occupying the land of the two holy places: A Message from Usama Bin Muhammad bin Laden unto his Muslim Brethren all over the world generally and in the Arab Peninsula specifically" (23 August 1996), in Yonah Alexander and Michael S. Swetnam, *Usama Bin Laden's al-Qaida*, 13.

31. In 1989, the vice-president of Parliament, Hojatol-Eslam Karoubi, proposed the creation of training camps for the "anti-imperialist struggle in the region." Quoted in the daily *Jomhouri-e Eslami* (Tehran), 7 May 1989, 9.

32. *Jomhouri-e Eslami* (Tehran), 7 May 1989, 11.

33. In this connection, it is worth noting that after the end of the Terror, the Declaration of the Rights of Man and the Citizen was not officially restored to constitutional status in France until 1946.

34. Howard Kurtz, "Interview Sheds Light on Bin Laden's Views," *Washington Post*, 7 February 2002, A12. Bin Laden gave this interview to Tayseer Alouni of the Arabic-language satellite television network al-Jazeera in October 2001.

35. Ali-Akbar Hashemi Rafsanjani, *Enqelabe va defa'e Moqadass* (Revolution and its sacred defense) (Tehran: Press of the Foundation of 15 Khordad, 1989), 63–64.

36. Russell Leigh Moses, *Freeing the Hostages: Reexamining U.S.–Iranian Negotiations and Soviet Policy, 1979–1981* (Pittsburgh: University of Pittsburgh Press, 1996), 174–75.

37. In an interview that ran in the Tehran daily *Jomhouri-e Eslami* on 4 November 1981 to mark the second anniversary of the embassy seizure, student-radical leader Musavi Khoeiniha remarked that the neutralization of Iranian liberals and democrats was the hostage-taking's most important result.

38. Ali-Akbar Hashemi Rafsanjani, *Enqelabe va defa'e Moqadass*, 64.

39. *Amnesty International Newsletter*, September 1982. The representative was Hadi Khosroshahi, another translator of Sayyid Qutb.

O sama bin Laden and al Qaeda are seen in the West as little more than barbaric throwbacks to a dark, ignorant age. The terrorist organization created by bin Laden is viewed as a movement defined by the ultra-violent medieval theology of fundamentalist Islam. The terrorists themselves are cast as unsophisticated thugs, brutish and predatory in their goals and methods. It is generally taken for granted that they are as crude as they are ruthless.

Nothing, it seems, could be farther from the truth. The terrorists, at least those about whom something is known, are often well educated and thoroughly comfortable with the modern world, especially modern technology. According to a recent study, 53 percent of the terrorists examined had university educations. Many even hold professional degrees, and some have received doctorates. An opinion piece in the *New York Times* rightfully urged Americans to give up "the soothing illusion that desperate automatons are attacking us rather than college graduates, as is often the case."*

The educations garnered by many al Qaeda operatives allow the organization to use and abuse the latest technologies to spread its message of jihad, or holy war. Cellular phones, global positioning systems, compact discs, the Internet, and—most importantly—television are used with great skill by radical Islamists and terrorists to reach out to Arab Muslims and speak to them in ways official sources cannot. Technological savvy allows Osama bin Laden and others of his ilk to communicate with the Muslim masses, which are commonly referred to as the Arab "street." It is this "street" to which the West must appeal if it hopes to counter the propaganda of hate and violence.

That is precisely the case made in the following essay by Dale Eickelman. Eickelman believes that the West, led by the United States, must win the media war against al Qaeda. Using the tools of public diplomacy, Eickelman argues, the West must address Arab Muslims directly and honestly. The Europeans and Americans must explain the stakes in the current "war on terror" and outline the benefits of rejecting extremism in favor of democracy.

NOTES

* Peter Bergen and Swati Panday, "The Madrassa Myth," *New York Times*, 14 June 2005, A19.

Bin Laden, the Arab "Street," and the Middle East's Democracy Deficit
DALE F. EICKELMAN

In the years ahead, the role of public diplomacy and open communications will play an increasingly significant role in countering the image that the Al Qaeda terrorist network and Osama bin Laden assert for themselves as guardians of Islamic values. In the fight against terrorism for which bin Laden is the photogenic icon, the first step is to recognize that he is as thoroughly a part of the modern world as was Cambodia's French-educated Pol Pot. Bin Laden's videotaped presentation of self intends to convey a traditional Islamic warrior brought up-to-date, but this sense of the past is a completely invented one. The language and content of his videotaped appeals convey more of his participation in the modern world than his camouflage jacket, Kalashnikov, and Timex watch.

Take the two-hour Al Qaeda recruitment videotape in Arabic that has made its way to many Middle Eastern video shops and Western news media.[1] It is a skillful production, as fast paced and gripping as any Hindu fundamentalist video justifying the destruction in 1992 of the Ayodhya mosque in India, or the political attack videos so heavily used in American presidential campaigning. The 1988 "Willie Horton" campaign video of Republican presidential candidate George H. W. Bush—in which an off-screen announcer portrayed Democratic presidential candidate Michael Dukakis as "soft" on crime while showing a mug shot of a convicted African-American rapist who had committed a second rape during a weekend furlough from a Massachusetts prison—was a propaganda masterpiece that combined an explicit although conventional message with a menacing, underlying one intended to motivate undecided voters. The Al Qaeda video, directed at a different audience—presumably alienated Arab youth, unemployed and often living in desperate conditions—shows an equal mastery of modern propaganda.

The Al Qaeda producers could have graduated from one of the best film schools in the United States or Europe. The fast-moving recruitment video begins with the bombing of the USS *Cole* in Yemen, but then shows a montage implying a seemingly coordinated worldwide aggression against Muslims in Palestine, Jerusalem, Lebanon, Chechnya, Kashmir, and Indonesia (but not Muslim violence against Christians and Chinese in the last). It also shows United States generals received by Saudi princes, intimating the collusion of local regimes with the West and challenging the legitimacy of many regimes, including Saudi Arabia. The sufferings of the Iraqi people are attributed to American brutality against Muslims, but Saddam Hussein is assimilated to the category of infidel ruler.

Many of the images are taken from the daily staple of Western video news—the BBC and CNN logos add to the videos' authenticity, just as Qatar's al-Jazeera satellite television logo rebroadcast by CNN and the BBC has added authenticity to Western coverage of Osama bin Laden.

Alternating with these scenes of devastation and oppression of Muslims are images of Osama bin Laden: posing in front of bookshelves or seated on the ground like a religious scholar, holding the Koran in his hand. Bin Laden radiates charismatic authority and control as he narrates the Prophet Mohammed's flight from Mecca to Medina, when the early Islamic movement was threatened by the idolaters, but returning to conquer them. Bin Laden also stresses the need for jihad, or struggle for the cause of Islam, against the "crusaders" and "Zionists." Later images show military training in Afghanistan (including target practice at a poster of Bill Clinton), and a final sequence—the word "solution" flashes across the screen—captures an Israeli soldier in full riot gear retreating from a Palestinian boy throwing stones, and a reading of the Koran.

THE THOROUGHLY MODERN ISLAMIST

Osama bin Laden, like many of his associates, is imbued with the values of the modern world, even if only to reject them. A 1971 photograph shows him on family holiday in Oxford at the age of 14, posing with two of his half-brothers and Spanish girls their own age. English was their common language of communication. Bin Laden studied English at a private school in Jidda, and English was also useful for his civil engineering courses at Jidda's King Abdul Aziz University. Unlike many of his estranged half-brothers, educated in Saudi Arabia, Europe, and the United States, Osama's education was only in Saudi Arabia, but he was also familiar with Arab and European society.

The organizational skills he learned in Saudi Arabia came in to play when he joined the mujahideen (guerrilla) struggle against the 1979 Soviet invasion of Afghanistan. He may not have directly met United States intelligence officers in the field, but they, like their Saudi and Pakistani counterparts, were delighted to have him participate in their fight against Soviet troops and recruit willing Arab fighters. Likewise, his many business enterprises flourished under highly adverse conditions. Bin Laden skillfully sustained a flexible multinational organization in the face of enemies, especially state authorities, moving cash, people, and supplies almost undetected across international frontiers.

The organizational skills of bin Laden and his associates were never underestimated. Neither should be their skills in conveying a message that appeals to some Muslims. Bin Laden lacks the credentials of an established Islamic scholar, but this does not diminish his appeal. As Sudan's Sorbonne-educated Hasan al-Turabi, the leader of his country's Muslim Brotherhood and its former attorney general and speaker of parliament, explained two decades ago, "Because all knowledge is divine and religious, a chemist, an engineer, an economist, or a jurist" are all men of learning.[2] Civil engineer bin Laden exemplifies Turabi's point. His audience judges him not by his ability to cite authoritative texts, but by his apparent skill in applying generally accepted religious tenets to current political and social issues.

THE MESSAGE ON THE ARAB "STREET"

Bin Laden's lectures circulate in book form in the Arab world, but video is the main vehicle of communication. The use of CNN-like "zippers"—the ribbons of words that stream beneath the images in many newscasts and documentaries—shows that Al Qaeda takes the Arab world's rising levels of education for granted. Increasingly, this audience is also saturated with both conventional media and new media, such as the Internet.[3] The Middle East has entered an era of mass education and this also implies an Arabic lingua franca. In Morocco in the early 1970s, rural people sometimes asked me to "translate" newscasts from the standard transnational Arabic of the state radio into colloquial Arabic. Today this is no longer required. Mass education and new communications technologies enable large numbers of Arabs to hear—and see—Al Qaeda's message directly.

Bin Laden's message does not depend on religious themes alone. Like the Ayatollah Ruhollah Khomeini, his message contains many secular elements. Khomeini often alluded to the "wretched of the earth." At least for a time, his language appealed equally to Iran's religiously minded and to the secular left. For bin Laden, the equivalent themes are the oppression and corruption of many Arab governments, and he lays the blame for the violence and oppression in Palestine, Kashmir, Chechnya, and elsewhere at the door of the West. One need not be religious to rally to some of these themes. A poll taken in Morocco in late September 2001 showed that a majority of Moroccans condemned the September 11 bombings, but 41 percent sympathized with bin Laden's message. A British poll taken at about the same time showed similar results.

Osama bin Laden and the Al Qaeda terrorist movement are thus reaching at least part of the Arab "street." Earlier this year, before the September terrorist attacks, United States policymakers considered this "street" a "new phenomenon of public accountability, which we have seldom had to factor into our projections of Arab behavior in the past. The information revolution, and particularly the daily dose of uncensored television coming out of local TV stations like al-Jazeera and international coverage by CNN and others, is shaping public opinion, which, in turn, is pushing Arab governments to respond. We don't know, and the leaders themselves don't know, how that pressure will impact on Arab policy in the future."[4]

Director of Central Intelligence George J. Tenet was even more cautionary on the nature of the "Arab street." In testimony before the Senate Select Committee on Intelligence in February 2001, he explained that the "right catalyst—such as the outbreak of Israeli–Palestinian violence—can move people to act. Through access to the Internet and other means of communication, a restive public is increasingly capable of taking action without any identifiable leadership or organizational structure."

Because many governments in the Middle East are deeply suspicious of an open press, nongovernmental organizations, and open expression, it is no surprise that the "restive" public, increasingly educated and influenced by hard-to-censor new media, can take action "without any identifiable leadership or organized structure." The Middle East in general has a democracy deficit, in which "unauthorized" leaders or critics, such as Egyptian academic Saad Eddin Ibrahim—founder and director of the Ibn Khaldun Center for Development Studies, a nongovernmental organization that promotes democracy in Egypt—suffer harassment or prison terms.

One consequence of this democracy deficit is to magnify the power of the street in the Arab world. Bin Laden speaks in the vivid language of popular Islamic preachers, and builds on a deep and widespread resentment against the West and local ruling elites identified with it. The lack of formal outlets to express opinion on public concerns has created the democracy deficit in much of the Arab world, and this makes it easier for terrorists such as bin Ladin, asserting that they act in the name of religion, to hijack the Arab street.

The immediate response is to learn to speak directly to this street. This task has already begun. Obscure to all except specialists until September 11, Qatar's al-Jazeera satellite television is a premier source in the Arab world for uncensored news and opinion. It is more, however, than the Arab equivalent of CNN. Uncensored news and opinions increasingly shape "public opinion"—a term without the pejorative overtones of "the street"—even in places like Damascus and Algiers. This public opinion in turn pushes Arab governments to be more responsive to their citizens, or at least to say that they are.

Rather than seek to censor al-Jazeera or limit Al Qaeda's access to the Western media—an unfortunate first response of the United States government after the September terror attacks—we should avoid censorship. Al Qaeda statements should be treated with the same caution as any other news source. Replacing Sinn Fein leader Gerry Adams' voice and image in the British media in the 1980s with an Irish-accented actor appearing in silhouette only highlighted what he had to say, and it is unlikely that the British public would tolerate the same restrictions on the media today.

Ironically, at almost the same time that national security adviser Condoleezza Rice asked the American television networks not to air Al Qaeda videos unedited, a former senior CIA officer, Graham Fuller, was explaining in Arabic on al-Jazeera how United States policymaking works. His appearance on al-Jazeera made a significant impact, as did Secretary of State Colin Powell's presence on a later al-Jazeera program and former United States Ambassador Christopher Ross, who speaks fluent Arabic. Likewise, the timing and content of British Prime Minister Tony Blair's response to an earlier bin Laden tape suggests how to take the emerging Arab public seriously. The day after al-Jazeera broadcast the bin Laden tape, Blair asked for and received an opportunity to respond. In his reply, Blair—in a first for a Western leader—directly addressed the Arab public through the Arab media, explaining coalition goals in attacking Al Qaeda and the Taliban and challenging bin Laden's claim to speak in the name of Islam.

PUTTING PUBLIC DIPLOMACY TO WORK

Such appearances enhance the West's ability to communicate a primary message: that the war against terrorism is not that of one civilization against another, but against terrorism and fanaticism in all societies. Western policies and actions are subject to public scrutiny and will often be misunderstood. Public diplomacy can significantly diminish this misapprehension. It may, however, involve some uncomfortable policy decisions. For instance, America may be forced to exert more diplomatic pressure on Israel to alter its methods of dealing with Palestinians.

Western public diplomacy in the Middle East also involves uncharted waters. As Oxford University social linguist Clive Holes has noted, the linguistic genius who thought up the first name for the campaign to oust the Taliban, "Operation Infinite Justice," did a major disservice to the

Western goal. The expression was literally and accurately translated into Arabic as *adala ghayr mutanahiya*, implying that an earthly power arrogated to itself the task of divine retribution. Likewise, President George W. Bush's inadvertent and unscripted use of the word "crusade" gave Al Qaeda spokesmen an opportunity to attack Bush and Western intentions.

Mistakes will be made, but information and arguments that reach the Arab street, including on al-Jazeera, will eventually have an impact. Some Westerners might condemn al-Jazeera as biased, and it may well be in terms of making assumptions about its audience. However, it has broken a taboo by regularly inviting official Israeli spokespersons to comment live on current issues. Muslim religious scholars, both in the Middle East and in the West, have already spoken out against Al Qaeda's claim to act in the name of Islam. Other courageous voices, such as Egyptian playwright Ali Salem, have even employed humor for the same purpose.[5]

We must recognize that the best way to mitigate the continuing threat of terrorism is to encourage Middle Eastern states to be more responsive to participatory demands, and to aid local nongovernmental organizations working toward this goal. As with the case of Egypt's Saad Eddin Ibrahim, some countries may see such activities as subversive. Whether Arab states like it or not, increasing levels of education, greater ease of travel, and the rise of new communications media are turning the Arab street into a public sphere in which greater numbers of people, and not just a political and economic elite, will have a say in governance and public issues.

NOTES

1. It is now available on-line with explanatory notes in English. See <http://www.ciaonet.org/cbr/cbr00/video/excerpts_index.html>.

2. Hasan al-Turabi, "The Islamic State," in *Voices of Resurgent Islam*, John L. Esposito, ed. (New York: Oxford University Press, 1983), p. 245.

3. On the importance of rising levels of education and the new media, see Dale F. Eickelman, "The Coming Transformation in the Muslim World," *Current History*, January 2000.

4. Edward S. Walker, "The New U.S. Administration's Middle East Policy Speech," *Middle East Economic Survey*, vol. 44, no. 26 (June 25, 2001). Available at http://www.mees.com/news/a44n26d01.htm.

5.   See his article in Arabic, "I Want to Start a Kindergarten for Extremism," *Al-Hayat* (London), November 5, 2001. This is translated into English by the Middle East Media Research Institute as Special Dispatch no. 298, Jihad and Terrorism Studies, November 8, 2001, at http://www.memri.org.

Bibliography

———⁕———

SECTION ONE: THE PROSPECTS FOR
DEMOCRACY IN THE MIDDLE EAST

Brumberg, Daniel. "The Trap of Liberalized Autocracy." *Journal of Democracy*, 13, 4 (October 2002): 56–68.

Cook, Steven A. "The Right Way to Promote Arab Reform." *Foreign Affairs*, (March/April 2005): 91–102.

Hawthorne, Amy. "Can the United States Promote Democracy in the Middle East?" *Current History*, 102, 660 (January 2003): 21–26.

Muravchik, Joshua. "Bringing Democracy to the Arab World." *Current History*, 103, 669 (January 2004): 8–10.

Ottoway, Marina and Thomas Carothers. "Think Again: Middle East Democracy." *Foreign Policy*, (November/December 2004). Available online. URL: http://www.foreignpolicy.com/story/cms.php?story_id=2705&print=1.

SECTION TWO: DEMOCRACY AND RELIGION

Filali-Ansary, Abdou. "Muslims and Democracy." In *Islam and Democracy in the Middle East*, ed. Larry Diamond, Marc F. Plattner, and Daniel Brumberg, 193–207. Baltimore: The Johns Hopkins University Press, 2003.

Fuller, Graham E. "The Future of Political Islam." *Foreign Affairs*, 81, 2 (March/April 2002): 48–60.

Keddie, Nikki R. "A Woman's Place: Democratization in the Middle East." *Current History*, 103, 669 (January 2004): 25–30.

Lewis, Bernard. "A Historical Overview." In *Islam and Democracy in the Middle East*, ed. Larry Diamond, Marc F. Plattner, and Daniel Brumberg, 208–219. Baltimore: The Johns Hopkins University Press, 2003.

Nasr, Vali. "The Rise of 'Muslim Democracy.'" *Journal of Democracy*, 16, 2 (April 2005): 13–27.

Norris, Pippa and Ronald Inglehart. "The True Clash of Civilizations." *Foreign Policy*, (March/April 2003). Available online. URL: http://www.foreignpolicy.com/story/cms.php?story_id=16&print=1.

Steinberg, Gerald M. "'Democratic Peace' and the Jewish Political Tradition." In *Democratization in the Middle East: Experiences, Struggles, Challenges*, ed. Amin Saikal and Albrecht Schnabel, 142–165. New York: United Nations University Press, 2003.

SECTION THREE: DEMOCRACY AND THE CHALLENGE OF EXTREMISM

Boroumand, Ladan and Roya Boroumand. "Terror, Islam, and Democracy." *Journal of Democracy*, 13, 2 (April 2002): 5–20.

Carothers, Thomas. "Promoting Democracy and Fighting Terror." *Foreign Affairs*, 82, 1 (January/February 2003): 84–97.

Eickelman, Dale F. "Bin Laden, the Arab 'Street,' and the Middle East's Democracy Deficit." *Current History*, 101, 651 (January 2002): 36–39.

Sources Cited

"03 March 2005: Rice Warns Syria, Iran to Meet International Obligations." Available online. URL: http://usinfo.state.gov/xarchives/display.html?p=washfile-english&y=2005&m=March&x=200503031846491CJsamohT0.885235&t=livefeeds/wf-latest.html.

"President Sworn-In to Second Term." Available online. URL: http://www.whitehouse.gov/news/releases/2005/01/20050120-1.html.

Allama Sir Abdullah Al-Mamun Al-Suhrawardy. *The Wisdom of Muhammad*. New York: Citadel Press, 2001.

Armstrong, Karen. *Islam: A Short History*. New York: Random House, 2000.

Ata, Abe W. "Opinion: Western Democracy Stillborn in Mideast." Available online. URL: http://www.metimes.com/print.php?Story ID=20050613-073346-9623r.

Barber, Benjamin R. *Fear's Empire: War, Terrorism, and Democracy*. New York: W.W. Norton and Company, 2003.

Bennis, Phyllis. "Bush on Middle East 'Democracy' and 'Ending Occupation' in Iraq." International Relations Center, *Foreign Policy in Focus*. Available online. URL: http://www.fpif.org/cgaa/talkingpoints/0311iraq.html.

Bergen, Peter and Swati Pandey, "The Madrassa Myth." *New York Times*, 14 June 2005, A19.

Brown, Richard D. *Modernization: The Transformation of American Life, 1600–1865*. Prospect Heights, Illinois: Waveland Press, 1976.

Diamond, Larry, Marc F. Plattner, and Daniel Brumberg, eds., *Islam and Democracy in the Middle East*. Baltimore: The Johns Hopkins University Press, 2003.

Huntington, Samuel P. *The Clash of Civilizations and the Remaking of World Order*. New York: Touchstone, 1996.

Roberts, J.M. *A History of Europe*. New York: Allen Lane, 1996.

Schnabel, Albrecht. "A Rough Journey: Nascent Democratization in the Middle East." In *Democratization in the Middle East: Experiences, Struggles, Challenges*, eds. Amin Saikal and Albrecht Schnabel, 1-22. New York: United Nations University Press, 2003.

Yacoubian, Mona, "Fostering Democracy in the Middle East: Defeating Terrorism with Ballots," statement before the U.S. House of Representatives Committee on Government Reform, Subcommittee National Security, Emerging Threats, and International Relations, May 17, 2005. Available online. URL: www.usip.org/aboutus/congress/testimony/2005/0517_yacoubian.html.

Further Reading

———— ⊗⊗⊗ ————

Books

Barzilai, Gad. *Wars, Internal Conflicts, and Political Order: A Jewish Democracy in the Middle East*. Albany, New York: State University of New York Press, 1996.

Carothers, Thomas and Maria Ottaway. *Uncharted Journey: Promoting Democracy in the Middle East*. Washington, D.C.: Carnegie Endowment for International Peace, 2005.

Deegan, Heather. *The Middle East and Problems of Democracy*. Boulder, Colorado: Lynn Rienner Publishers, 1994.

Kamrava, Mehran. *Democracy in the Balance: Culture and Democracy in the Middle East*. New York: Chatham House Publishers, 1998.

Muravchik, Joshua, et al. *Democracy in the Middle East: Defining the Challenge*. Washington, D.C.: Washington Institute for Near East Policy, 1993.

Trofimov, Yaroslav. *Faith at War: A Journey on the Frontlines of Islam, From Baghdad to Timbuktu*. New York: Henry Holt and Company, 2005.

Web Sites

Basham, Patrick and Christopher Preble. "The Trouble with Democracy in the Middle East." Available online. URL: http://www.cato.org/dailys/11-30-03.html.

Gerges, Fawaz. "Is Democracy in the Middle East a Pipedream?" Available online. URL: http://yaleglobal.yale.edu/display.article?id=5622.

Hughes, John. "Whispers of Democracy Across the Middle East." Available online. URL: http://www.csmonitor.com/2003/1022/p11s01-cojh.html.

Index

About the Editor

─────◦∞∞◦─────

JOHN C. DAVENPORT holds a Ph.D. from the University of Connecticut and currently teaches at Corte Madera School in Portola Valley, California. Davenport is the author of several biographies, including one of Muslim leader Saladin, and has written extensively on the role of borders in American history. He lives in San Carlos, California, with his wife, Jennifer, and his two sons, William and Andrew.

Photo Credits

─────◦∞∞◦─────